# SUPERNATURAL PROUST

# SUPERNATURAL PROUST

Myth and Metaphor in
*A la recherche du temps perdu*

*Margaret Topping*

UNIVERSITY OF WALES PRESS
CARDIFF
2007

© Margaret Topping, 2007

All rights reserved. No part of this book may be reproduced, stored in a retrieval system, or transmitted, in any form or by any means, electronic, mechanical, photocopying, recording or otherwise, without clearance from the University of Wales Press, 10 Columbus Walk, Brigantine Place, Cardiff, CF10 4UP.
*www.wales.ac.uk/press*

**British Library Cataloguing-in-Publication Data**
A catalogue record for this book is available from the British Library.

ISBN 978-0-7083-1866-9

The right of Margaret Topping to be identified as author of this work has been asserted by her in accordance with sections 77 and 79 of the Copyright, Designs and Patents Act 1988.

Typeset by Florence Production Ltd, Stoodleigh, Devon
Printed in Great Britain by Antony Rowe Ltd, Wiltshire

*To David and Nicola*

# CONTENTS

*Acknowledgements* ix
*Abbreviations* xi

## INTRODUCTION 1

Myth and the supernatural 1
Myth and the Self: understanding and invention 4
Myth and communication: Self meets Other 5
Myth and time: memory and transcendence 7
Statistical occurrences of myth and the supernatural in *A la recherche du temps perdu* 12

## I MAGIC AND FAIRYTALE 24

Introduction: the novel as fairytale 24
Fairytale romances 29
*Les Mille et Une Nuits* proustiennes 42
The magical mundane 55
    The apparently supernatural 56
    The fairy queen 59
    The feigned supernatural 64
    The everyday supernatural 65

## II ARTISTIC LEGENDS: PERFORMANCE, MUSIC AND TEXT 74

Introduction 74
Punch and Judy: ritual and repetition 76
La Fontaine: mockery and morals 81

| | | |
|---|---|---|
| Wagner's *Parsifal* and *Tristan and Isolde*: text/music/text | | 91 |
|    A *Proustian* Parsifal   92 | | |
|    *The cult of Wagner*   101 | | |
|      Tristan and Isolde: *towards aesthetic independence*   104 | | |
|      *From Wagnerian synthesis to Proustian redemption*   108 | | |
| *Pelléas et Mélisande*: a model of aesthetic synthesis | | 113 |
| Closing the cycle: 'That's the way to do it' | | 115 |

## III  RITUALS AND BELIEFS        118

| | |
|---|---|
| Introduction | 118 |
| Superstition and anxiety | 119 |
| Spiritualism, communication and 'l'interpénétration des âmes' | 130 |
| Magic and the occult: from possession to exorcism | 142 |
| Divination, destiny and the stars | 150 |

## CONCLUSION        161

## NOTES        165

## BIBLIOGRAPHY        207

## INDEX        214

# ACKNOWLEDGEMENTS

I am grateful to the School of European Studies at Cardiff University for granting me a sabbatical to pursue this research, and to the editors of *Essays in French Literature* for giving me permission to reproduce here the text of an article, '*Les Mille et Une Nuits* proustiennes', which appeared in issue 35/36 (November 1998–9) of the journal. Thanks also go to Nicola for providing me with valuable insights into bereavement, to David for all his support, and to Sarah Lewis at University of Wales Press for her patience and advice. Finally, I should like to thank Professor Alison Finch who, once again, gave generously of her time and ideas in reading the manuscript of this book.

# ABBREVIATIONS

Individual titles in *A la recherche du temps perdu*:

AD   *Albertine disparue*
G    *Le Côté de Guermantes*
JF   *A l'ombre des jeunes filles en fleurs*
P    *La Prisonnière*
S    *Du côté de chez Swann*
SG   *Sodome et Gomorrhe*
TR   *Le Temps retrouvé*

# INTRODUCTION

## Myth and the supernatural

Ghosts, fairies and sorcerers are conjured up in the pages of *A la recherche du temps perdu*, while legendary quests, paranormal 'bumps in the night', evocations of the dead, and rituals, both superstitious and occult, mingle with these spellbinding figures to infuse Proust's masterpiece with all the mysteries of the supernatural.[1] Such allusions imply an existence beyond the natural, empirical world; they hint at a power that seems to violate or transcend natural forces; they lead us out of the realm of the logical and mundane, and into that of the magical, the miraculous and the divine. It is in these hidden resonances that the eclectic spectrum of sources discussed in the pages that follow finds its underlying unity.

Part I of the study transports us into a deceptively carefree, magical domain by exploring a range of familiar fairytales from East and West. Not only do these tales provide a strikingly apt interpretative template for *A la recherche*, but they are also subject to a suggestive metaphorical retelling by the author. My own and others' psychoanalytical readings of Perrault's 'fairytale romances' offer a vision of stasis to mirror the narrator/protagonist's (potential) non-progression. Turning eastward, the *Mille et Une Nuits* seems, on the surface, to provide him with a fittingly exotic locus of escape from the pressure to progress. Yet these tales of enchanting alterity are gradually transformed from a quasi-intellectual excuse for inaction – the reading of which will assuage the exhortations of mother and grandmother to work – into the spur for an involuntary evolution to awareness and, ultimately, to creative activity on the part of the narrator. These sources are thus stripped by Proust of the veneer of levity and escapism with which they are associated for the young narrator/protagonist in anticipation of their metaphorical reinvention in the hands of the mature narrator/writer.

In entering the province of the legends of performance, music and text – the inevitable stopping point for a figure seeking transcendent truth in art – Part II accompanies the narrator/protagonist on his mythical quest for the realization of his vocation. Whether consciously or otherwise, he confronts an alluring array of legendary figures, each offering models for emulation or imitation. The overarching paradigm of the narrator's journey in itself possesses the supernatural flavour of an Arthurian quest for the Holy Grail, and, indeed, at the most distant point on his metaphorical path, it is Wagner's *Parsifal* that the narrator/protagonist will unravel both aesthetically and in terms of its dramatization of a mythical quest. This is, however, a quest which may be hindered by temptation and obstruction at the hands of the sorcerer Klingsor and the chimerical Flower Maidens.[2] Side by side with *Parsifal* stands an alternative model of transcendence for the narrator/protagonist, namely Wagner's *Tristan and Isolde*, in which a magical love-potion propels the two protagonists towards the eventual attainment of their quest: a mystical, otherworldly union in death. Roger Scruton, in his recent study of *Tristan and Isolde*, highlights the contrasting models of heroism and redemption embodied in *Parsifal* and *Tristan*:

> Heroes of compassion (*agape*) renounce their desires for the sake of others, and thereby redeem and renew the social order. Such is Parsifal [. . .] Heroes of erotic love (*eros*) exist outside the social order in a state of exalted solitude; but they too long either to redeem or be redeemed through an act of loving sacrifice. Redemption comes when, having found the love that meets their inner need, they are carried onward by it to extinction.[3]

We shall see how Proust's narrator navigates an independent path between these two models.[4] Yet not all the vicarious identities he entertains are as 'lofty' as those presented by Wagner. At the other end of the aesthetic scale, as conventionally understood, the legendary, if not exemplary, Polichinelle enacts his ritualistic set-pieces in the fantastical realm of the puppet theatre, tempting the narrator/protagonist with the attractions of the frivolous.[5] Unravelling the nature of, and charting the narrator's progress through, the intermediary stages on his journey from Polichinelle to *Parsifal* are La Fontaine's celebrated *Fables*, their anthropomorphic basis granting access to an existence outside the natural world which, in turn, provides a privileged space for insight into the natural world. By introducing La Fontaine's world of talking animals into the novel – often only in the veiled form of a fleeting reference by a character – Proust as *moraliste* subtly exposes human motivations and emotions to the reader and, ultimately, to the narrator/protagonist whose evolution they also chart.

As this 'separation' of writer and character implies, my discussion also charts a dual evolution. Complementary to the narrator/protagonist's mythical quest through the legends of performance, music and text, the narrator-soon-to-be-writer's exposure to the various aesthetic media in which these legends are played out suggests models for stylistic and generic experimentation. This may culminate in the development of a *novelistic* aesthetic, but the style of this novel nonetheless owes much to other textual, visual and sonic forms. Thus, where the protagonist appears gradually to ascend and successively to transcend an aesthetic hierarchy of legendary models, the writer is enacting a carnivalesque deconstruction of this conventional hierarchy. Magpie-like, Proust collects the gleaming stylistic treasures he sees in a whole range of genres, both 'high' and 'low', ultimately transforming and renewing them in his own work.

Part III extends this dual paradigm by exploring the various metaphysical rituals and beliefs which tempt the narrator/protagonist – above all, in moments of emotional crisis – and which are woven into the novel as metaphor by the mature narrator/writer. Magic, the occult, superstition, spiritualism, divination and astrology all provide the (young) narrator/protagonist with glimpses of a power, governing his own and others' lives, that lies beyond the natural world, an existence beyond his knowledge and understanding. For the mature writer, in contrast, these worlds offer a metaphorical intertext, the unity of which lies in its common basis in the supernatural. The writer will challenge the genuinely supernatural power of these rituals and beliefs, and he will debunk the credulity and/or self-deception of his younger, intradiegetical self, but he will also celebrate and embody in his own writing their metaphorical power both to renew vision and to communicate hidden 'truths'; their power, in other words, to make the familiar unfamiliar and the unfamiliar familiar.

The commonality that unites this sweep of sources is, moreover, profounder than the shared foundation in the supernatural detailed above, for Proust's handling of such seemingly diverse interaesthetic realms points, implicitly, to the existence of what Ruth Nanda Anshen terms 'a primordial unitive power [. . .], a common humanity more fundamental than any unity of dogma'.[6] That all of these sources can complement one another in their collective dramatization of the narrator's dual quest implies Proust's apprehension of their essential syncretism. Indeed, this transcendence of (artificial) boundaries within the domain of the supernatural chimes, more generally, with the collapsing of binary oppositions – be they between heterosexual and homosexual desire, East and West, cruel and kind, good and evil, high and low – that is so integral to Proust's philosophical and aesthetic outlook.

Anthropologists and psychoanalysts have argued that a number of common mythical structures underlie all drives to believe in the supernatural. The draw of the transcendent lies at the heart of the apparently artless medium of fairy-tale as much as of the metaphysical dramas played out in Wagner's operas, for myth-making and the invention of legend and fairytale have been argued to be inherent human tendencies. Jung, for example, claims that:

> On objectera que les penchants mythologiques des enfants leur ont été inculqués par l'éducation. C'est là une objection oiseuse. Les hommes se sont-ils jamais entièrement libérés du mythe? [. . .] Il est donc possible de priver un enfant des contenus des mythes anciens: on ne peut lui enlever le besoin de mythologie et encore moins l'aptitude à la créer. On peut affirmer que, si l'on réussissait à supprimer d'un seul coup toute tradition dans le monde, toute la mythologie et toute l'histoire religieuse recommenceraient à leur début avec la génération suivante.[7]

What, then, are the preoccupations that seduce us into myth-making and legend-creation? What are the spiritual concerns to which we grant plastic expression in myth, legend or ritual? What are the essential mythical structures that underlie all the sources examined in this study? Mythographers have responded to these questions from a variety of perspectives.[8] However, the theories of Mircea Eliade, with their emphasis on creation, re-creation and renewal through a return to origins, seem, above all, to offer a compelling template for an analysis of Proustian mythopoeia.[9] A close reading of Eliade's exploration of the drives underlying myth highlights a number of unifying strands. These are the aspirations and preoccupations that, he argues, unite humanity, and that we may detect, represented in microcosm, in Proust's narrator's quest for the absolute.

## Myth and the Self: understanding and invention

According to Eliade, legends, myths, rituals, and the systems of philosophical and spiritual belief that they embody, arise in response to a need not only to understand where we come from and what constitutes us existentially, but also to have 'models for human behaviour'. It is this that grants 'meaning and value to life'.[10] Myths thus offer an account of creation, a sacred story that, as Eliade is careful to underline, is also a 'true history' and one that deals with realities: 'The cosmogonic myth is "true" because the existence of the World is there to prove it; the myth of the origin of death is equally true because man's mortality proves it, and so on.'[11] Yet their sphere extends beyond this chronicle of origins, for myths also explain humanity's subsequent development. Indeed, by revealing 'exemplary models for all human rites and all significant human activities', they chart the processes of our past and future self-creation.[12]

In playing out the developmental dilemmas and conflicting impulses acting on the narrator/protagonist through fairytale, Proust is at once exploiting all the richly distinctive resonances of this particular source – its fusion of the *populaire* and *savant*, its burlesque elements, its potent symbolism, its duality of tone which, like Proust's own, oscillates almost imperceptibly between the naive and the knowing – and echoing the desire for exemplary models of behaviour that underlies many myths.[13]

However, it is, above all, in the artistic legends explored in Part II of the book that the narrator finds the 'point de repère' for his existential scrutiny and for his own (self-)invention. As with fairytale, opposing drives are voiced through La Fontaine's fables and, while not overtly moralizing, their aim to 'instruire' as much as 'plaire' identifies them as a mirror of human nature that aids the narrator in understanding his earlier self and defining his future self.[14] Similarly, Wagner's *Parsifal* and *Tristan and Isolde* chart their protagonists' and, metaphorically, the narrator's development to Selfhood; they also offer alternative models of attaining the absolute and, in both, although most tangibly in *Parsifal*, meaning and value are accorded to life through a symbol, the Holy Grail, and its associated narrative. Once again, Proust exploits the unique inflections of the original sources – Wagner's sacred narratives and lofty subject-matter contrast with La Fontaine's playful touch in expressing the moralist's lucid vision of humanity's pre-eminently worldly concerns[15] – but the same drives are drawn out of both by Proust. Indeed, in writing the Self, Proust is consciously experimenting with different genres, tones and registers, exploiting a philosophical unity within aesthetic diversity.

## Myth and communication: Self meets Other

A preoccupation with communication defines the second strand that may be drawn out of Eliade's analysis of myth. The primordial desire to make contact with the world, with all that is not Self, is dogged by a seemingly insurmountable alterity. Mythical thinking is a response to this difficulty, a means of encouraging the individual not to 'feel shut up in his[/her] own mode of existence'.[16] By depicting common human experiences, dilemmas and emotions, and offering exemplary models for their resolution, myths subtly imply that the essence of the existence of the Other resembles that of the Self. Indeed, myth's reliance on archetypes and archetypal modes of behaviour highlights the commonalities which may lie behind the perception of difference, be that cultural or existential. For instance, an erosion of the binary opposition between Europe and Asia that lies at the heart of Edward Said's understanding of the western construction of the 'Orient' underlies Proust's handling of the *Mille et Une Nuits*.[17] A rethinking of apparent cultural difference here uncovers unexpected concurrences in the patterns of desire, for the West offers a vision of eroticism which is at least as 'exotic' as that associated, in Orientalist discourse, with a stereotyped East. On a broader level, too, individuality and isolation are transcended, as is further reinforced by Proust's recourse to the fables of La Fontaine: in granting a voice to the animal world, La Fontaine broadens the applicability of his message beyond a single human consciousness and experience.[18] Myth thus enables communication both by granting plastic expression to spiritual ideas/ideals and by its recourse to the common language of symbol.

Myth's reliance on symbols for communication and for an understanding of the Self has further implications, for what are fables, legends and fairytales if not myths that have *evolved into* symbols? Products of a process of demythicization, they are myths that have been stripped of their literal religious meanings to become allegories, the hidden significance of which must be sought out.[19] In key respects, this book charts a similar transition from *mythos* to *logos*: the narrator seems gradually to abandon the magical thinking of his younger self in favour of an increasingly empirical apprehension of each new person and situation he encounters. As a result, the naive young protagonist who invests Mme de Guermantes with the supernatural aura of a fairy queen, or the bereaved lover who – in the prime example of mythical thought aimed at overcoming isolation and achieving communication – contemplates spiritualism as a conduit to the now-dead Albertine, evolves into the writer who exploits myth as symbol. Following the process of demythicization described above, the sacred thus becomes literary, and genuine belief is transformed into metaphor, the significance of which the reader must disentangle. In this, the movement of the novel at least appears to chime with the theory of a progression from magic to religion to science famously proposed by Sir James Frazer as a macrocosmic template for the evolution of all human societies:[20]

> We may illustrate the course which thought has hitherto run by likening it to a web of three different threads – the black thread of magic, the red thread of religion, and the white thread of science, if under science we may include those simple truths, drawn from the observation of nature, of which men in all ages have possessed a store. Could we then survey the web of thought from the beginning, we should probably perceive it to be at first a chequer of black and white, a patchwork of true and false notions, hardly tinged as yet by the red thread of religion. But carry your eye further along the fabric and you will remark that, while the black thread and the white chequer still run through it, there rests on the middle portion of the web, where religion has entered most deeply into its texture, a dark crimson

stain, which shades off insensibly into a lighter tint as the white thread of science is woven more and more into the tissue. To a web thus chequered and stained, thus shot with threads of diverse hues, but gradually changing colour the farther it is unrolled, the state of modern thought, with all its divergent aims and conflicting tendencies, may be compared. Will the great movement which for centuries has been slowly altering the complexion of thought be continued in the near future? Or will a reaction set in which may arrest progress and even undo much of what has been done? To keep up our parable, what will be the colour of the web which the Fates are now weaving on the humming loom of time? Will it be white or red? We cannot tell.[21]

If genuine belief becomes metaphor, and myth becomes art, then the reciter of myth assumes the identity of artist; indeed, in many 'primitive' societies, only a select few individuals are permitted to recite myths – usually those known for their mnemonic capacity, their imagination or their literary talent.[22] Filtered through the prism of such individuals' creativity, myths are elaborated to bring about a renewal of culture.[23] Proust's metaphorical handling of established legends, fables and fairytales identifies him as the dynamic architect of a corpus of reinvented myths, providing a sharp contrast with, for example, the repetitively sterile or absurdly excessive reciters of La Fontaine's fables that the narrator encounters in the novel.[24] M. de Cambremer provides an ideal illustration of the former, Rachel of the latter. Just as habit impedes a renewed vision of the world, therefore, so, too, can a passive recitation of myth, of the kind typified by M. de Cambremer, be unproductive for the artist. Rachel's recitation at the princesse de Guermantes's party may be more energetic, but the fact that it is ridiculously overdone both exposes her as a travesty of the authentic reinventor of myth and debunks one of the most pervasive modern myths, that of the artist:[25] in the earlier nineteenth century, the myth of the artist was that of an isolated, damned figure, but by the time of Rachel's performance, the myth had evolved to prize avant-gardism above all. As Eliade states, 'the more daring, iconoclastic, absurd, and inaccessible [the artist] is, the more he[/she] will be recognized, praised, spoiled, idolatrized'.[26] An authentically inventive engagement, in contrast, may not only be aesthetically fertile; it may also enable the 'reciter' and his/her material to transcend the specific temporal moment.

## Myth and time: memory and transcendence

A preoccupation with time and the associated concept of memory characterizes a third and final undercurrent in mythical thinking. For Eliade, the dynamic recitation, or reinvention, of myth reconstitutes, and thus makes one contemporary with, the 'strong' time of the original mythical event: 'these ceremonies [. . .] suspend the flow of profane time, of duration, and project the celebrant into a mythical time, *in illo tempore*'.[27] Having emerged out of 'profane, chronological time', one enters 'a "sacred Time" '.[28] Indeed, '[m]erely by listening to a myth', Eliade argues, 'man forgets his profane condition, his "historical situation" as we are accustomed to call it'.[29] Yet this retelling is by no means an eternal and unchanging representation of the same event; it does not equate to cultural immobility. It is, rather, a means of constantly 'conquering the World, organizing it, transforming the landscape of nature into a cultural milieu'.[30] Indeed, it promotes creativity, for in becoming contemporary with a 'strong' past time – which amounts to being confronted with an assurance that certain actions have already been accomplished – individuals may overcome doubts and fears about what *they* have to do. The existence of an exemplary model, in other words, stimulates 'creative innovation', and although retaining its mystery, the world is nonetheless rendered more familiar, intelligible and transparent.[31] The echoes of Proustian metaphor and involuntary memory in this superimposition of past and present moments are also unmistakable, and I shall return to these in the course of this book.

The sources on which Proust draws embody both fruitful and sterile models of mythical re-enactment/retelling. Uncovering unexpected correspondences between polar opposites on the conventional aesthetic hierarchy, correspondences that are reminiscent of Bakhtin's carnivalesque 'suspension of all hierarchical rank, privileges, norms and prohibitions', both Punch and Judy and the Brethren of the Knights of the Grail depicted in Wagner's *Parsifal* dramatize the unproductive appeal of static ritual.[32] The equally unlikely bedfellows of Perrault's fairytales and Wagner's operas are likewise allied in opening up symbolic routes to the attainment of the narrator's quest. As we shall see, Perrault's tales represent just one trigger for the narrator's initiation into an active re-creation and subsequent transmission of myth which leave behind his earlier submission to fairytale enchantment; Wagner's operas similarly propel him forwards, by providing models for the transcendence of profane, chronological time, albeit models which the narrator cannot simply emulate; he must, rather, actively re-create them and thus create himself. As Eliade suggests, though, the availability of exemplars of success may counter the narrator's fear and irresolution when faced with projected action.

In making one contemporary with the primordial mythical event, the recitation – or reinvention – of myth marks a return to origins which, in traditional cosmogony myths and rituals, is also perceived as a means of renewal. If regeneration is to occur, however, the destruction of what has degenerated is necessary. The return to origins is thus inseparable from eschatology myths which embody both the perfection and the certainty of a new beginning at the end of each natural cycle.[33] Proust's own dynamic recitation of myth in metaphor likewise prompts a form of renewal: that is, a renewal of vision both for the reader and, symbolically, for the narrator/protagonist whose development these images chart. For the reader, for example, Proust uncovers the fairytale magic that lies beneath the apparently mundane, while the narrator/protagonist will pass through, and learn from, cycles of experience before he can become creative.[34] These cycles of experience are granted expression through metaphorical cycles reminiscent of those embodied in myth. By way of illustration, the mytho-metaphorical paradigm of his changing attitude towards Mme de Guermantes opens with an ingenuous young narrator/protagonist who perceives only the perfection of the beginnings in his initial apprehension of the woman loved. A degeneration in perception follows as he is gradually released from this state of naive enchantment. Finally, mythical renewal is achieved in the work of the narrator/writer who re-creates these origins in metaphor.

The overarching cyclical movement of Proust's novel thus taps into the foundations of mythical thinking, and this is replicated on the microcosmic level of individual sources. A conspicuous example is offered by Proust's recourse to astrology and the planets as a metaphorical intertext, but on a more symbolic level, sources such as Wagner's *Parsifal* also dramatize a return to origins which brings with it regeneration: the conclusion of the opera leads us full circle as Parsifal returns to the Brethren of the Knights of the Grail after a long absence, but as in *A la recherche*, when the narrator returns to Paris in *Le Temps retrouvé*, everything has changed. In different ways, however, what has degenerated will, in both cases, be renewed.

Proust's handling of fairytale also prompts a very twentieth-century study of origins, for Perrault's narratives are open to a psychoanalytical reading in the context of the narrator's development. For both Freud and Proust, memory marks a return to origins which, as with mythical ritual, may be seen as a form of healing:[35] a release from present suffering, in the case of Freud, ultimately translates, in Proust's universe, into a transcendence of the present moment through (involuntary) memory and its literary correlative, metaphor.[36]

We begin to sense, therefore, that mythical ritual, time, memory and metaphor form a still nebulous bond, but this bond comes into sharper focus if we delve further into the conviction common to many belief systems that ritual abolishes temporal distances between past and present. This concept is especially prevalent in Hindu and Buddhist thought where the dissolution of temporal boundaries aims to relieve humanity of the 'pain of existence in time'.[37]

To be released from the burden of time, one must recollect; indeed, it is through anamnesis that mastery over one's present and future may be attained.[38] This return to origins is sometimes instantaneous – and thus reminiscent of Proustian involuntary memory – and sometimes gradual, as when the detail of past experience is wilfully recalled.[39] But, as Proust's novel illustrates, ultimately a fusion of the two is necessary if one is to transcend time (through the work of art).[40] This is a precarious business, for recollection could so easily have evaded the protagonist. The theme of the narrowly missed fate recurs throughout this study, most notably in the context of fairytale. The interpretation of *Sleeping Beauty*, by theorists such as Bettelheim, as a cautionary tale highlighting the dangers of a prolonged period of (developmental) dormancy, illustrates, by extension, the risks of being distracted from one's true desires or, indeed, the risk of forgetting one's true Self. While these obstacles to self-realization are here explored primarily through fairytale, however, it is surely significant that imagery of binding, chaining, captivity and sleep signifies precisely this same risk in a whole range of mythical traditions.[41] Conversely, images of release and awakening symbolize the realization of one's true identity, the transcendence of the human condition and, ultimately, the promise of redemption.[42] In Buddhist scriptures, this conflict between remembering and forgetting is commonly expressed through the tale of a yogi who falls into oblivion because of the love of a woman whose prisoner, in effect, he becomes.[43] That Proust's metaphorical Sleeping Beauty is Albertine and that the narrator is as much Albertine's prisoner as she is his, only underlines the perceived syncretism in the author's mind of such apparently diverse sources. It further reinforces Proust's challenge to the conventional aesthetic hierarchy: sacred myth and childhood tale coincide.

In teasing out, in this introductory discussion, a number of the common currents in mythical (and Proustian) thinking that unite an apparently eclectic range of sources – the need to understand and create the Self; the desire for communication; and the importance of time and memory – I have touched on specific traditions of mythical thought which will not be addressed in detail in the following analysis, notably eastern religions such as Buddhism. To omit these sources is not to eclipse their importance or relevance to Proust's supernatural vision, but to recognize, rather, that other critics have extended this area of Proust studies with a breadth and depth of insight that cannot be matched in a study which proposes to explore an already extensive – but, in critical terms, neglected – range of fairytales, legends, rituals and beliefs. I shall therefore confine myself to directing the reader to others' work in these areas.[44]

Few of the sources discussed here have been the object of critical attention. Indeed, only Wagner's operas have detained critics for long. Aspects of this interaesthetic relationship to have interested Proust scholars include: the musicality of *A la recherche*, in particular the interweaving of recurrent motifs by both writer and composer;[45] the thematic parallels between Parsifal's and the narrator's quests and, by extension, between Kundry and the women loved in *A la recherche*;[46] and the possibility of redemption both for the narrator-as-Parsifal and for others.[47] Yet the implications of these associations are open to development, as are other aspects of Proust's handling of Wagner such as its comic effects or the consciously cultivated thematic reminiscences of *Tristan and Isolde* that may be detected in Proust's narrative.[48] All the studies alluded to here have, nonetheless, provided illuminating insights into Proust's recourse to Wagner and thus a conceptual springboard for my analysis. Where the discussion that follows differs from existing critical works that touch on these supernatural sources is in its emphasis on such features as the conscious oscillation between literal and metaphorical that characterizes Proust's handling of them; the often unexpected and, at times, humorous manipulations that they undergo when transformed into metaphor; and the aesthetic tensions produced by, for example, Proust's comic or parodic handling of tragic sources, his harnessing of profound metaphysical dramas to the most trivial of contexts. The individual sources discussed here are also viewed as elements within a wider network of 'supernatural' images and references. Such references are diffused throughout the novel in such a way that, on first reading, the interrelatedness of individual occurrences may not be immediately discernible to the reader. Yet Proust's vision of the supernatural has its own coherence and plays a fundamental role in dramatizing the narrator's mythical quest for transcendence and ultimate evolution to creation.[49] To recognize this coherence and deliberateness is not, however, to reduce the rich catholicity of Proust's vision to an easily digestible unity; incongruity, exuberant abundance and a refusal of closure characterize Proust's handling of these sources as much as do pattern and structure, and all find their place within this singularly intricate work, the novelistic embodiment of the dramatist's maxim: 'I am human so nothing human is strange to me.'[50]

This focus on metaphorical transformation, combined with the extended analysis of fairytale in Part I, will doubtless conjure up Claude Vallée's *La Féerie de Marcel Proust* in the reader's mind. Vallée's work undoubtedly provides a suitable lens through which to view the nature and effects of Proustian myth-making, but it follows a different path from the exploration of the world of fairytale here. 'La féerie' is understood, by Vallée, in the sweeping sense of the fairytale-like metamorphoses which Proust generates through metaphor, not in terms of specific fairytale narratives such as the *Mille et Une Nuits* or Perrault's *Contes de ma mère l'oye*. Yet Vallée's observations on the functions and effects of metaphor as a device have been influential. By purifying the objects of comparison of all that does not indicate similarity,[51] by engendering 'des mariages hasardés',[52] by variously reifying, denaturing, distorting, dematerializing and dehumanizing people or objects, metaphor, Vallée argues, enables the communication of sensation, a repoeticization of the habitual, and thus a renewal of vision.[53] This, for Vallée, constitutes Proust's 'féerie'. Indeed, it is metaphor per se, with its Ovidian power of metamorphosis, that creates a sense of mystery and the supernatural, according to Vallée. How much more potent, then, are metaphors of the supernatural.

## Statistical occurrences of myth and the supernatural in *A la recherche du temps perdu*

The reader may well be wondering what statistics can tell us about Proust's vision of the supernatural. How can mathematical analyses enrich literary criticism? And yet, a precise overview of both the distribution of individual sources throughout the novel and the modes of manipulation they undergo enables us to supplement an intuitive sense of the novel's movement with empirical evidence of the transitions and returns that define its mythical structures. The following tables, key features of which are briefly drawn out here, thus pave the way for, and support, the nuanced interpretations offered in later parts of the book.

Before progressing any further, though, a few words are needed on the criteria adopted in generating these tables. Limitations have necessarily been imposed on the scope and boundaries of the sources discussed in the study and counted here: in considering the legendary in Part II, for example, one might wish for an exploration of what assumes the proportions of contemporary legend within the fictional universe of the novel – Odette's bad reputation offers just one instance (*S* I 308) – but to include all such references would distract us from the pivotal theme of the narrator's mythical journey which, culminating as it does in the attainment of the absolute through aesthetic production, should naturally involve the influence of others' aesthetic production. Part II and the statistics relating to it are thus confined to the legends of performance, music and text. Similarly, in Part III, while the category 'spiritualism' draws in all explicit evocations of ghosts and of spiritualist practice, it does not extend to the many hints at a separation of body and spirit that permeate the novel. It includes, rather, only strong suggestions of a spirit's return to the loved one in order to communicate a message. The narrator's note to his mother, which Françoise delivers in the build-up to the 'drame du coucher', represents just such a scenario, for the description of the narrator putting on his 'suaire de chemise de nuit' identifies his dismissal from the table and his mother's presence as a form of death; thus, for this 'spirit', 'mon petit mot allait [. . .] me faire du moins entrer invisible et ravi dans la même pièce qu'elle, allait lui parler de moi à l'oreille' (S I 29–30).

As to the method for calculating total numbers of references, whether literal or metaphorical, if they could stand independently, they were counted individually. This includes the component parts of extended metaphors. Provided they were not simply descriptive extensions of the initial image with no value except via their association with that preceding image, then each was counted. For example, while the following passage forms a coherent extended metaphor, it is, nonetheless, made up of seven component images (identified in italics), each of which could stand meaningfully on its own:

> Toute cette activité vertigineuse se fixait en une calme harmonie. Je regardais les tables rondes dont l'assemblée innombrable emplissait le restaurant, *comme autant de planètes, telles que celles-ci sont figurées dans les tableaux allégoriques d'autrefois* [1]. D'ailleurs, *une force d'attraction irrésistible s'exerçait entre ces astres divers* [2] et à chaque table les dîneurs n'avaient d'yeux que pour les tables où ils n'étaient pas, exception faite pour quelque riche amphitryon, lequel ayant réussi à amener un écrivain célèbre, s'évertuait à tirer de lui, *grâce aux vertus de la table tournante* [3], des propos insignifiants dont les dames s'émerveillaient. L'harmonie de *ces tables astrales n'empêchait pas l'incessante révolution* [4] des servants innombrables, lesquels parce qu'au lieu d'être assis, comme les dîneurs, ils étaient debout, évoluaient dans une zone supérieure [. . .]. Assises derrière un massif de fleurs, deux horribles caissières, occupées à des calculs sans fin, *semblaient deux magiciennes* [5] occupées à prévoir *par des calculs astrologiques* [6] les bouleversements qui pouvaient parfois se produire *dans cette voûte céleste* [7] conçue selon la science du Moyen Âge. (*JF* II 167–8)

Seven images are thus counted.[54] In contrast, the phrase 'ces tables astrales n'empêchait pas l'incessante révolution [. . .]' constitutes only one image, despite its two metaphorical components, for without the presence of 'tables astrales', the image of a 'révolution' would lose much of its metaphorical value: it is merely a descriptive extension of the initial image. Direct repetitions *are* counted, however, on the grounds that they point to a conscious intensification of the original image on Proust's part. Talking to his grandmother on the telephone from Doncières, for example, the narrator describes how, 'quand j'amenai à moi le récepteur, ce morceau de bois se mit à parler comme Polichinelle; je le fis taire, ainsi qu'au guignol, en le remettant à sa place, mais, comme Polichinelle, dès que je le ramenais près de moi, il recommençait son bavardage' (*G* II 432–3). While the sentence and metaphorical association on which it is constructed would be entirely comprehensible without the repetition of 'comme Polichinelle', Proust's reiteration of the phrase conveys the frustratingly inescapable chatter to which the narrator is repeatedly subject on picking up the receiver. Having its own individual function, therefore, the repetition is counted separately.

Loosely evocative terms such as 'apparition', 'transformation' or 'métamorphose' are included only where the context indicates a strong supernatural character.[55] The same criterion is applied in relation to occurrences of 'charme', 'charmer', 'enchantement', 'enchanter' and their derivatives.[56] Given the frequency with which these terms appear in the novel – in many cases characterized by a meaning that is more social than magical – to include all would be to inflate artificially the patterns of distribution discussed here.[57] Nonetheless, the oscillation between worldly and supernatural in the handling of these terms is integral to the narrator's encounter with fairytale.[58] For this reason, social uses of the terms will also be addressed in the relevant section of the study. In contrast, every literal mention of the composers or writers who occupy us here is counted. This principle extends to their works as well as to other key narratives such as the *Mille et Une Nuits*.

Categorization by source can itself present challenges. A term such as 'surnaturel', for example, or a character's metaphorical incarnation as 'fée' or 'génie' could find a home within a number of categories. The following principles are thus applied: 'surnaturel' is classified according to the context in which the reference appears, as are ambiguous evocations of magic,[59] while 'génie' and 'fée' are associated with the narratives in which they most commonly appear: the 'génie' is situated in the world of the *Mille et Une Nuits*, therefore, and as the 'fée', whether good or bad, tends to exert her influence within Perrault's fairytales, it is here that she is included. With the exception of these potentially ambiguous terms, only explicit references to the two precursor texts appear in these categories.

Table 1 provides a comprehensive tally of all supernatural references to appear in *A la recherche*, according to the broad sources into which this study is divided. It includes both literal allusions and figures of speech. As is immediately evident, the worlds of both magic and fairytale, and rituals and beliefs are represented in significant numbers. The pervasive presence of magic and fairytale only confirms the atmosphere of mystery and fantasy that characterizes perception in the novel, whether the genuine enchantment of the young narrator/protagonist or the stylistic spells woven by the mature narrator/writer. Perhaps more surprising is the numerical challenge posed to the realm of magic and fairytale by the rituals and beliefs at the centre of such metaphysical 'systems' as spiritualism, superstition or the occult. Given the varying emphases

**Table 1 Distribution by general source**

|  | I: Magic and fairytale | II: Artistic legends | III: Rituals and beliefs |
|---|---|---|---|
| A la recherche | 333 | 116 | 313 |

of these latter on ill omens, bad luck and death, however, their currency within the novel only underscores the extent to which Proust's vision is dark as much as it is light. Furthermore, as the breakdown of sources by volume in Table 2 illustrates, this numerical near-coincidence in representation between the sources discussed in Parts I and III of the study is matched by a comparable distribution throughout the volumes. With a few notable exceptions, broadly similar rises and falls chart our progress through each volume, and magic and fairytale assert as strong a presence in the final volume of the novel as rituals and beliefs.

We can already see, therefore, that our intuitive perception of the movement of the novel in terms of a straightforward progression from *mythos* to *logos* is open to question. Albeit to different effect, magic, ritual and belief are woven into the culmination of the narrator's evolution no less than they defined the beginning of his journey. The conspicuous departure from this pattern of comparability is the considerable number of references to rituals and beliefs in *Albertine disparue* (thirty-three) in comparison with the number of 'Magic and fairytale' allusions (only fourteen). As later tables show, this is explained by the substantial proportion of literal allusions to spiritualism in what is a relatively non-metaphorical volume; indeed, the complete absence of legendary figures in this volume reinforces its static nature, for if the legends of performance and text represent stages on the narrator's quest and potential models for

**Table 2 Distribution by general source, by volume**

|  | I: Magic and fairytale | II: Artistic legends | III: Rituals and beliefs |
|---|---|---|---|
| S | 35 | 2 | 40 |
| JF | 50 | 1 | 41 |
| G | 79 | 23 | 67 |
| SG | 53 | 33 | 43 |
| P | 38 | 31 | 42 |
| AD | 14 | – | 33 |
| TR | 64 | 26 | 47 |

emulation and/or 'traps' of imitation, then their omission here signals the provisional halt to the narrator's journey in the face of bereavement. If this is the case, though, why should *La Prisonnière* – also a static volume in terms of the narrator's development – include a relatively large proportion of legends drawn from the worlds of performance, music and text? As revealed in Table 3, however, twenty-three of the thirty references counted are to Wagner or his works and the remaining seven to *Pelléas et Mélisande*. Moreover, all the allusions to Wagner are literal, rather than metaphorical, as are two of those to *Pelléas et Mélisande*. This predominance of literal references to the music that the narrator hears being performed may reflect his lack of engagement with his quest. However, a more productive interpretation would point to an absorption of aesthetic ideas and influence that gradually enables his active and independent evaluation of Vinteuil's work – via Wagner's *Tristan and Isolde* – in this volume.[60] Although this evaluation may not, in *La Prisonnière*, be connected, in the narrator's mind, with his own future status as 'creator', it nonetheless marks an evolution which is initially put on hold, but ultimately advanced, by the processes of grief in *Albertine disparue*.

Table 2 is also marked by a paucity of references to artistic legends in both *Du côté de chez Swann* and *A l'ombre des jeunes filles en fleurs* (two and one respectively). Yet this chimes with the sheltered life of a young narrator whose exemplary models are, at this stage, limited to the restrictingly specific at one end of the spectrum, in the form of individual figures such as Bergotte, or the impenetrably monolithic, in the form of 'the Artist', at the other. This is a narrator imbued with the strains of magical thinking, and while a significant rise in the number of legendary figures can be detected by *Le Côté de Guermantes*, over a third of these, as Table 3 reveals, are allusions to puppet theatre which serve to highlight the static rituals of social interaction. They are thus not incompatible with the provisional identity of a narrator distracted from his quest by social preoccupations. Indeed, the abundance of evocations of magic and fairytale in this volume attests to the narrator's state of enchantment, even entrancement.

The narrator is progressively released from this enchantment through a process of disillusionment which is well underway even in the later parts of the novel's primary volume of idealization of the social world, *Le Côté de Guermantes*; and yet, general evocations of magic and fairytale re-emerge in significant numbers in *Le Temps retrouvé*. Despite surface similarities, however, these differ from those appearing in earlier volumes, acquiring subtle new inflections which distance the narrator/protagonist from his earlier self. Re-evaluative returns to his own ingenuous state of enchantment are common, for example;[61] and widening further the gulf between present self and earlier

**Table 3 Distribution by individual source, by volume**

| | I: Magic and fairytale[62] | | | II: Artistic legends | | | | | | III: Rituals and beliefs | | | |
|---|---|---|---|---|---|---|---|---|---|---|---|---|---|
| | Perr. | 1001 | Gen. | P/J | F | T/I | P | Wag. | P/M | S/S | Sp. | Div. | Mg. |
| **S** | 7 | 9 | 19 | 1 | 1 | — | — | — | — | 11 | 18 | 1 | 10 |
| **JF** | 4 | 17 | 29 | — | — | — | 1 | — | — | 7 | 10 | 16 | 8 |
| **G** | 24 | 24 | 31 | 8 | 4 | 1 | 4 | 6 | — | 2 | 20 | 34 | 11 |
| **SG** | 22 | 6 | 25 | 1 | 6 | 1 | 2 | 9 | 14 | — | 22 | 13 | 8 |
| **P** | 6 | 12 | 20 | — | 1 | 6 | 1 | 16 | 7 | 1 | 13 | 18 | 10 |
| **AD** | 2 | 9 | 3 | — | — | — | — | — | — | 2 | 12 | 10 | 9 |
| **TR** | 8 | 18 | 38 | 6 | 12 | — | — | 8 | — | 5 | 11 | 24 | 7 |

**Key to sources**
Perr. = Perrault; *1001* = *Mille et Une Nuits*; Gen. = fairytale (general); P/J = Punch & Judy/puppetry; F = La Fontaine; T/I = *Tristan and Isolde*; P = *Parsifal*; Wag. = Wagner (general); P/M = *Pelléas et Mélisande*; S/S = Superstition; Sp. = spiritualism; Div. = Divination, destiny and the planets; Mg. = Magic and the occult

magical thinking, both we and the narrator are witness to other characters' submission to enchantment.[63] Ironic reinventions of magical sources – discussed in Part I in terms of the 'feigned supernatural' – are also prominent, while Proust's evocation of the 'apparently supernatural' enables us to enjoy such experiences as the power of involuntary memory in terms of a magical transportation into another time,[64] or the surprise of the narrator at the seemingly abrupt arrival of old age at the 'bal costumé'.[65] Through these images, therefore, the mature narrator/protagonist defines his present self in opposition both to his past self and to others, while the narrator/writer exploits the literary potential of these images as a means to renew vision.

The distribution throughout the novel of other mythical paradigms similarly reflects the culmination of the narrator's self-creation in *Le Temps retrouvé*. A relative profusion of references to superstitious belief in the first two volumes is dictated by the superstitious women who inhabit them, notably Odette, and by their lovers' superstitions surrounding their sexual (mis)conduct.[66] Yet if such amorous preoccupations have faded by the final volume, to what do we attribute their renewed presence in this context? A careful scrutiny of the seemingly divergent evocations of superstition in *Le Temps retrouvé* uncovers a unifying strand: Elstir is the only person to grieve for M. Verdurin because of his superstitious attachment to his models (*TR* IV 349); Mme de Guermantes maintains a superstitious loyalty to traditional codes of etiquette and to 'les liens du sang' (*TR* IV 430); it is these that the narrator imagines will dictate the nature of her grief over Saint-Loup's death; finally, people of Mme de Guermantes's long acquaintance remain superstitiously attached to the conviction that she is witty just as they do to a favourite baker (*TR* IV 582). What all of these allusions to superstitious belief embody is a largely irrational attachment to the past and a likely or actual failure to rethink or re-evaluate on the basis of present realities and experience. They therefore offer a fitting counterpoint to the now developed narrator, for although superstitious belief is also attributed to him in this last volume, it is the superstition itself, and with it earlier patterns of behaviour and thinking, that are consigned to the past:

> Non pas que je prétendisse refaire, en quoi que ce fût, *Les Mille et Une Nuits*, pas plus que les *Mémoires* de Saint-Simon, écrits eux aussi la nuit, pas plus qu'aucun des livres que j'avais aimés dans ma naïveté d'enfant, superstitieusement attaché à eux comme à mes amours [. . .]. (*TR* IV 620)[67]

The pattern of allusions to Wagner and Debussy appears to invert this paradigm of sustained re-emergence in *Le Temps retrouvé*: while repeated exposure to these composers' works through both performances and conversation intensifies their presence in the predominantly social volume of *Sodome et Gomorrhe*, this largely 'surrogate' appreciation is displaced by the development of the narrator's own aesthetic opinions on both Wagner's and Debussy's work in *La Prisonnière* and by a typically static, but nonetheless necessary, period of dormancy in *Albertine disparue*.[68] Such references are then notably absent from *Le Temps retrouvé*. Indeed, the majority of evocations of Wagner, the only artistic legend to appear in this final volume, feature in the words of Saint-Loup, not of the narrator. Their absence here thus consciously reinforces the realization that transcendence cannot be achieved by means of a vicarious quest.

Finally, the interpretation of *Albertine disparue* as a period of developmental, and thus metaphorical, dormancy appears to be belied by the relatively frequent appearance of the *Mille et Une Nuits* in this volume (nine references in comparison to two images from Perrault and three general magic/fairytale references).[69] Of the nine, however, two are to the 'Sésame', the words or phrases that release the flood of painful memories and suspicions relating to Albertine. They therefore represent a dark subversion of the source in which the 'Sésame' releases not treasure, but pain. The remaining images describe the narrator's experiences in Venice and these, too, in keeping with the mood of this part of the text, are granted a more sinister accent than in other volumes of the novel. Venice has become a locus of disorientation where, at the hands of a 'mauvais génie' (*AD* IV 230), the narrator is unable to find his way, unable to 'possess' the city as he was unable to 'possess' Albertine. Indeed, with its evocations of streets that rise up unexpectedly, of unnamed women resembling

**Table 4 Distribution of literal (L) and metaphorical (M) references, by source and volume**

| | I: Magic and fairytale | | | | | | II: Artistic legends | | | | | | | | | | | | III: Rituals and beliefs | | | | | | | |
|---|---|---|---|---|---|---|---|---|---|---|---|---|---|---|---|---|---|---|---|---|---|---|---|---|---|---|
| | Perr. | | 1001 | | Gen. | | P/J | | F | | T/I | | P | | Wag. | | P/M | | S/S | | Sp. | | Div. | | Mg. | |
| | L | M | L | M | L | M | L | M | L | M | L | M | L | M | L | M | L | M | L | M | L | M | L | M | L | M |
| S | – | 7 | 4 | 5 | – | 19 | 1 | – | – | – | – | 1 | – | – | – | – | – | – | 10 | 1 | – | 18 | – | 1 | – | 10 |
| JF | – | – | 4 | 12 | – | 29 | – | – | – | – | – | – | – | 1 | – | – | – | – | 7 | – | 2 | 8 | – | 16 | – | 8 |
| G | – | 24 | 5 | 24 | – | 31 | – | – | 8 | 2 | 2 | 1 | – | 4 | 3 | 3 | – | – | 2 | – | 2 | 18 | 3 | 31 | – | 11 |
| SG | – | 22 | 2 | 6 | – | 25 | – | 1 | – | 4 | 2 | – | 2 | 1 | 6 | 3 | 14 | – | – | – | 5 | 17 | 6 | 7 | 1 | 7 |
| P | – | – | 6 | 10 | – | 20 | – | – | – | – | 1 | 6 | 1 | – | 16 | – | 2 | 5 | 1 | – | 1 | 12 | 4 | 14 | – | 10 |
| AD | – | 2 | – | 9 | – | 3 | – | – | – | – | – | – | – | – | – | – | – | – | 2 | – | 11 | 1 | 5 | 5 | 2 | 7 |
| TR | – | 8 | 2 | 16 | – | 38 | – | 6 | 11 | 1 | – | – | – | – | 3 | 5 | – | – | 3 | 2 | 1 | 10 | 2 | 22 | 1 | 6 |

**Key to sources**

Perr. = Perrault; *1001* = *Mille et Une Nuits*; Gen. = fairytale (general); P/J = Punch & Judy/puppetry; F = La Fontaine; T/I = *Tristan and Isolde*; P = *Parsifal*; Wag. = Wagner (general); P/M = *Pelléas et Mélisande*; S/S = Superstition; Sp. = spiritualism; Div. = Divination, destiny and the planets; Mg. = Magic and the occult

**Table 4a Distribution of literal and metaphorical references, by volume**

|    | Literal | Metaphorical |
|----|---------|--------------|
| S  | 15      | 62           |
| JF | 14      | 78           |
| G  | 13      | 156          |
| SG | 44      | 85           |
| P  | 33      | 78           |
| AD | 20      | 27           |
| TR | 23      | 114          |

witches who are glimpsed in the light of a window on a dark night, the emphasis of the volume is on the unknown and, by extension, the unknowable.

As one might expect, and as Tables 4 and 4a confirm, the ratio of metaphorical to literal references consistently favours the former and, indeed, that ratio is itself broadly similar in each of the volumes. Yet there are a few salient exceptions. In *Le Côté de Guermantes*, for example, a disproportionately high number of metaphorical figures appear, but, as we have seen, this is the prime volume of illusion and wilful myth-making; as if to reinforce this, metaphorical references in this volume are predominantly unmediated.[70] *La Prisonnière* also stands out on account of the relatively large proportion of literal allusions to figure in it, yet this is surely attributable to the repeated introduction of Wagner and Debussy, the importance of which I have already suggested. Finally, we note that, in *Albertine disparue*, the numbers of literal and metaphorical allusions are atypically similar, departing from the ratio of five or six metaphorical references to every literal reference in most other volumes.[71] All the literal examples in this penultimate volume are, in addition, drawn from the sources explored in Part III. The effect of such a distribution is in keeping with the movement of the novel, however, underlining the fact that this volume is dominated, not by a metaphorical quest for transcendence, but by a literal search for strategies to cope with grief and with the sense of impotence generated by the narrator's ongoing suspicion surrounding Albertine's sexual identity.

The final table (Table 5) reveals which of the characters, other than the narrator, have recourse to myth, whether in the form of literal allusions or metaphorical rewritings. These are negligible in number, and yet noteworthy features emerge. Charlus, for example, is the most prominent 'myth-maker' in the novel apart, of course, from the narrator/writer himself. Moreover, none of his manipulations of supernatural sources is literal, underlining Charlus's

**Table 5 Distribution of references (both literal and metaphorical) voiced other than by the narrator**

|  | S | JF | G | SG | P | AD | TR |
|---|---|---|---|---|---|---|---|
| Berg. | – | Div. (1) | – | – | – | – | – |
| Brich. | – | – | – | Sp. (1) | Div. (1)/ | – | Gen. (1) |
|  | – | – | – | – | Perr. (1)/ | – | – |
|  | – | – | – | – | Mg. (2) | – | – |
| M. de C. | – | – | – | F (2) | – | – | – |
| Mme de C. | – | – | – | – | P/M (1)/ | – | – |
|  | – | – | – | – | P (1)/ | – | – |
|  | – | – | – | – | F (1) | – | – |
| Ch. | – | – | 1001 (5) | 1001 (1)/ | Mg. (1)/ | – | Gen. (1) |
|  | – | – | – | Sp (1) | Perr. (1)/ | – | – |
|  | – | – | – | – | Gen. (1) | – | – |
| Elst. | Mg. (1) | – | – | – | – | – | – |
| Fr. | – | – | – | – | Perr. (1) | – | – |
| Gon. | – | – | – | – | – | – | F (1)/ |
|  | – | – | – | – | – | – | 1001 (1) |
| Leg. | Gen. (1) | – | F (1) | – | – | – | – |
| Od. | F (1) | – | – | – | – | – | – |
| Or. | – | – | Gen. (1)/ | – | Sp. (1) | – | Gen. (1) |
|  | – | – | Perr. (1)/ | – | – | – | – |
|  | – | – | Wag. (4) | – | – | – | – |
| SL | – | – | Div. (1)/ | – | – | – | Wag. (4) |
|  | – | – | Wag. (1) | – | – | – | – |
| Mme V. | – | – | – | Mg. (1) | – | – | – |
| Mme de V. | – | Mg. (1) | – | – | – | – | – |
| Other | Sp. (1) | – | Perr. (1)/ | P/M (1)/ | – | – | – |
|  | – | – | F (1) | Sp. (1)/ | – | – | – |
|  | – | – | – | Mg. (1) | – | – | – |

Note: The number of occurrences of each source is provided in brackets. 'Other' includes references by minor characters such as the comtesse de Monteriender, the Ambassadress of Turkey, the historian of the Fronde, the Scandinavian with imperfect French and Mme Cottard.

**Key to characters**
Berg. = Bergotte; Brich. = Brichot; M. de C. = M. de Cambremer; Mme de C. = Mme de Cambremer; Ch. = Charlus; Elst. = Elstir; Fr. = Françoise; Gon. = the Goncourt brothers; Leg. = Legrandin; Od. = Odette; Or. = Oriane; SL = Saint-Loup; Mme V. = Mme Verdurin; Mme de V. = Mme de Villeparisis

aesthetic invention and potential creativity. In contrast, the supposedly aesthetically sensitive Mme de Cambremer's recourse to myth – in the form of artistic legends – reveals a distinct lack of invention, for her references to operatic works are, without exception, literal. Ironically, her husband, who defers to his wife's intellectual superiority, is the one who betrays a level of creativity, for he at least uses his favoured source, La Fontaine, metaphorically.[72] To return to Charlus, it is also, of course, significant that more than half of his evocations of the supernatural are inspired by the *Mille et Une Nuits* (six out of eleven), an exotic world associated in western perception with the erotic. That the majority of these images are unmediated (five out of six) further casts him in the role of wilful fantasist. Saint-Loup's choice of metaphorical source is equally evocative in the context of his sexuality. His outspoken admiration of Wagner during the war in itself situates him in the counter-current to accepted tastes, and his dramatization of the air battles over Paris as a 'Ride of the Valkyries' – for *The Valkyrie* is the opera to which Saint-Loup repeatedly refers – embodies an ideal of female virility which seems to prefigure the narrator's understanding, and encapsulate Proust's creation, of Saint-Loup's sexuality.

The narrator/protagonist of *A la recherche* is on a mythical and supernatural quest, just as the narrator as would-be writer has embarked on a literary quest that leads him, through experimentation, to a carnivalesque syncretism of form and style. Many archetypes are encountered on his journey, and in negotiating a path through them, Proust fuses high and low art, *populaire* and *savant*, music and text. Laurence Coupe's perspective on the re-creation of myth evokes Proust's own project. Coupe proposes that:

> The very act of remembering, and re-creating [myths] in secular, aesthetic terms [is] an act of emancipation: not in the Enlightenment sense of rational progress, but in a new spirit of 'ludic imagining'. [It] is an ethics of 'otherness' [. . .] meant in a triple sense. Firstly, the myth recalls and projects an 'other' world. Secondly, the myth reminds us that there is always something else, something 'other', to be said or imagined. Thirdly, the myth, as a play of past paradigm and future possibility, gives expression to the 'other', to those persons and causes excluded from the present hierarchy. Thus we might come to understand myth, 'fragile' as it is, as a disclosure rather than a dogma: as a narrative whose potential always evades the given order, with its illusion of truth. Though we will continue to be 'rotten with perfection', in Burke's phrase, we may come to see that it is the task of myth constantly to imply, but always to resist, completion. Myth might then be appreciated as that narrative mode of understanding which involves a continuing dialectic of same and other, of memory and desire, of ideology and utopia, of hierarchy and horizon, and of sacred and profane.[73]

Coupe's analysis signals a progressive release from both existing models of transcendence and existing models of writing, not least, as we shall see in the course of this study, through aesthetic synthesis. It is this release from the vicarious path that frees the narrator/protagonist to become a creator, and an often ludic reinventor, of myth, and it is this independent creator who will uncover new ways of thinking, who will challenge conventional perspectives, and who will, thus, open up creative possibilities for the reader. The narrator as reader of myth becomes a writer of myth whose narrative may be read and potentially reinvented in turn. Reflecting the myth of the Eternal Return, in other words, mythography leads to mythopoeia for the narrator, ultimately, and ideally, stimulating the cycle's recurrence in the reader.

# I
# MAGIC AND FAIRYTALE

### Introduction: the novel as fairytale

*A la recherche du temps perdu* is a novel of fairytale and enchantment, rich in marvels, mystery and surprise. To mention the Proustian fairytale is to conjure up such well-known images as Mme de Guermantes's fairy status, the 'demeure enchanté' inhabited by the Swanns (*JF* I 501) or the supernatural exoticism of the *Mille et Une Nuits*. In essence, it conjures up the 'enchantements d'imagination' (*JF* II 93) which have the power to endow people or experiences with a 'magie illusoire' (*TR* IV 301) or to repoeticize an everyday reality that habit has rendered stale.[1] But the fairytale structure of *A la recherche* extends far beyond these familiar tropes: not only is the text suffused with general evocations of the 'fantastique', the 'surnaturel' and the startling 'apparitions' which both delight and terrify,[2] but some of the most celebrated fairytales from East and West – fairytales that have entered the European cultural consciousness – sustain and stimulate the main thematic paradigms of the novel. Turning eastward, such figures as 'Ali-Baba', 'Zobéide' and 'le Dormeur éveillé' emerge from the *Mille et Une Nuits* to enter the pages of *A la recherche*, while Proust needed to look no further than France itself for 'le Petit Chaperon rouge', 'Grisélidis', 'le Chat botté', 'la Barbe-Bleue', 'la Belle au bois dormant' and, last but not least, 'le Petit Poucet'. On a subtextual level, too, the attentive reader may detect, in Proust's text, such enchanted narratives as Perrault's *Cendrillon* or *Riquet à la houppe*. These potently symbolic fairytales both enrich and transcend the immediate contexts in which they are evoked, creating a metaphorical undercurrent which contributes to the broader movement of the novel as a whole; for as one noted theorist of the fairytale, Max Lüthe, has argued, despite the many conceivable interpretations of individual tales, what is common to all, as in Proust's novel, is a quest for the absolute:

What is shown directly [. . .], obvious to every eye, is the fascination with the beautiful, the longing for the ultimate degree in beauty, for the absolute. It is likewise indisputable that, in contrast to this absolute, this superlative beauty, there is something ugly, a distorted form which at times pushes the beautiful aside and takes its place [. . .]. The king (in other versions, the prince), whom we can look upon as the representative of mankind in general, is confronted with the polarity between matchless value and absolute worthlessness. He strives for the one, but, at least temporarily, cannot get away from the other.[3]

The longed-for absolute, in Proust, is an aesthetic-cum-spiritual one which, like the fairytale hero, the narrator will tread an arduous path to attain. Indeed, Lüthe's evocation of polarity mirrors the coexistence of the sublime and the trivial, the lofty and the base, the simultaneous pull of the mundane and the ideal (whether genuine or imagined) which is intrinsic to *A la recherche*.

These oppositions and frustrations, as experienced by both the narrator and other characters, are encapsulated in Lüthe's analysis of the structure of the fairytale which, he argues, is 'characterized by the basic *framing tension* (*Rahmen-Spannung*) Lack/Striving for remedy, behind which stands the pattern Happiness/Disturbance/Happiness restored' (p. 56). Within *A la recherche*, the fundamental 'Lack/Striving for remedy' tension is clearly reflected in all the narrator's social, amorous and aesthetic endeavours, while the 'Happiness/Disturbance/Happiness restored' schema marks the novel's overarching transition from the narrator's childhood contentment in Combray to the intense pleasures of involuntary memory and the realization of his vocation in *Le Temps retrouvé*. Of course, neither of these states of happiness is unequivocal for the narrator, as Lüthe's neatly formulated paradigm may suggest;[4] and despite the novel's circular structure, its culmination does not mark a *return* to the narrator's childhood happiness. Echoing Eliade's theories, the cyclical return to the past in the form of a recitation or re-enactment of myth(ical events) should be dynamic and creative, not passively repetitive.[5] Like the fairytale hero, therefore, the narrator will undergo trials, overcome obstacles and evolve as a result of these experiences.

Within this global framing tension, Lüthe identifies a variety of 'linking tensions' which generate the narrative movement and instigate the protagonist's development. Among these tensions figure such oppositions as:

Beautiful and ugly, good and bad, success and failure, helplessness/perplexity and successful outcome, emergency and rescue, enchantment and disenchantment, reward and punishment, gold and pitch, death and resuscitation, appearance and reality, high and low, magnificent and dirty, small and large, real and unreal. (p. 95)

In Proust, such polarities as good and bad, beautiful and ugly, magnificent and dirty, even real and unreal, are commonly embodied in a single figure, creating a mode of characterization based on an authentic inconsistency.[6] Such psychological paradoxes lie at the heart of Jung's analysis of fairytale which argues that different characters in the tale represent different aspects of an individual psyche: to externalize the contradictory impulses of the id, ego or superego in the form of a literal duality (or, indeed, multiplicity) of character is, for Jung, to create a forum in which to resolve psychological conflict;[7] and, indeed, the recurrence of twins in Perrault's and others' fairytales only reinforces this idea of a coexistent sameness and difference.[8] We shall see, in the following section, how Proust's handling of fairytale reflects Jung's theories, for he frequently aligns the narrator with a variety of (seemingly opposing) fairytale characters. We should not forget, however, that opposites may also coincide in a single person in fairytale. As in the case of the servant girl who is, in fact, a princess,[9] the genre is built on unexpected revelations which chime with the images of duality and disguise underpinning Proust's presentation of key themes in the novel.

Of all the linking tensions which characterize fairytale as a genre, Lüthe argues that the conflict between appearance and reality predominates and that this conflict tends to centre on the 'unpromising', a category within which three main groupings stand out: unpromising heroes and heroines; unpromising helpers; and unpromising things (p. 125). Thus, for example, the neglected stepdaughter, Cinderella, is the unlikely bride for the prince, while the diminutive, and therefore underestimated, Tom Thumb outwits all adversaries. The tension between appearance and reality is, of course, a familiar theme in Proust, but less familiar is its conceptualization in terms of the 'unpromising'. An analysis of the fairytale structure of the novel thus opens up new perspectives on this persistent dynamic. That Proust introduces a fairytale image to describe one of his unpromising artists – the sporting friend of the 'jeunes filles' – also hints at his keen awareness of the recurrent structures that characterize the genre and anticipates the work of later theorists of the fairytale: once a 'brute épaisse', the narrator wonders whether some 'cataclysme physiologique avait éveillé en lui le génie assoupi comme la Belle au bois dormant' (*AD* IV 185). Vinteuil, believed by Swann to be a 'vieille bête', provides a further illustration of the unlikely creator;[10] and if we recall that among the 'unpromising things' which typify fairytale for Lüthe are apparently unaccomplishable tasks, then the narrator himself becomes the archetypal unpromising artist whose ambition to create appears doomed to failure.

Although a fundamental manifestation of it, the conflict between appearance and reality in both fairytale and *A la recherche* also extends beyond the unpromising. As Lüthe proposes:

> The cardinal theme of the conflict between appearance and reality is reflected in the change of situations, conditions of existence, and forms of appearance into radically different ones, changes presented in the form of sudden transformations, enchantments and disenchantments, and also in the rising and falling of personal fortunes, in the shift from poverty to riches, or from servant status to kingdom, and in many another. (p. 133)

In such varied forms as the narrator's evolving perceptions, the revolution in the social status of Mme Verdurin and Odette, or the physical changes wrought by time as starkly laid bare at the 'bal costumé', Proust's novel offers a strikingly apt illustration of Lüthe's taxonomy of the fairytale. Conversely, the appropriateness of this source to Proust's own vision of the evolutions, at times potential, at times inevitable, that Self, Other or social collective may undergo is also underlined. As Marina Warner colourfully argues, with an eclecticism that only substantiates the commonality of mythical structures across cultures and epochs:

> Shape-shifting is one of fairy tale's dominant and characteristic wonders: hands are cut off, found and reattached, babies' throats are slit, but they are later restored to life, a rusty lamp turns into an all-powerful talisman, a humble pestle and mortar becomes the winged vehicle of the airy enchantress Baba Yaga, the beggar changes into the powerful enchantress and the slattern in the filthy donkeyskin into a golden-haired princess. More so than the presence of fairies, the moral function, the imagined antiquity and oral anonymity of the ultimate source, and the happy ending (though all these factors help towards a definition of the genre), metamorphosis defines the fairy tale.[11]

As the preceding analysis has shown, fairytale offers a fitting metaphorical paradigm for the narrator's search for the absolute and for the oppositions he will gradually resolve in order to attain that goal, but to what extent does the fairytale hero provide an interpretative template for the narrator himself? Often an only child, the youngest child or a stepchild, the fairytale hero is an isolated figure. This position of isolation grants him a special status (whether positive or negative) and may also imply an ability to 'detach' himself from the home, either because of family conflict or in order to perform a task. The fairytale hero is further isolated, as Lüthe argues, in that he 'does not know what means he can use to overcome the difficulties which he encounters'.[12] Indeed,

> the fairytale hero, even if he is a dragon-slayer, is time and again shown as one in need of help, often as one who is helpless, who sits down on the ground and weeps because he has no idea what to do. The fairytale hero is a deficient creature. He has no specific abilities; unlike the animals, which have inborn instincts, he is not equipped by nature for special tasks.[13]

Proust certainly chooses to give his narrator no siblings. Both this and his Romantic hypersensitivity endow him with a 'special' status, but that status is double-edged: the narrator is cherished by mother and grandmother (and, in this regard, is not the typically 'detachable' hero), but his nervous disposition engenders an attitude of indulgence which isolates him from the conventional path and expectations exemplified by his father. As for the characterization of the fairytale hero as a helpless and deficient creature, this is the identity that the young narrator/protagonist, who believes he is in need of help to appreciate the aesthetic and who believes he does not possess the abilities required for the literary vocation, assumes for himself. But, as Eliade points out, fairytale possesses an unmistakeable 'structure initiatique'; thus, 'le conte reprend et prolonge l'"initiation" au niveau de l'imaginaire'.[14] Only by undergoing this initiation, with all its tests, its 'luttes contre le monstre, obstacles en apparence insurmontables, énigmes à résoudre, travaux impossibles à accomplir', will the fairytale protagonist develop into a fairytale hero ('Les Savants', p. 891). For Lüthe too, initiation is intrinsic to the human condition, and adversaries and antagonists are thus necessary stimuli to 'development, self-realization, and the actualization of possibilities'.[15]

This path of initiation marks the fairytale hero out as a 'creature of detours'. Not only does s/he act in opposition to expectations, but the fairytale hero also transgresses boundaries and opens forbidden doors; s/he changes direction and follows diversions which symbolize the processes of development and change and thus signpost the hero's progression. Such active engagement with the external world may justify Lüthe's description of the fairytale hero as 'a traveler, a doer', rather than 'a ponderer, an investigator, or a philosopher' (p. 141); yet the distinction between these two identities is more fluid in Proust's narrative where we detect a productive and ever-changing interplay of the two. The young narrator's intellect, for instance, unhappily distinguishes him (in his view) from the *jeune filles*' seemingly instinctive existence, as ponderer envies (the perceived pleasures of the) doer.[16] The later narrator, in contrast, laments his status as a doer rather than a ponderer – frivolous 'socialite' versus the revered artist. In reality, of course, even the socialite is a ponderer, absorbing and analysing what he witnesses and experiences, and ultimately providing the material for the work of art.

Vallée describes Proust's novel as 'une littérature magique', explaining how: '[e]lle choque la raison, trouble l'entendement, dérègle l'homme et tient la porte ouverte aux Génies. Le texte de Proust est comme l'atelier d'Elstir "le laboratoire d'une sorte de nouvelle création du monde"' (p. 61). This, he argues, is achieved by the fairytale-like metamorphoses which Proust generates through metaphor. And yet, the literal world of fairytale also resonates throughout

*A la recherche*, ranging from explicit re-creations of individual tales to faint, but persistent, traces of others. As we have seen, the recurring structures and characteristics of the genre can also be overlaid on to the broader narrative movement of Proust's novel: both embody the pursuit for an absolute, both are built on tensions and oppositions, and, in both, fulfilment is achieved through the overcoming of obstacles and trials. Moreover, the successful execution of these trials entails a progression towards self-realization for the isolated, self-doubting hero. For Eliade and, indeed, for Proust, fairytales externalize archetypal human experiences and dilemmas.

Yet this is no simple imitation of the structures of fairytale, as Proust's blending of identities which Lüthe is careful to separate ('doer' and 'ponderer') has already hinted. Proust's is, rather, a dynamic reinvention of the genre which, above all, explores the nature of social, sexual and aesthetic desire. The three sections that follow explore the various permutations of Proust's re-creation of this source. The first, focusing on Perrault's narratives, draws on interpretations of fairytale elaborated by developmental psychologists in order to illustrate, among other conclusions, how Proust debunks the idealized popular image and familiar trope of the 'fairytale romance'. This symbolic reading also reveals how obsessive *sexual* desire equates to stasis and negates the possibility of achieving the object of the narrator's *aesthetic* desire. The second section, '*Les Mille et Une Nuits* proustiennes', charts the processes of the narrator's evolution, the necessity of which was perceived on a symbolic level through the western tales analysed in the first section. Social and aesthetic desire here intermingle with the narrator's enforced confrontation with homosexual and lesbian desire. Proust's handling of the *Mille et Une Nuits* is further distinguished from that of Perrault's fairytales in that the former is not only an extradiegetical source of metaphor, but also an intradiegetical trigger that propels the narrator along the path to self-realization as artist. As the (re-)creation of the writer, in contrast, Perrault's tales remain largely outside the 'action'. The final section turns to the culmination of this evolution. In exploring the 'Magical mundane', we perceive a familiar reality through new eyes, the embodiment of the narrator-as-writer's aesthetic doctrine in metaphor.

## Fairytale romances

*Beauty and the Beast, Cinderella, Sleeping Beauty*: in narratives such as these the figure of the 'fairytale romance' finds its origins, culminating as these tales do in marriage and enduring bliss. Trials must, of course, be undergone before this joyful resolution: the Beast suffers an enchantment while Beauty learns to see beyond external appearance, Cinderella is abused by her wicked stepmother and stepsisters, and Sleeping Beauty is condemned to a trance of one hundred years. But, in these last two tales at least, and indeed in many others, love occurs instantaneously and reciprocally; no courtship is required, and marriage and lifelong happiness ensue.[17] Affairs of the heart thus seem far from tangled. But to describe the seemingly perfect relationship as a 'fairytale romance' is to consign to some dusty corner the darker side of the genre, for both well- and lesser-known fairytales abound in images of unwilling seductions, forbidden love and the objectification and control of women.

Perrault's *Grisélidis*, for instance, whose eponymous heroine Proust associates with the solitary homosexual at the beginning of *Sodome et Gomorrhe*, dramatizes the threat of incest, for Griselda's husband proposes to marry his own daughter. The spectre of incest also looms over another of Perrault's celebrated tales, *Peau d'Âne*, in which the king's incestuous love for his daughter prompts her to flee her home. The implicit association suggested by Proust between an incestuous scenario and homosexuality may appear to insinuate that the latter is as unnatural a practice as the former, but a closer examination of the image of the solitary homosexual-as-Griselda may tell a more ambiguous story: 'le solitaire ne pourra plus aller lui demander l'heure des trains, le prix des premières, et avant de rentrer rêver dans sa tour, comme Grisélidis, il s'attarde sur la plage, telle une étrange Andromède qu'aucun Argonaute ne viendra délivrer' (*SG* III 27–8). The tone here is not without sympathy or compassion. Moreover, in his gender-crossing dual incarnation as both Griselda and the Andromeda of Greek mythology, the solitary homosexual is presented as sharing the fate of mythical figures destined to be sacrificed despite their innocence of any crime.[18] Andromeda is to be devoured by a sea-monster in order to appease Poseidon, while Griselda is the victim of her husband's paranoia and mistrust of women. In order to test her fidelity, he separates her from her daughter, locks her away from society,[19] threatens to marry another woman whom he knows to be his daughter and returns Griselda to her humble origins as a shepherdess.[20] Through each of these trials, the heroine remains virtuous, patient and loyal to her husband. Thus, although the fairytale which Proust evokes in relation to the solitary homosexual bears the taint of a forbidden love, the homosexual himself is not linked to the guilty party. Indeed, the opposite is true: he is virtuous Griselda. What, then, is the significance of this web of metaphorical reference which associates homosexuality with a source depicting the juxtaposition, or coexistence, of virtue and unnatural love? Arguably, to borrow the terms of contemporary perception, censure of homosexuality can go hand in hand with compassion for those 'afflicted' with this 'disease'.[21] From this perspective, the homosexual's solitary status, if interpreted as a symbol of celibacy and restraint, comes to signify virtue. Given that Perrault shows the threat of unnatural love being averted as a result of the heroines' probity in both *Grisélidis* and *Peau d'Âne*, Proust's image may constitute a caution to the solitary homosexual: if he remains patient and virtuous like Griselda, the temptations of 'unnatural' love may be avoided and he may be 'cured' of his 'disease'.[22] Proust's ambivalence regarding his own sexual orientation is well documented and is evident in the novel in the subtly multifaceted metaphors he uses in portraying homosexuality. Tinged with images of degradation and disease, his vision of it is doubtless a product of his time.[23] But this combines with a sympathetic inflection, and the Griselda figure can certainly be read as a valorization of the qualities the homosexual's orientation has forced him to acquire, if not of his homosexuality itself. One might counter that Proust's focus on the character of Griselda, the symbol of virtue, betrays a desire to accentuate the homosexual's innocence of any 'crime'. However, what is left unsaid, but implied by the fairytale intertext, points to a more complex attitude on Proust's part: a visceral uneasiness born of his own identity and contemporary perspectives provides the unsteady underpinning for an intellectual acceptance of same-sex desire.[24]

The Griselda image does not only serve to imply Proust's ambivalent attitude towards homosexuality; it is also one vehicle for his quasi-scientific scrutiny of homosexual types and, indeed, of all desire, for, as one theorist of the fairytale, Jean-Pierre Mothe, has proposed, *Grisélidis* is a sado-masochistic tale, in which the king's sadistic impulses find their mirror image in Griselda's willing submission to his cruelties.[25] The fact that the only overtly sexual scenes of sado-masochism in the novel are homosexual – Mlle Vinteuil and her lover's desecration of Vinteuil's image (*S* I 158–61) and Charlus's willing subjugation to physical violence in Jupien's 'Temple de l'Impudeur' (*TR* IV 411) – may suggest an imbalance of presentation between homosexual and heterosexual desire in the direction of caricature and condemnation of the former.[26] However, this may readily be countered by the fact that not only is Griselda's masochism neither sexual nor fetishistic – she is guilty, to quote Mothe, of no more than 'masochisme moral'[27] – but all the relationships portrayed by Proust, whether heterosexual or homosexual (or, indeed, social or aesthetic), cast the lovers in the constantly shifting roles of sadist, masochist or sado-masochist. All the lovers experience the pleasure of making the loved one suffer (albeit not physically), while themselves submitting to the same cruelty from the loved one. Apparent stereotype-confirmation thus deconstructs itself as all desire is shown to be based on similarly 'perverse' impulses and, with this deconstruction, the ideal of the 'fairytale romance' collapses.

Through the fairytale intertext, Proust plays with, and challenges, the reader, defying him/her to see beyond the too simple interpretation of any metaphorical source and, by extension, any sexual identity. We might usefully recall here Laurence Coupe's formulation of myth in terms of a reimagining of otherness,[28] invoking alongside it Marina Warner's celebration of how 'the wonders that create the atmosphere of fairy tale disrupt the apprehensible world in order to open spaces for dreaming alternatives' (p. xvi). Proust's attitude to homosexuality is not one of categorical acceptance, as his handling of Perrault's tales has subtly implied, but his reworking of these same tales seems also to challenge conventional perceptions and interpretations. It thus marks a rejection of categorical thinking. By drawing out the complex currents which lie beneath the surface of Proust's apparently straightforward handling of a deceptively simple genre, we can therefore appreciate both the plurality and the commonality of Proustian desire and, indeed, more generally, the plurality of Proust's vision.

These abstract concepts are granted tangible form in Proust precisely by means of a fairytale image of metamorphosis. Describing the replacement of the prince de Guermantes by three women as Morel's company at the brothel where he is spied on by Jupien and Charlus, Proust writes: 'on avait prévenu Morel que deux messieurs avaient payé fort cher pour le voir, on avait fait sortir le prince de Guermantes métamorphosé en trois femmes' (*SG* III 467). In accordance with Jung's theory, this magical metamorphosis externalizes the (emotional, psychological, bodily) multiplicity of Morel's desire. That Proust has chosen to entertain Morel with *three* women is, moreover, significant, for this number, which is a recurrent feature in fairytale (three wishes, three visits to the ball), is the first to represent true plurality. Its use here thus hints at the multifacetedness of Morel's sexual incarnations as subsequently revealed to Charlus by the 'en être' letter (*P* III 720). Three is also, of course, the figure of mediated desire.[29]

The overtly sexual scenes of sado-masochism mentioned above guide us into the realms of another fairytale source, for the narrator, witnessing these expressions of desire, assumes the role of voyeur gazing on a forbidden sight. In Perrault's *La Barbe-Bleue*, Bluebeard hands over to his new wife the keys to all the rooms in his house, explaining that while he is away on business, she may have free access to every room but one, the key to which (in itself, a sado-masochistic act[30]) he nonetheless gives her. Should she enter this forbidden room, he warns that his anger will know no bounds. The only mention of this tale in *A la recherche* occurs in a reference to the magic lantern in *Du côté de chez Swann*. On this occasion, however, Proust does not directly state that the image of Bluebeard appears on the magic lantern and subsequent descriptions of the lantern make no reference to this character. After a detailed description of Golo and Geneviève de Brabant, we find no more than the fleeting allusion to Bluebeard that follows:

> Et dès qu'on sonnait le dîner, j'avais hâte de courir à la salle à manger où la grosse lampe de la suspension, ignorante de Golo et de Barbe-Bleue, et qui connaissait mes parents et le bœuf à la casserole, donnait sa lumière de tous les soirs; et de tomber dans les bras de maman que les malheurs de Geneviève de Brabant me rendaient plus chère, tandis que les crimes de Golo me faisaient examiner ma propre conscience avec plus de scrupules. (S I 10)

Bluebeard is almost entirely confined to the realms of the unsaid.[31] Moreover, the question of guilt raised by the narrator at the end of the extract quoted above feeds the sense of the forbidden already implied by Bluebeard's 'unspeakable' status.[32] And it is not only his insertion into Proust's text that secures his identity as an outsider, for this is already established by the socio-historical context for Perrault's own tale. Once a sign of virility, beards were, as Marina Warner explains, '[w]ell out of fashion by the court of the Sun King'. '[T]he beard of Perrault's villain', she continues, therefore betokens:

> an outsider, a libertine, and a ruffian. The very word in French – *barbe* – looks as if it is related to *barbare*, barbarian, though the etymology remains fanciful. [. . .] And it becomes the custom, beginning with the first woodcuts of the first edition, and continuing in the watercolours by Arthur Rackham and later artists, to portray Bluebeard as an Oriental, a Turk in pantaloons and turban, who rides an elephant, and grasps his wife by the hair when he prepares to behead her with his scimitar. [. . .] By the blueness of the protagonist's beard, Perrault intensifies the frightfulness of his appearance: Bluebeard is represented as a man against nature, either by dyeing his hair like a luxurious Oriental, or by producing such a monstrous growth without resorting to artifice. (pp. 242–3)

A web is thus woven, in the popular imagination and in Proust, between voyeurism, (homo)sexuality, marginality and exoticism. The paradigm linking the first three of these is our concern here, as it is the forbidden view at the centre of the tale of *La Barbe-Bleue* which draws them together. The strand which equates the erotic with the exotic will be unravelled in the following section.

In Perrault's account, Bluebeard's wife cannot resist the temptation to look inside the forbidden room, just as the narrator's experiences of voyeurism are at once horrifying and compelling. What Bluebeard's wife sees, however, appears to bear no relation to the scenes witnessed by the narrator: a row of women (Bluebeard's previous, overly curious wives) with their throats cut and surrounded by a pool of fresh blood rather than the dried blood one would expect. In her shock, Bluebeard's latest wife drops the key – the quintessential phallic symbol[33] – and, by some supernatural trick, is unable to wash off the blood which then stains it, thus betraying her guilt to her husband and sealing her doom. Seemingly a long way from the sexual scenes witnessed by the narrator, the image of blood which dominates the vision offered to Bluebeard's wife in fact finds subtle parallels in Proust's text. The bleeding Charlus, for instance, is the willing counterpart of Bluebeard's victims, the old scars the narrator sees which are reopened and exacerbated with every new assault echoing the fresh blood in Bluebeard's forbidden room. The link established in the tale between blood and phallic symbol also seems to betoken a potentially violent and certainly male-driven desire. As for the scene at Mlle Vinteuil's house, the absence of blood and any equivalent to the phallic key symbolizes what the at once bemused and fascinated narrator does not yet understand about both the 'mystery' of womanhood and the many permutations of human desire.[34] In a further rethinking of otherness, the Self–Other gaze is thus inverted, as it is the narrator, as much as the marginalized homosexuals whose pleasure he witnesses, who experiences the identity of outsider, both to knowledge and to their desire.

Both Bluebeard's prohibition on his current wife and the punishment inflicted on previous wives for disobeying what we assume to be the same interdiction are symptoms of a desire to control the woman loved. Indeed, the fact that Bluebeard keeps his slaughtered wives locked up in a room transforms them, for Mothe, into his ideal, 'des femmes chosifiées, réduites à l'état d'objets'.[35] The desire to control, which arises from jealousy and paranoia, is also the trigger for the action in *Grisélidis*. As we are told of the king, 'Ce tempérament héroïque / Fut obscurci d'une sombre vapeur / Qui, chagrine et mélancolique, / Lui faisait voir dans le fond de son cœur / Tout le beau sexe infidèle et trompeur'. Any appearance of virtue is merely '[un] déguisement', '[un] personnage'.[36] Suspicion thus motivates all of his actions. Despite this fundamental similarity between the two tales, however, they diverge in one essential respect: Griselda is innocent, remaining virtuous despite all tests of her fidelity and obedience to her husband, while Bluebeard's wife is guilty, literally of curiosity about the forbidden room, metaphorically of sexual infidelity, for this is the commonest interpretation of the tale. ' "Bluebeard" ', argues Bruno Bettelheim, 'is a tale about sexual temptation. [. . .] The behavior of Bluebeard's wife suggests two possibilities: that what she sees in the forbidden closet is the creation of her own anxious fantasies; or that she has betrayed her husband, but hopes he won't find out' (p. 301). The sexual symbolism of the tale, notably the key entering the lock and the blood that stains it, points conclusively, for Bettelheim and others, to her infidelity.[37]

These two poles of innocence and guilt represent the paradigm swing of possibilities, first, for Swann and, later, for the narrator in their relationships with, and perceptions of, Odette and Albertine, and these fluctuations are expressed, among other sources, through images drawn from the world of fairytale. Thus, for example, on Swann's pleasure in Odette's show of kindness towards him, we read: 'et il lui gardait de ce regard *enchanteur* et bon autant de reconnaissance que si elle venait de l'avoir réellement et si ce n'eût pas été seulement son imagination qui venait de le peindre pour donner satisfaction à son désir' (*S* I 298, my italics). Swann's susceptibility to this charming Odette suggests her continuing power to cast a spell on him, but the second part of the extract quoted highlights the narrator's, and doubtless Swann's, awareness that enchantments are temporary and essentially an illusion in which the lover is often consciously complicit. In its very fabrication, the fairytale is thus unwoven.

Perrault's tale *Riquet à la houppe* sounds the magical echo of Proust's presentation of the subjectivity of desire. Although not explicitly mentioned by Proust, this story of the ugly but clever Riquet, whose fairy godmother has granted him the ability to pass on his wit to whoever loves him, and of the Princess who is beautiful but stupid and has the equivalent power to pass on her beauty to whoever loves her, finds its clear reflection in Proust's theory of desire: the loved one may not possess any 'objective' beauty or other qualities; it is the lover's transforming vision alone that endows him/her with these qualities. When the princess finally reciprocates Riquet's love, immediately,

> Riquet à la houppe parut à ses yeux l'homme du monde le plus beau, le mieux fait et le plus aimable qu'elle eût jamais vu. Quelques-uns assurent que ce ne furent point les charmes de la Fée qui opérèrent, mais que l'amour seul fit cette Métamorphose. (p. 187)

A similar transformation marks the denouement of *La Belle et la Bête*, as the Beast is metamorphosed into a handsome prince. There is, however, one key difference between the culmination of these two tales, for if the Beast's transformation is a genuinely supernatural one – a curse is lifted – the ending of *Riquet à la houppe* is prompted by no magical power. Indeed, it seems that Riquet will remain as ugly to the outside world as he has become beautiful in the eyes of the princess who now loves him: this is merely a perceptual shift on the part of the lover. These two narratives thus embody the simultaneous pull of the natural and supernatural. Riquet's story illustrates that subjective vision has the 'magical' power to transfigure *without* the aid of witch or fairy. This power is ultimately realized, in more general aesthetic terms, by the narrator-as-writer; but for the narrator/protagonist, embroiled in the painful realities of his relationship with Albertine, *Riquet à la houppe*'s celebratory vision of the transformative power of individual perception remains in the realm of the potential. Only in retrospect – through a mythical return to, and retelling of, the experiences that contribute to the narrator's (self-)creation – will this become possible. Although he quickly realizes that his relationship with Albertine will not, as in the tale of Beauty and the Beast, undergo a miraculous, supernatural transformation, the narrator will continue, for the duration of their relationship, to deploy the natural power of the mind and emotions to transfigure the loved one to self-deceiving ends. At times, even this task appears unaccomplishable to him. Once again, therefore, Proustian desire denies the permanent happy ending of the fairytale, and the struggle, between extremes, to transform the loved one into a variously beautiful, intelligent or loving woman carries on.[38]

As early as the narrator's first meeting with Albertine, we find traces of an inversion of the positive 'transformations' undergone by 'Riquet à la houppe' and his princess, for it signals Albertine's metamorphosis *away* from the idealized image of her that the narrator possessed prior to this meeting:

> Au moment où notre nom résonne dans la bouche du présentateur, surtout si celui-ci l'entoure comme fit Elstir de commentaires élogieux – ce moment sacramentel, analogue à celui où dans une féerie, le génie ordonne à une personne d'en être soudain une autre –, celle que nous avons désiré d'approcher s'évanouit, d'abord comment resterait-elle pareille à elle-même puisque [. . .] dans les yeux hier situés à l'infini [. . .] le regard conscient, la pensée inconnaissable que nous cherchions, viennent d'être miraculeusement et tout simplement remplacés par notre propre image peinte comme au fond d'un miroir qui sourirait? (*JF* II 227)

The dynamic interplay of qualities which we find in *Riquet à la houppe* is absent here, and the image of Self being transposed on to Other becomes an obstruction to objectivity. The impact of Albertine's transformation is developed a few pages later:

> Dès ce premier jour, quand en rentrant je pus voir le souvenir que je rapportais, je compris quel tour de muscade avait été parfaitement exécuté, et comment j'avais causé un moment avec une personne qui, grâce à l'habileté du prestidigitateur, sans avoir rien de celle que j'avais suivie si longtemps au bord de la mer, lui avait été substituée. (*JF* II 229–30)

The narrator is either unable or reluctant to articulate the nature of her transformation, but metamorphosis in fairytales, and, indeed, in Proust, always marks out the extremes. Thus, one can assume a shift from idealization to a negative reality. The immediacy of this shift from inaccessible perfection to the disenchantment of the knowable is only accentuated by the fairytale metaphor, the forum in which such complete and instantaneous transformations can occur. The intensity of emotions such as disappointment and the sudden and extreme volte-face they can induce are thus fittingly voiced through this metaphorical paradigm. Moreover, Proust's choice of the conjuror as the agent of this transformation – rather than, for example, a fairy godmother – hints at the illusions and deceptions on which the relationship will be built and of which the narrator will, like the conjuror's audience, be the largely willing victim.

These fairytale transformations are extended in *La Prisonnière* in which the story of *Sleeping Beauty* (*La Belle au bois dormant*) comes into play. The tale is not directly evoked by Proust in this context, but reference to it is made in the drafts for *Albertine disparue*. In a discussion of the 'châtelains de Mérouville', we find the following:

> la trame des sensations que revêtaient ces personnages dont les noms étaient prononcés devant le buffet aux massepains s'était cassée et ils n'étaient plus vêtus que du reflet rose et bleuâtre de la robe d'aurore ou du clair de lune des personnages de contes de fées, comme tout ce pays qui s'étendait au loin dans les champs au-dessus de Combray quand on avait dépassé la porte du parc Swann, avec tous ces châteaux et ces fermes où je n'étais jamais allé, noyés dans la vapeur bleuâtre qui est celle des lointains, offrant çà et là dans sa géographie que j'avais tant voulu, que j'allais pouvoir approfondir, la ferme du Petit Poucet et le château de la Belle au bois dormant. (IV 712-3)

This relatively underdeveloped image plays into a general association between the aristocracy and what is, to the narrator, the equally unreal and inaccessible world of fairytale. It does not point to any nuanced handling of individual tales. But the resonances of the story of Sleeping Beauty that one detects in the presentation of Albertine in *La Prisonnière* are so conspicuous – particularly in the context of the narrator's vision of her sleeping – as to suggest an evolved appreciation and, indeed, re-invention of the tale. Certainly, reference to *Sleeping Beauty* can illuminate our own interpretations of this key volume. The first such link is created by the description of Albertine's breathing while asleep as 'féerique':

> J'écoutais cette murmurante émanation mystérieuse, douce comme un zéphyr marin, féerique comme ce clair de lune, qu'était son sommeil. [. . .] Ce que j'éprouvais alors c'était un amour devant quelque chose d'aussi pur, d'aussi immatériel,

d'aussi mystérieux que si j'avais été devant les créatures inanimées que sont les beautés de la nature. (*P* III 578)

Later, too, her sleep is likened to a 'monde merveilleux et magique' (*P* III 621). The narrator's love for Albertine is, as we have seen with reference to other fairytales, dependent on (and destroyed by) a desire to control her and to reduce her plurality.[39] However, by the later stages of her/their captivity in *La Prisonnière*, it is only in her sleeping state that the narrator feels any attraction towards her and only then does he experience any sense of ascendancy over her:

> Elle avait rappelé à soi tout ce qui d'elle était en dehors, elle s'était réfugiée, enclose, résumée, dans son corps. En la tenant sous mon regard, dans mes mains, j'avais cette impression de la posséder tout entière que je n'avais pas quand elle était réveillée. Sa vie m'était soumise, exhalait vers moi son léger souffle. (*P* III 578)[40]

The story of *Sleeping Beauty* is thus the idealized template that the narrator would wish to impose on Albertine's existence. While asleep, Albertine is, like Sleeping Beauty, trapped in stasis and thus 'fixable' for the narrator. Like her fairytale counterpart, who is surrounded by a wall of thorns which prevent suitors from drawing near, Albertine is also, of course, physically confined within the narrator's apartment. But if, in the Proustian scenario, Albertine is allied to the fairytale heroine, what is the narrator's role? In keeping with Jung's reading of the different characters in a fairytale as representative of the different parts of an individual psyche, his is a dual role: he is both the evil fairy who casts the spell which will trap her in stasis and the 'prince' who loves her when she is asleep. The narrator thus plays the roles of both 'good' and 'evil', as they are presented in the original source. Proust thereby subtly underlines the counter-productive measures undertaken by the lover and the perversity of his actions. The symbolic parallels which, in fairytale, link enclosure to a denial of knowledge extend this 'self-sabotage'. As discussed below, Sleeping Beauty remains isolated while she develops the maturity required to cope with the knowledge her encounter with the world will bring. More explicitly, in the tale of Bluebeard, the eponymous protagonist assumes a God-like role, prohibiting knowledge as in the Garden of Eden: his forbidden room calls to mind the tree of the knowledge of good and evil in Genesis.[41] But in attempting, through enclosure, to deny Albertine knowledge (of other women, of other forms of sexual gratification), the narrator effectively becomes both torturer and victim, condemning himself, arguably more than Albertine, to intellectual immobility.[42] Perrault's moral on the fatal effects of curiosity in women is thus transposed, in an implied rewriting of the gender dynamic at work in the tale, on to the narrator: his tunnel-vision preoccupation with discovering Albertine's misdeeds exposes him to a perilous fate. Enclosure, like the images of being devoured that recur in fairytale, also represents sexual possession; and in this respect, too, the narrator and Albertine's common imprisonment denotes a mutual possession, not the unequal dominance of woman by man, 'enclosed' by 'encloser', that the narrator hopes for. In fact, it is, paradoxically, Albertine who enjoys greater sexual power over the narrator than he enjoys over her, for her sexuality always eludes him; and like Bluebeard, whose wife acquires knowledge by entering the forbidden room despite all his measures to restrain her, the narrator's attempts to contain Albertine are thwarted.

Bettelheim's psychoanalytical reading of *Sleeping Beauty* interprets the period of sleep as that of adolescent passivity or withdrawal into the self, a period which paves the way for physical and emotional maturity. It is only, as Bettelheim argues, when

> Sleeping Beauty has finally gained both physical and emotional maturity and is ready for love, and with it for sex and marriage, [that] that which had seemed impenetrable gives way. The wall of thorns suddenly turns into a wall of [. . .] beautiful flowers, which opens to let the prince enter. (p. 233)

One may apply this reading of the tale to the narrator's idealization of the sleeping Albertine in that her sleep represents a form of restoration of innocence, an impression of pre-sexuality, but one which is destroyed the moment she awakens: like that of Sleeping Beauty, Albertine's awakening is a sexual awakening, upon which all the narrator's anxieties about her sexuality and fidelity return.[43]

Albertine's literal sleeping state can thus be filtered through the fairytale of *Sleeping Beauty*, but as the concurrence of the princess's entrapment within the wall of thorns and Albertine's physical imprisonment suggests, the entire period of *La Prisonnière* is a dormant one in developmental terms, not only for Albertine, but also for the narrator. It is not, however, an unproductive one. To return to Bettelheim's analysis, he argues that: ' "The Sleeping Beauty" tells us that a long period of quiescence, of contemplation, of concentration on the self, can and often does lead to highest achievement' (p. 226). Albertine's fate subsequent to *La Prisonnière* can hardly be described in terms of her 'highest achievement', but this volume nonetheless culminates in her awakening to a form of agency and activity: she makes the decision to escape her prison. Similarly, this symbolic dormant period highlights the possible consequences of withdrawal for the narrator, as symbolized by sleep. Bettelheim explains how withdrawal 'leads to a dangerous, deathlike existence when it is embraced as an escape from the vagaries of life. The entire world then becomes dead to the person' (p. 234).[44] Unlike Albertine, however, the narrator is unable to 'awaken' and free himself from her, even though he understands the necessity of doing so long before she is revived into action. In fact, in those moments when she is not fulfilling the role of his ideal Sleeping Beauty – that is, when the wakeful Albertine resurrects his jealous torment – the narrator attempts to escape, with the help of Françoise, into another fairytale: of the young dairymaid whom Françoise finds to run the narrator's errands, she says: '"Elle pourra très bien porter la lettre de Monsieur et faire les courses si ce n'est pas trop loin. Monsieur va voir, elle a l'air d'un Petit Chaperon Rouge."' (*P* III 647). Once again, the narrator plays a dual role, thus highlighting his competing impulses: he is at once the mother who sends Little Red Riding Hood on errands and the wolf who wishes to devour her. Indeed, the note of caution in Françoise's statement ('si ce n'est pas trop loin') marks an implicit recognition of danger which mirrors Perrault's moral. The former, non-sexual role marks an attempted resurrection of the pre-knowledge/pre-seduction Albertine, as displaced on to the innocent dairymaid, while the latter, of course, represents a sexual desire. This duality is reinforced in the episode at the beginning of *Albertine disparue* when the narrator receives a visit from the police following a complaint by the parents of another young girl whom he invited into his apartment and cradled in his lap: 'je la berçai quelque temps sur mes genoux' (*AD* IV 15). Perrault's own moral reveals that he intended the narrative to be a cautionary tale for young girls and their parents:

> On voit ici que de jeunes enfants, / Surtout de jeunes filles / Belles, bien faites, et gentilles, / Font très mal d'écouter toute sorte de gens, / Et que ce n'est pas chose étrange, / S'il en est tant que le loup mange. / Je dis le loup, car tous les loups / Ne sont pas de la même sorte; / Il en est d'une humeur accorte, / Sans bruit, sans fiel et sans courroux, / Qui privés, complaisants et doux, / Suivent les jeunes Demoiselles / Jusque dans les maisons, jusque dans les ruelles; / Mais hélas! qui ne sait que ces Loups doucereux, / De tous les Loups sont les plus dangereux. (p. 145)

If the narrator's attraction to the dairymaid can be seen as a displaced desire for an idealized, pre-sexual Albertine, then the various possible interpretations of Little Red Riding Hood's willing compliance with the wolf's requests raise important questions. Bettelheim himself proposes that she is 'either [. . .] stupid or wants to be seduced' (p. 169), while other theorists have highlighted the erotic nature of the questions she asks of the wolf once in bed with him.[45] These diverse interpretations only serve to underline how the narrator's desire to return Albertine to the apparent innocence of a Little Red Riding Hood will inevitably be frustrated by the equivocal actions of, and thus uncertainty surrounding, the heroine of the tale herself.

Whatever Little Red Riding Hood's role in her fate, innocence is devoured and the idealized image represented by this fairytale figure extinguished, at least in Perrault's telling of the tale.[46] Other versions of the story, such as that of the Brothers Grimm, present a different conclusion, with Little Red Riding Hood and her grandmother rescued from the wolf's stomach by a woodcutter. As an originally oral tradition, different versions and alternative outcomes are always possible in fairytale; the affinities with Proust's vision are clear. Narrowly missed fates are commonplace in both fairytale and *A la recherche*, and the narrator's experience of, for example, Sleeping Beauty might well have had the happy ending characteristic of many fairytales. However, had his relationship ended in fairytale romance and marriage, had he not been freed from Albertine, the novel, like Swann's aesthetic self-realization, might never have been completed. The fairytale cycle is thus necessarily closed by the end of *Albertine disparue* with a recognition of the narrator's indifference to Albertine in the form of a reference to a devouring monster that recalls the wolf of *Little Red Riding Hood*: 'La mort n'agit que comme l'absence. Le monstre à l'apparition duquel mon amour avait frissonné, l'oubli, avait bien, comme je l'avais cru, fini par le dévorer' (*AD* IV 222). Building on versions of the tale such as that of the Brothers Grimm, the narrator's obsession with Albertine will be devoured by forgetfulness, only to be revived much later in their literary and mythical retelling.

Marie-Louise von Franz sums up the significance of fairytales as follows:

> Fairy tales are the purest and simplest expression of collective and unconscious psychic processes. Therefore their value for the scientific investigation of the unconscious exceeds that of all other material [. . .]. [They] represent the archetypes in their simplest, barest and most concise forms [. . .]. All fairy tales endeavor to describe one and the same psychic fact, the archetype of the Self.[47]

The preceding pages have demonstrated not only that modern psychoanalytical readings of the fairytales Proust evokes in the novel shed new light on his construction of the Self, and in particular the desiring Self, but also that Proust himself approached and exploited the genre with the eyes of the psychoanalyst.[48] The interpretative potency of Proust's handling of these tales – some of which are present explicitly, others as a pervasive undercurrent – implies that he has consciously exploited the psychological conflicts and the sexual symbolism he detected in the genre in order to play out the dualities and desires of his characters. But this is not, as we have seen, a simple imitation of the original source, a direct transposition of its structures on to Proust's novelistic universe, for Proust rewrites these tales as much as he replicates them. Most notably, the 'happily ever after' that characterizes the majority of fairytales is largely missing from Proust's vision. If, however, as theorists such as Bettelheim have argued, fairytales provide a kind of ideal template, the aim of which is to demonstrate, on an unconscious level, for the child who reads them, the exemplary resolution of psychological or sexual conflict, we must remind ourselves that Proust is presenting not an ideal model for resolution, but a reality. Moreover, if we set aside the far-fetched scenarios and the miraculous *fairy godmother ex machina* ending of many tales, what is left is an emotional and psychological honesty. As Marina Warner comments:

> The disregard for logic, all those fairytale non-sequiturs and improbable reversals, rarely encompasses the emotional conflicts themselves: hatred, jealousy, kindness, cherishing retain an intense integrity throughout. The double vision of the tales, on the one hand charting perennial drives and terrors, both conscious and unconscious, and on the other mapping actual, volatile experience, gives the genre its fascination and power to satisfy. (p. xvii)[49]

Drawing on the familiar archetypes of fairytale, Proust unmasks the authentic complexities of human nature. Perrault's original text may recognize these complexities, but they are necessarily clothed in an unambiguous didacticism for the benefit of his youthful readership. Proust teases out and reworks the elaborate resonances of this deceptively artless genre. In doing so, he offers a challenge to binary and categorical thinking. The following section illustrates how this challenge is extended in the narrator's, Proust's and, indeed, the reader's engagement with the *Mille et Une Nuits*.

## *Les Mille et Une Nuits* proustiennes

The widespread traces of interconnection between the *Mille et Une Nuits* and the narrator's own grand artistic project culminate in a final, determined rejection of this symbol of childhood nostalgia in the last pages of the novel:

> Moi, c'était autre chose que j'avais à écrire, de plus long, et pour plus d'une personne. Long à écrire. [. . .] Si je travaillais, ce ne serait que la nuit. Mais il me faudrait beaucoup de nuits, peut-être cent, peut-être mille. Et je vivrais dans l'anxiété de ne pas savoir si le Maître de ma destinée, moins indulgent que le sultan Sheriar, le matin quand j'interromprais mon récit, voudrait bien surseoir à mon arrêt de mort et me permettrait de reprendre la suite le prochain soir. Non pas que je

prétendisse refaire, en quoi que ce fût, *Les Mille et Une Nuits*, [. . .] pas plus qu'aucun des livres que j'avais aimés dans ma naïveté d'enfant, superstitieusement attaché à eux comme à mes amours, ne pouvant sans horreur imaginer une œuvre qui serait différente d'eux. Mais, comme Elstir Chardin, on ne peut refaire ce qu'on aime qu'en le renonçant. [. . .] Ce serait un livre aussi long que *Les Mille et Une Nuits* peut-être, mais tout autre. (*TR* IV 620–1)

Yet the extract also suggests that the work may have provided thematic and structural models for *A la recherche*: for example, the active participation of Sheriar, Schéhérazade's listener, in the thematic framework of the *Mille et Une Nuits* is reflected in the dynamic role the narrator ascribes to his own readers; there is an obvious association between Sheriar and the narrator's death, and the storytelling which both the narrator and Schéhérazade hope will keep these threats at bay; the stories of both are composed at night; and last, but not least, the two works have in common their considerable length.[50] The dynamic between the two texts goes far beyond a sudden and unforeseeable rejection of one, the purpose of which is to make way for the other, however. To be sure, the *Mille et Une Nuits* as the symbol of the narrator/protagonist's earlier naivety about, and misunderstanding of, art – a stage at which art is the unchallengeable monument that takes the place of his independent evolution – must be, and is, renounced, but subtle intertextual traces evoke the very texture of the *Mille et Une Nuits* throughout *A la recherche*: there are stories within stories; internal repetitions; hints and reminiscences; and parallel, but ultimately intertwining, narratives. Moreover, both well- and lesser-known tales from the *Mille et Une Nuits* are woven into *A la recherche* in the form of metaphorical rewritings of these original sources. The 'tensions' between old and new context that result are vehicles for the expression of ironies, pleasures, anxieties and the kinds of truths which, throughout the novel, Proust almost greedily roots out through metaphorical association. The narrator may have renounced the collection insofar as it represents a period of aesthetic immaturity, but he has also retold aspects of it. Victor Graham has even suggested that the title of *A la recherche* may be a metaphor plucked from the *Mille et Une Nuits*. He quotes an extract from 'Le Dormeur éveillé', a tale which is explicitly referred to by Proust in the novel: 'L'autre moitié [of an inherited fortune] qui consistait en une somme considérable en argent comptant, fut *destinée à réparer tout le temps qu'il croyait avoir perdu* sous la dure contrainte où son père l'avait retenu jusqu'à sa mort (Graham's italics, 'Mille et Une Nuits', p. 92). Setting aside this possible source for the title of Proust's work, a pattern emerges whereby the *Mille et Une Nuits* is repeatedly transposed on to the same contexts in *A la recherche*. Exploiting the Orientalist myth of exotic sexual licence, Proust introduces the collection of tales in relation to sexuality and, specifically, homosexuality. Second, and by no means independent of this first context, the stylistic and narrative twists and turns of the earlier work are also written into *A la recherche* as markers of complexity and, indeed, sources of perplexity for the narrator. But the tales of the *Mille et Une Nuits* are markers of unexpected revelation as often as they are signs of impenetrability, and once again, this, the third context, frequently overlaps with the first and second: for example, the *Mille et Une Nuits*, as we shall see, provides a metaphorical framework which will map out the narrator's aesthetic development from naive incomprehension to independent creation, that is, from perplexity to revelation.

As Graham explains, however, 'the *point de départ* for this particular theme in *A la recherche du temps perdu* [is] the allusion to the plates in the home of Tante Léonie at Combray which [are] painted with scenes from the *Mille et Une Nuits*' (ibid., p. 92). It is here, therefore, that we shall begin. The tales are evoked in the context of what the narrator imagines would be his great-aunt's incredulity, were she to discover that Swann is the favourite of the Faubourg Saint-Germain:

> cela eût paru aussi extraordinaire à ma tante qu'aurait pu l'être pour une dame plus lettrée la pensée d'être personnellement liée avec Aristée dont elle aurait compris qu'il allait, après avoir causé avec elle, plonger au sein des royaumes de Thétis, dans un empire soustrait aux yeux des mortels et où Virgile nous le montre reçu à bras ouverts; ou – pour s'en tenir à une image qui avait plus de chance de lui venir à l'esprit, car elle l'avait vue peinte sur nos assiettes à petits fours de Combray – d'avoir eu à dîner Ali-Baba, lequel quand il se saura seul, pénétrera dans la caverne, éblouissante de trésors insoupçonnés. (*S* I 17–18)

We later discover which of the tales the plates depict: '*Aladin ou la Lampe Merveilleuse* [. . .], *Ali-Baba, le Dormeur éveillé* [et] *Simbad le Marin embarquant à Bassora avec toutes ses richesses*' (*JF* II 257–8), the only other tale specifically referred to in the novel being *L'Histoire de la belle Zobéide* (*TR* IV 411).[51] At this early stage, the *Mille et Une Nuits* would *seem* to be the unequivocally reassuring – if slightly tacky[52] – accessory to the childhood world of Combray and, indeed, one to which the narrator returns in later life as a comforting escape from present anxiety. However, the fact that the anxieties which he will later try to evade in these childhood tales are invariably fears about Albertine's sexual orientation, and that the tales referred to in the context of Léonie's plates are frequently used in the novel in relation to homosexuality, taints their sweetness and underlines the futility of his attempt at flight. Moreover, when we look beyond the parallel here being drawn between Swann's access to the aristocracy and Ali-Baba's access to the thieves' den, to Ali-Baba's other appearances in the novel, we will see that Proust's repeated reincarnations of the Persian merchant will retrospectively, and by association, cast a further shadow over the supposed idyll of the *Mille et Une Nuits* version of Combray. All of this contributes to, and prepares for, the narrator's ultimate self-realization as artist.

If we are to make the leap of logic from the Swann/Ali-Baba image to the tarnishing of the idyll of Combray, however, we must first explore the various incarnations of Ali-Baba in the novel and the train of association which links them. The parallel between entry into the world of the aristocracy and entry into the thieves' den is reiterated later in the novel in the form of Charlus's claim, made to the young narrator, that only his 'Sésame' will ensure the latter's entry into the salons of the aristocracy; but elsewhere this very 'Sésame' also becomes the means of entry into Jupien's 'Temple de l'Impudeur'.[53] Jupien explains to the narrator:

> Si jamais vous étiez curieux, un soir, de voir, je ne dis pas quarante, mais une dizaine de voleurs, vous n'avez qu'à venir ici; pour savoir si je suis là vous n'avez qu'à regarder la fenêtre de là-haut, je laisse une petite fente ouverte et éclairée, cela veut dire que je suis venu, qu'on peut entrer; c'est mon Sésame à moi. Je dis seulement Sésame. Car pour les lys, si c'est eux que vous voulez, je vous conseille d'aller les chercher ailleurs. (*TR* IV 411–12)

The 'Temple de l'Impudeur' and the aristocracy are thus associated through the common reference to the 'Sésame' which is required if one is to be granted access to them. The suggestion in the novel that the aristocracy is the bastion of homosexuality, and the series of *Mille et Une Nuits*-esque revelations as to the sheer number of aristocrats who turn out to be homosexual, have thus been hinted at through the subtle intertwining, in the course of the novel, of the aristocracy, homosexuality and the story of Ali-Baba. By introducing the same tale in different metaphorical contexts, truths are implied before they are stated, fully to appreciate the ironies of which we must return to page one and begin reading again. A second intertextual layer, Ruskin's *Sesame and Lilies* – translated, of course, by Proust himself as *Sésame et les lys* – only enhances the ironic effect, for whereas Ruskin had used the magic formula of the 'Open Sesame' to describe the treasures of the mind which are opened up to the reader of great books, Jupien is offering access to quite different treasures. Jupien's subversion of Ruskin's meaning, combined with the almost coquettish promise of 'je ne dis pas quarante, mais une dizaine de voleurs' marks a wryly humorous, because incongruous, juxtaposition.

This brief overview of the winding course followed by the figure of Ali-Baba throughout *A la recherche* has given the reader a foretaste of the deliberateness and the persistence of Proust's use of this source. Clearly, though, a number of thematic strands intertwine in this web of hints and reminiscences which, though relying on a single tale, has transported us far from the world of Combray. Or so it would seem, for these subtle associative overlaps are, in fact, part of a unified vision which encompasses the narrator's evolution from Combray to creation. To appreciate this unity, let us now disentangle each strand in turn.

We saw, first of all, that the 'purity' of the *Mille et Une Nuits* as depicted on Léonie's plates – 'purity' in the sense that they were the symbol of childhood innocence and relative lack of turmoil – were later to be 'tainted' by virtue of their appearance in the context of anxieties over Albertine's suspected lesbianism:

> Mais bientôt la saison battit son plein; c'était tous les jours une arrivée nouvelle et à la frequence subitement croissante de mes promenades, remplaçant la lecture charmante des *Mille et Une Nuits*, il y avait une cause dépourvue de plaisir et qui les empoisonnait tous. (*SG* III 234)

The attempt at flight into an anxiety-free past is thwarted by unrelenting pressure in the present, and this setting, which combines the narrator's paradigm swing of emotions over Albertine with the intellectual inactivity of Balbec that results from it, also serves indirectly to extend one of the principal thematic strands of the novel, namely the narrator's aesthetic evolution. Several pages earlier, we find the narrator questioning Albertine on the issue of her sexual preferences and being momentarily reassured by her – only momentarily, however, as the immediate result of their conversation is his conclusion that: 'J'aurais dû partir ce soir-là sans jamais la revoir' (*SG* III 229). A paragraph of fluctuation and indecision follows, while the subsequent paragraph reads:

> Tranquillisé par mon explication avec Albertine je recommençai à vivre davantage auprès de ma mère. Elle aimait à me parler doucement du temps où ma grand-mère était plus jeune. Craignant que je ne me fisse des reproches sur les tristesses dont j'avais pu assombrir la fin de cette vie, elle revenait volontiers aux années où mes premières études avaient causé à ma grand-mère des satisfactions que jusqu'ici on m'avait toujours cachées. Nous reparlions de Combray. Ma mère me dit que là-bas du moins je lisais et qu'à Balbec je devrais bien faire de même, si je travaillais pas [*sic*]. Je répondis que pour m'entourer justement des souvenirs de Combray et des jolies assiettes peintes j'aimerais relire *Les Mille et Une Nuits*. Comme jadis à Combray quand elle me donnait des livres pour ma fête, c'est en cachette, pour me faire une surprise, que ma mère me fit venir à la fois *Les Mille et Une Nuits* de Galland et *Les Mille Nuits et Une Nuit* de Mardrus. Mais après avoir jeté un coup d'œil sur les deux traductions, ma mère aurait bien voulu que je m'en tinsse à celle de Galland, tout en craignant de m'influencer à cause du respect qu'elle

avait de la liberté intellectuelle, de la peur d'intervenir maladroitement dans la vie de ma pensée, et du sentiment qu'étant une femme, d'une part elle manquait, croyait-elle, de la compétence littéraire qu'il fallait, d'autre part elle ne devait pas juger d'après ce qui la choquait les lectures d'un jeune homme. En tombant sur certains contes elle avait été révoltée par l'immoralité du sujet et la crudité de l'expression. (SG III 229–30)

The *Mille et Une Nuits* and, more specifically, the different French translations of it are thus not only linked to, but represent, various stages in the narrator's intellectual and aesthetic development. The 'tamer' Galland translation becomes the symbol of a period when the narrator appreciated art more or less exclusively via the mediation of third parties; in the case of his mother, this was a sanitizing mediation which remains a potential influence on the narrator, despite his mother's determined attempt at impartiality.[54] The Mardrus translation, on the other hand, would appear to signal a potential step towards intellectual, aesthetic and emotional independence. At this stage, though, the narrator does not make a choice between the two versions: 'Pourtant ma mère me remit les deux ouvrages et je lui dis que je les lirais les jours où je serais trop fatigué pour me promener' (SG III 231). This postponement of a decision is thus a metaphorical marker of the narrator's flight from his own aesthetic vocation. Activity represents an avoidance of reading, and reading is a means to avoid writing, while the mother's, and previously the grandmother's, pride in his appetite for books provide a further ballast to the narrator's unconvincing self-deception.

The next association between Albertine's suspected lesbianism and the *Mille et Une Nuits* significantly modifies the relationship between the two, for the tales of the *Mille et Une Nuits* have themselves metamorphosed from being the, albeit imperfect, asylum from fears about Albertine's sexuality to being synonymous with the lies she tells when probed on this question. In the wake of one of these interrogations, the narrator claims that he could have extracted the truth about her relationship with Léa from Albertine:

il m'eût suffi de rassembler devant mon amie, en une synthèse, ses affirmations contradictoires pour la convaincre de ses fautes [. . .]. Mais elle aurait encore mieux aimé dire qu'elle avait menti quand elle avait émis une de ces affirmations, dont ainsi le retrait ferait écrouler tout mon système, plutôt que de reconnaître que tout ce qu'elle avait raconté dès le début n'était qu'un tissu de contes mensongers. Il en est de semblables dans *Les Mille et Une Nuits*, et qui nous y charment. Il nous font souffrir dans une personne que nous aimons, et à cause de cela nous permettent d'entrer un peu plus avant dans la connaissance de la nature humaine au lieu de nous contenter de nous jouer à sa surface. (P III 652)

Not only has the *Mille et Une Nuits* become synonymous with Albertine's lies, it has also become the instrument of the narrator's enforced confrontation with reality rather than the soothing balm he had intended it to be. The narrator does not *have* to extract the truth from Albertine; it becomes visible, despite his efforts, through the *Mille et Une Nuits*, and, in the process, the precarious balance between the 'sanitized' world of Combray and the licentious world of Balbec finally collapses in unwilling and uncomfortable resignation. Because both of these worlds find a reflection in the *Mille et Une Nuits*, the two cannot be conveniently separated, and one cannot provide a straightforward refuge from the other. The narrator is therefore forced 'plus avant dans la connaissance de la nature humaine', obliged to recognize that in reality – and in the *Mille et Une Nuits* – the joyful and the painful, the sublime and the grotesque coexist. He realizes, too, that his earlier attempts, in life and in reading, to compartmentalize experience into opposites and to block out all but the enchantment were nothing more than 'playing on the surface'.

As if to support this realization, the passage discussed above marks a change as regards the handling and means of integration of the tales – a change which will be repeated in most, if not all, of the subsequent uses of the *Mille et Une Nuits* in the novel. In this last example, Proust's handling of the source has evolved from a purely external association between the events surrounding or involving the narrator and his reading of the *Mille et Une Nuits*, to a rewriting of the *Mille et Une Nuits* within the narrative of *A la recherche*, a rewriting which fuses together tales from the Arabian Nights and the situations lived out by Proust's characters: the *Mille et Une Nuits* is no longer simply a book the narrator reads. As if to prove that he is not just playing on the surface, Albertine *becomes* a character from the collection of tales; her lies *become* the very stories the narrator read as a child, just as Charlus is later transformed, as if by a sorcerer, into the dogs in the tale of Zobéide. The *Mille et Une Nuits* no longer offers an escape from reality, for these tales of the East have become the very substance of the narrator's own modern, western reality. By 'reapplying' familiar childhood stories to an entirely different and seemingly incongruous context, a new and revealing light can be shed on the society the narrator inhabits and the characters he frequents. The immediate effects of these metaphorical transpositions can be to show that an apparently insipid reality does possess its own magic, that it can take unexpected and logic-defying directions and that characters can be transformed as if supernaturally. But in the longer term – and quite apart from their contribution to the denouement of the novel – these metaphorical transpositions also help to infuse *A la recherche* with a unity in which what is explicitly stated at a textual level is subtly heralded, nuanced or reinforced through the subtextual associations generated by networks of imagery such as these. Perhaps nowhere is this more apparent than in the character of Charlus, a paradoxical figure who both perpetuates orientalist myths of exotic sexuality in, for example, seeing Bloch as Oriental and therefore exotic/erotic, and also unwittingly embodies them.

The association between Albertine's sexuality and the *Mille et Une Nuits* was an indirect one that played – again indirectly – on the orientalist myth which equates the East with sexual licence and/or deviance. It did not, therefore, represent a particularly surprising appropriation of the source. In contrast, the metaphorical transpositions that cast Charlus in a role from the *Mille et Une Nuits* are significantly more unexpected and unconventional, as if Proust were using this subtle rewriting of the *Mille et Une Nuits* not only to herald, nuance or reinforce certain characteristics, but also to collapse orientalist myths and stereotyped distinctions between East and West; for, in Charlus, Proust offers us a vision of western reality which, in terms of 'exoticism', matches anything offered by the East, at least as it is depicted in the *Mille et Une Nuits*.

The various roles from the collection of tales ascribed to characters such as Charlus and Jupien have already been hinted at. By virtue of uttering the 'Sésame', both would appear to be likened to the virtuous figure of Ali-Baba, although a degree of ambiguity remains as to the exact nature of this association, given that, in the tale of Ali-Baba, the eponymous hero is not the only character to utter the magical formula: the greed-driven Kassim, Ali-Baba's brother, whose vice leads to a violent death at the hands of the thieves, also uses the 'Sésame', as does, of course, the ruthless leader of the band of thieves. Charlus and Jupien could therefore be any of these figures. Surely, though, this ambiguity represents a deliberate means of underscoring the fact that these *are* multifaceted characters who can be ruthless or greedy as well as virtuous or altruistic. As in the western fairytales discussed previously, the characters in the original *Mille et Une Nuits* are necessarily one-dimensional types – symbols of virtue or greed or evil – so that the didactic function of the tales is immediately penetrable. In Proust's new *Mille et Une Nuits*, in contrast, characters regain a more convincing multidimensionality, the necessity of which was realized by Proust's narrator, at least in part, through the comparison drawn between Albertine's lies and these well-known tales.

This multidimensionality of character acquires a special poignancy when we consider Charlus's homosexuality, for he, like other homosexuals in the novel, is depicted as incarnating more than one persona and as disguising his authentic self – he is the 'homme-femme' whose true identity, that of 'une femme', is fleetingly glimpsed only in unguarded moments. It is no accident, therefore, that he should be written into the tale of Ali-Baba and the forty thieves, for it is not only profuse in disguises, both literal and figurative (two of the thieves dress themselves as local townspeople to try to discover the identity of the intruder, as does their leader as an oil-merchant and later as a shop-owner; Kassim's wife wears a mask of friendship to root out her sister- and brother-in-law's secret; and the servant Marjanah adopts the façade of a sensual entertainer as a means to kill the disguised thief), but all these dualities are reinforced by a grotesquely literal division of Self in the shape of the punishment meted out to Kassim by the thieves: he is chopped into six pieces which are subsequently stitched together to create the impression of unity. These resonances are general ones, however, so let us turn our attention to specific instances of Charlus's transportation into the *Mille et Une Nuits*.

We find ourselves in *Le Temps retrouvé*, in Paris, in wartime, at night, a setting already rich in possibilities for enchantment. The narrator encounters M. de Charlus on the trail of two 'zouaves' but, significantly, he cannot initially make out the identity of the figure who interrupts this pursuit to approach him:

> Une seconde je me demandai qui me disait bonjour: c'était M. de Charlus. [. . .] M. de Charlus était arrivé aussi loin qu'il était possible de soi-même, ou plutôt il était lui-même si parfaitement masqué par ce qu'il était devenu et qui n'appartenait pas à lui seul mais à beaucoup d'autres invertis, qu'à la première minute je l'avais pris pour un autre d'entre eux [. . .]. (*TR* IV 343)

Only a *Nuits*-esque realization – the suddenness of which is conveyed in the abrupt apposition of '[u]ne seconde je me demandai qui me disait bonjour' and 'c'était M. de Charlus' – resolves the self hidden behind Charlus's much-transformed exterior. The lengthy conversation which then ensues between the narrator and Charlus concludes with the latter shaking the former's hand by way of farewell 'en continuant pendant quelques instants à me la malaxer' (*TR* IV 388). The narrator observes:

> Chez certains aveugles le toucher supplée dans une certaine mesure à la vue. Je ne sais trop de quel sens il prenait la place ici. Il croyait peut-être seulement me serrer la main, comme il crut sans doute ne faire que voir un Sénégalais qui passait dans l'ombre et ne daigna pas s'apercevoir qu'il était admiré. Mais dans ces deux cas le baron se trompait, il péchait par excès de contact et de regards. 'Est-ce que tout l'Orient de Decamps, de Fromentin, d'Ingres, de Delacroix n'est pas là-dedans?' me dit-il, encore immobilisé par le passage du Sénégalais. 'Vous savez, moi je ne m'intéresse jamais aux choses et aux êtres qu'en peintre, en philosophe. D'ailleurs je suis trop vieux. Mais quel malheur, pour compléter le tableau, que l'un de nous deux ne soit pas une odalisque!'
>
> Ce ne fut pas l'Orient de Decamps ni même de Delacroix qui commença de hanter mon imagination quand le baron m'eut quitté, mais le vieil Orient de ces

> *Mille et une Nuits* que j'avais tant aimées, et me perdant peu à peu dans le lacis de ces rues noires, je pensais au calife Haroun Al Raschid en quête d'aventures dans les quartiers perdus de Bagdad. (ibid.)[55]

Both the text and the context of this extract conspire to lend it a significance which underlies and yet transcends its immediate meaning. First is the strong suggestion made by the narrator that Charlus's conduct – whether in shaking his hand or looking at the 'Sénégalais' – has an intensity which surpasses innocent courtesy or curiosity. Second is the substance of the conversation they have just had, for it is here that Charlus, in a state of agitated excitement, draws a three-way parallel between wartime Paris – visualized as swarming with young German soldiers for whom he expresses, in imagination, a highly ambivalent admiration – the destruction of Pompeii and the fates of the biblical cities of Sodom and Gomorrah. Third is what follows their conversation, for after bidding Charlus farewell, the narrator, although as yet unaware of the purpose of the establishment, witnesses Saint-Loup going into Jupien's 'Temple de l'Impudeur'. In other words, the first explicit reference to the *Mille et Une Nuits* in a context involving Charlus is both shot through with, and framed by, suggestions of an exotic and, according to contemporary mores, deviant form of sexuality. These then pave the way for a further retrospective irony; for although, in this extract, the narrator maintains a sharp distinction between Charlus's 'Orient de Decamps' and his own 'vieil Orient de ces *Mille et une Nuits* que j'avais tant aimées', the parallel he then draws between himself and the 'calife Haroun Al Raschid en quête d'aventures dans les quartiers perdus de Bagdad' leads us in a metaphorical circle back to Charlus and specifically to his masochistic pleasures: the next vision we have of Charlus is his being beaten in Jupien's 'Temple de l'Impudeur' – a vision which prompts the narrator to evoke the tale of Zobéide beating two bitches who are, in fact, her sisters transformed by the spell of a genie. The Tale of Zobéide is summarized in the notes to the Pléiade edition as follows:

> Le calife Haroun Al Raschid, accompagné de Giafar son grand vizir, se promène la nuit, incognito, dans les rues de Bagdad. Il est intrigué par des voix, des rires, de la musique qui viennent de la maison de la belle Zobéide. Elle les accueille gracieusement mais se met ensuite à fouetter cruellement deux chiennes noires dont elle essuie finalement les larmes. Zobéide révèle alors que ses deux sœurs l'ayant trahie ont été changées en chiennes par une fée, qui l'a obligée, sous peine de subir la même métamorphose, à leur donner chaque soir cent coups de fouet. (IV 1244)

While the 'calife Haroun Al Raschid' may provide a frame for many of the tales from the *Mille et Une Nuits*, of those which Proust draws on in the novel,

Zobéide is the only character whom the caliph, like the narrator, stumbles upon. Proust has thus set up a distinction between Charlus's purely aesthetic and/or intellectual Orient and the narrator's Orient of the Arabian Nights, only to collapse it by revealing that the narrator's Orient in fact leads straight back to Charlus, himself cast as one of the characters from this collection of tales. In so doing, Proust exposes the fallacy of Charlus's protestations of innocent interest in young men. But this is an irony which we are able to appreciate only when we read on to the narrator's encounter with Jupien after having witnessed this display of masochism, for it is here that the figure of Zobéide is evoked:

> 'En attendant, dis-je à Jupien, cette maison est tout autre chose, plus qu'une maison de fous, puisque la folie des aliénés qui y habitent est mise en scène, reconstituée, visible. C'est un vrai pandemonium. J'avais cru comme le calife des *Mille et Une Nuits* arriver à point au secours d'un homme qu'on frappait, et c'est un autre conte des *Mille et Une Nuits* que j'ai vu réalisé devant moi, celui où une femme, transformée en chienne, se fait frapper volontairement pour retrouver sa forme première.' Jupien paraissait fort troublé par mes paroles, car il comprenait que j'avais vu frapper le baron. (*TR* IV 411)

The nature of the sisters' betrayal of Zobéide – so consumed were they by jealousy at the love of Zobéide and a beautiful young man that they threw the lovers overboard, causing the young man's death – finds an immediate parallel in Charlus's own extreme jealous rages; and the elements of disguise and metamorphosis which lie at the heart of the tale reach far into the psyche of Proust's homosexual characters.[56] The Charlus/'chienne' image also includes further rewritings of the tale of Zobéide that combine with other metaphorical associations in the novel to nuance the bald fact of his homosexuality. These are not, as the Pléiade editors may be suggesting, unintentional deformations of the source caused by Proust's quoting from memory (IV 1244), for they are too richly allusive to be coincidental. Most obviously, the image casts Charlus in a female role, a common by-product of metaphors relating to homosexuality in the novel; while Zobéide's sisters have undergone a single transformation from woman to beast, Charlus's is a double metamorphosis, from man to woman to dog, an end-state which also underlines his gradual degradation in the last volume of the novel to an animal-like condition. A second inversion of the original source is, of course, that these floggings are a source of sexual pleasure for Charlus – he is beaten 'volontairement'; moreover, he is beaten so that he can 'retrouver sa forme première' whereas, in the tale of Zobéide, there is no suggestion that beating the dogs will ever restore them to their original form. On the contrary, Zobéide reluctantly beats them for fear that she, too, will be turned into a dog if she does not. In Proust's new version of the tale, in contrast, this violence is a means for Charlus to realize his true self.

The reintroduction of the tale of Ali-Baba immediately after this reference to Zobéide, in the form of Jupien's 'Sésame', can deflect any further suggestions of arbitrariness, for as well as underlining the indirect link between homosexuality and the aristocracy highlighted earlier, the tale includes a number of details which allow Proust to enlarge his already potent mythology of exotic sexuality. An element of black humour, in the form of Charlus's desire for villainous young men to be employed by Jupien to indulge his appetites and the largely unconvincing attempts of those employed to appear suitably ruthless enhances the basic parallel between the 'Temple de l'Impudeur' and the thieves' den. Ironically, the young men may be more akin to the tender-hearted Zobéide, who comforts the dogs after beating them, than to the cold and cruel criminals Charlus dreams of. The influence of the Mardrus, as opposed to the Galland, translation also comes to light here, for not only does the Mardrus version generally grant greater prominence to the erotic than the Galland, but Mardrus's version of the tale of Ali-Baba also contains a likely reference to homosexual activity between an older man and a young boy. Kassim's wife, having discovered a gold dinar stuck to the bottom of the measure she had lent Ali-Baba's wife, is furious at the idea of her brother- and sister-in-law possessing untold wealth. She therefore summons her husband from his shop and 'dès que l'essouflé Kassim eut franchi le seuil de la maison, elle l'accueillit par des exclamations furibondes, tout comme si elle l'avait surprise en train de triturer quelque jeune garçon'.[57]

The *Mille et Une Nuits* sends out tendrils to all parts of the novel, backwards to the world of Léonie's plates and to Combray, and forwards to evocations of the Orient in the context of art and, ultimately, involuntary memory. All of these are entwined with the figures and exploits of Albertine and Charlus, and subtly foreshadow and reinforce what is elsewhere said either directly or via other networks of imagery. Tadié argues that most of the earlier contexts in which the tales appear 'ne portent pas sur l'essentiel et demeurent latérales' and that they alone do not justify the privileged position occupied by the *Mille et Une Nuits* (p. 226). To unearth the nature of the deeper relationship between the two works, therefore, Tadié takes as his starting point that: 'Le monde dans lequel [Proust] plonge son héros a ceci de commun avec les contes arabes que c'est un monde enchanté. Pas toujours assurément, l'existence y est souvent plate et ordinaire, mais un moment survient où tout s'abolit devant une apparition miraculeuse' (ibid.). This world of unknown riches remains beyond our apprehension unless some unexpected chance renders it visible. This chance ('hasard') is, according to Tadié, involuntary memory. Of particular importance for the narrator's artistic vocation is, of course, the series of involuntary memories which surprise him just before the final Guermantes *soirée* in *Le Temps retrouvé*, and, in fact, Tadié identifies an intensification of implicit allusions to the *Mille et Une Nuits* in the final volume of the novel which prepares for this culmination. The third of these involuntary memories is released by the napkin which returns the narrator to Balbec, and, in a clear reference to the tale of Aladdin, specifically to the genie which can transport him from China to Africa just as involuntary memory can transport the narrator from Paris to Balbec or Venice or Combray, he writes: 'mais aussitôt, comme le personnage des *Mille et Une Nuits* qui sans le savoir accomplissait précisément le rite qui faisait apparaître, visible pour lui seul, un docile génie prêt à le transporter au loin, une nouvelle vision d'azur passa devant mes yeux' (*TR* IV 447). A pure moment experienced as if outside time is expressed through the suggestion of being whisked away in sudden flight and, with these 'vagues d'interventions "surnaturelles"', says Tadié, 'les nouvelles *Mille et Une Nuits* sont nées' (p. 228).

The significance of these moments and the eloquent role played by the *Mille et Une Nuits* in their expression are unquestionable, but we ought not to play down the importance of the many other evocations of the collection of tales in the novel. We have already seen the way in which much earlier introductions of the *Mille et Une Nuits* have a bearing on the gradual movement towards the narrator's realization of his creative vocation, and, indeed, the *Mille et Une Nuits* is directly transposed on to the context of art some time before the involuntary memories of *Le Temps retrouvé*. In *La Prisonnière*, for instance, the *Mille et Une Nuits* is already expressing moments of pure joy experienced, like involuntary memories, as if outside time. The narrator may not yet fully grasp their implications, but these experiences nonetheless represent a stage which is crucial to the denouement of the novel. In *La Prisonnière*, the tales of the *Mille et Une Nuits* act as markers of a labyrinthine but magical complexity, the intricacies of which, for the moment, remain just beyond the narrator's full apprehension. Hearing the Vinteuil Septet for the first time, for example, he grapples with the feeling of disorientation:

> Où le situer? Dans l'œuvre de quel auteur étais-je? J'aurais bien voulu le savoir et, n'ayant près de moi personne à qui le demander, aurais bien voulu être un personnage de ces *Mille et Une Nuits* que je relisais sans cesse et où dans les moments d'incertitude surgit soudain un génie ou une adolescente d'une ravissante beauté, invisible pour les autres, mais non pour le héros embarrassé, à qui elle révèle exactement ce qu'il désire savoir. (*P* III 753)

His wish is rewarded, as the genie or ravishing adolescent assumes the form of 'la petite phrase de Vinteuil': 'Or à ce moment, je fus précisément favorisé d'une telle apparition magique' (ibid.). However, the ultimate *Nuits*-esque revelation can, as Tadié suggests, come only in *Le Temps retrouvé*, when the narrator is finally able to make the necessary link between pleasures such as these and his own writing. The luxurious intricacy of the Septet remains a source of wonder, though:

> Une page symphonique de Vinteuil, connue déjà au piano et qu'on entendait à l'orchestre, comme un rayon de jour d'été que le prisme de la fenêtre décompose avant son entrée dans une salle à manger obscure, dévoilait comme un trésor insoupçonné et multicolore toutes les pierreries des *Mille et Une Nuits*. (P III 758)

The *Mille et Une Nuits* has thus come full circle, for it has regained the status it first enjoyed in Combray: once again, this collection of tales is the symbol of an unquestionable source of pleasure. There is a difference, though, and a crucial one at that, for the pleasure expressed by reference to the *Mille et Une Nuits* and provoked here by contact with the work of art, and later in the related context of the involuntary memories of *Le Temps retrouvé*, is now endowed with an authenticity and a transcendence which, in the *Mille et Une Nuits* version of Combray, was, in retrospect, merely transience and illusion. There could be no easy shortcut from the *Mille et Une Nuits* of Combray to the *Mille et Une Nuits* of *Le Temps retrouvé*, however. This symbol had first to lose its lustre; it had to be re-evaluated and reapplied – whether to Albertine, to Charlus or to art – before the final realization with which this discussion opened could be reached. Having also come full circle, therefore, we might conclude that in the course of making his journey from Combray to creation, Proust, as much as Balzac, succeeded in creating 'les *Mille et Une Nuits* de l'Occident', that is, a familiar world infused with an unexpected magic.

## The magical mundane

For critics Jacques Barchilon and Peter Flinders, fairytale diverges from legend in that magical or supernatural elements seem entirely natural within the fairytale universe.[58] Fairytale characters neither flee nor doubt their soundness of mind when confronted with witch, ogre or fairy godmother, as we might reasonably expect were these latter to appear in a realist narrative. Yet this is precisely the forum into which Proust transports them, presenting familiar surroundings and experiences as under the sway of supernatural, fairytale forces. Reality is not altered by these fairytale enchantments; only, as we succumb to the writer's spell, our perception of it, for this is a spell wrought by style and, above all, in Proust, by metaphor. My discussion of 'Fairytale romances' drew on psychoanalytical readings of the familiar western fairytales which are evoked in *A la recherche* in order to create an interpretative template for the narrator/protagonist's development. In contrast, 'Les *Mille et Une Nuits* proustiennes' transported us into the 'action' by focusing on the narrator/protagonist as a *reader* of fairytale. The *Mille et Une Nuits* was shown to be, at first, an intradiegetical prop. This exotic other initially represents escape from the pressure on the narrator, which is so characteristic of the familiar world of the Self, to pursue his intellectual and creative ambitions. However, the role of these tales gradually evolves to provide an enforced stimulus to the processes of evolution that will lead to the narrator's self-realization as artist. Where the '*Mille et Une Nuits* proustiennes' explored the readerly, therefore, this final section turns to the writerly, to the culmination of the processes charted in earlier sections. Leaving behind the spellbound credulity of the young protagonist, we turn here to the mature metaphorical construction of the writer. As we shall see, the former may still be written into the text as fairytale, but it is the writer who weaves the illusions that enchant his young narrator/protagonist and, indeed, his reader.

Three models provide us with a means to explore the range of tones, functions and effects generated by the author's metaphorical appropriation of fairytale: the apparently supernatural, the feigned supernatural and the everyday supernatural. The boundaries between these three models inevitably blur. To illustrate their interaction, therefore, the figure of the fairy queen – as variously incarnated in *A la recherche* through metaphor – will provide the material for a 'case study' of quintessentially Proustian fluctuation and ambiguity.

### THE APPARENTLY SUPERNATURAL

Born of a sense of the genuinely marvellous, fairytale images of the apparently supernatural, in Proust, commonly relate to new technologies. The telephone, for instance, is an 'admirable féerie' which has the, as yet unfathomable, capacity to transport others into our presence as if by magic (G II 431). An inflation of this technological advance, the passage in which the phrase quoted above is embedded nonetheless implies, with a self-ironizing accent, that, like the characters in fairytale, we all too quickly come to see the magical as routine:[59]

> Et pourtant l'habitude met si peu de temps à dépouiller de leur mystère les forces sacrées avec lesquelles nous sommes en contact que [. . .] je ne trouvais pas assez rapide à mon gré, dans ses brusques changements, l'admirable féerie à laquelle quelques instants suffisent pour qu'apparaisse près de nous, invisible mais présent, l'être à qui nous voulions parler [. . .]. (ibid.)

Playing on a polarity that the world of fairytale manages to reconcile, for this world is at once routine for its characters and magical for its readers, Proust both prompts a renewal of vision and simultaneously highlights how this freshness of perspective can so easily fade.

If the telephone loses some of its lustre, the apparently supernatural powers of the car are, in contrast, preserved, arguably on account of the potent metaphorical associations that this mode of travel acquires in Proust's novel. Both *Sodome et Gomorrhe* and *La Prisonnière* highlight the narrator and Albertine's amazement at this delightfully spontaneous new form of transport:

> [...] prisonniers aussi hermétiquement enfermés jusque-là dans la cellule de jours distincts que jadis Méséglise et Guermantes, et sur lesquels les mêmes yeux ne pouvaient se poser dans un seul après-midi, délivrés maintenant par le géant aux bottes de sept lieues, vinrent assembler autour de l'heure de notre goûter leurs clochers et leurs tours, leurs vieux jardins que le bois avoisinant s'empressait de découvrir. (*SG* III 386)

Invested with the symbolic power to reconcile the apparently irreconcilable – as represented here by Guermantes and Méséglise – the car can also effect a dissolution of conventional temporal boundaries: travellers are no longer imprisoned within 'la cellule de jours distincts'. The terms in which Proust expresses these revelations inspired by car travel conjure up unmistakably his descriptions of the power of involuntary memory as finally unravelled in *Le Temps retrouvé*. The car is thus not only a medium for physical travel; it is also transformed into the symbol of a metaphorical journey, that being the narrator's quest for his vocation. William Carter highlights the fact that:

> these machines not only changed the way people moved through space but also how they perceived themselves and the world. People had the impression of living not only at a much faster pace but also more intensely than at any previous time in history. The French Cubist painter Fernand Léger observed that a 'modern man registers a hundred times more sensory impressions than an eighteenth-century artist'.[60]

Both literally and figuratively, the car enables an expansion of the artist's vision. But, at the time of these wondrous excursions with Albertine, Proust's narrator is not yet an artist and, although the car enables prodigious physical progress, the narrator remains a prisoner of time, trapped, as the allusive presence of *Sleeping Beauty* in the text implies, in the dormant state that equates to his relationship with Albertine. As a locus for the resolution of contradictory psychological impulses, therefore, fairytale fittingly dramatizes the 'powerful Proustian dialectic of statis and kinesis'.[61] This dialectic, according to Carter, is generated by the narrator's confusion of erotic desire and the desire to travel. And, indeed, the narrator's desire to speed along in a car with Albertine by his side is, in no small part, fused with a desire to keep apace with, and control of, this 'bacchante à bicyclette' (*JF* II 228). The narrator's own realization of the metaphorical value of car travel is therefore delayed. Preoccupied, in *La Prisonnière*, with those distant, exotic worlds, such as Venice, that Albertine's presence prevents him from exploring, the narrator fails to realize the extent to which an unfamiliar perspective on the familiar can feed the artist's vision. As one noted theorist of travel, Jean-Didier Urbain, argues,

> it is 'easier to be in unfamiliar surroundings than to make one's own surroundings familiar', since defamiliarisation is a form of disorientation at home, an experience of endoticism that is much more difficult to achieve because it is a matter of creating a feeling of elsewhere in the here and now rather than actually going to experience it in another time or place by transporting your body far away or into an enclave of the past.[62]

In the creation of a fairytale universe and, perhaps, above all, in the creation of a Proustian *Mille et Une Nuits*, the narrator/writer will ultimately effect this exoticization of the everyday.

The narrator's current status as an unpromising artist, yet also his potential to overcome the barriers to achieving that identity, are subtly underlined by the intertextual presence in this extract of the story of Tom Thumb, for Tom Thumb is the quintessential unpromising hero whose tale tells of triumph over adversity despite the seeming unlikelihood of success or the obstacles one faces. The tale of this lilliputian character is summoned up in the figure of the giant with seven-league boots, and this implied reference further extends the metaphorical paradigm which interlaces car travel with the journey to one's vocation.[63] Not only do the boots evoke the great distances covered, whether on a physical or creative quest, but also their extraordinary power to shrink or expand to fit whoever wears them draws attention to the freedom of this mode of travel: the journey is dictated by the traveller, not by the preordained path of the railway line. In its broadest sense, therefore, the car represents independence from a fixed path, be that of thought or experience. This is a necessity, as Coupe has shown, for the powerful reinventor of myth.[64] As if to reflect this, the car which takes the narrator and Albertine home after an outing in *La Prisonnière* follows a winding route: 'Et elle s'engagea pour le retour dans de petites allées sinueuses où les arbres d'hiver, habillés de lierre et de ronces, comme des ruines, semblaient conduire à la demeure d'un magicien'

(*P* III 680). This meandering path evokes the detours that the narrator, like the fairytale hero, will explore, whether in society or in his relationship with Albertine. And yet, even when distracted by these diversions, hope remains: this meandering path promises to lead, at least tentatively ('semblaient conduire'), to a supernatural destination ('la demeure d'un magicien'). Before the nature of the narrator's ultimate, 'supernatural' destination is defined and attained by him, however, he will negotiate the different manifestations of the supernatural that he encounters on his path. These include the lure of the magician's power, hinted at here, and this and other forms of supernatural power that tempt him will be explored in Part III of the book. Before achieving his goal, he will also evolve an independent understanding of the supernatural, elaborating a personal vision of transcendence through artistic production.

## THE FAIRY QUEEN

Significant among the detours taken by Proust's fairytale hero is the path which introduces him to the fluctuating figure of the fairy queen:

> alors chaque château, chaque hôtel ou palais fameux a sa dame ou sa fée comme les forêts leurs génies et leurs divinités les eaux. Parfois, cachée au fond de son nom, la fée se transforme au gré de la vie de notre imagination qui la nourrit; c'est ainsi que l'atmosphère où Mme de Guermantes existait en moi, après n'avoir été pendant des années que le reflet d'un verre de lanterne magique et d'un vitrail d'église, commençait à éteindre ses couleurs, quand des rêves tout autres l'imprégnèrent de l'écumeuse humidité des torrents.
>
> Cependant, la fée dépérit si nous nous approchons de la personne réelle à laquelle correspond son nom, car, cette personne, le nom alors commence à la refléter et elle ne contient rien de la fée; la fée peut renaître si nous nous éloignons de la personne; mais si nous restons auprès d'elle, la fée meurt définitivement et avec elle le nom [. . .]. (*G* II 311)

This is arguably the most explicit declaration to appear in *A la recherche* of the transformative power of the imagination and the processes of illusion and disillusion on which the novel is constructed. The passage also establishes Mme de Guermantes as the novel's undisputed 'fairy queen', and, indeed, the majority of references to fairies in the novel are allusions to this character: the church at Combray, the first site with which the young narrator associates her, is 'une vallée visitée des fées' (*S* I 60); his first vision of Mme de Guermantes in this context describes 'un plissement de la robe de la fée' (*S* I 173); she inhabits 'des lieux [. . .] féeriques' (*G* II 335); her voice evokes 'la plainte poétique d'une fée' (ibid.); she is capable of working enchantments;[65] and even the frequent use of the term 'apparition' to describe her arrivals invests them with a trace of the supernatural.⁶⁶ She is not the novel's only fairy, however. Mme de Villeparisis, Robert de Saint-Loup and Mme Verdurin are, to quite different effect, granted this same incarnation.

Mme de Villeparisis acquires the magical potency of a fairy in the narrator's eyes in the course of his first visit to Balbec, a status prompted by her unexpected acquaintance with his grandmother:

> Tandis que cette Mme de Villeparisis était bien la véritable, elle n'avait pas été victime d'un enchantement qui l'eût dépouillée de sa puissance, mais était capable au contraire d'en mettre un à la disposition de la mienne qu'il centuplerait, et grâce auquel, comme si j'avais été porté par les ailes d'un oiseau fabuleux, j'allais franchir en quelques instants les distances sociales infinies – au moins à Balbec – qui me séparaient de Mlle de Stermaria. (*JF* II 45)⁶⁷

The transgression of social boundaries and the possibility of social mobility are well-known features of fairytale. Mme de Villeparisis is thus the quintessential fairy godmother, albeit unconsciously endowed with the power to grant the narrator, like Cinderella, the appearance of a higher social standing. In this regard, she provides an unwittingly benevolent foil to Mme de Guermantes's more ambivalent appearance in this role. If the fairy loses her charm when approached, however, myth and reality must be incompatible. In writing Mme de Villeparisis into this role, therefore, Proust is also embedding within the image the clue that the narrator's hopes regarding her power will inevitably be dashed. What the narrator does not realize, of course, is that the 'distances sociales infinies' he perceives are, in fact, as mythical as the fabulous birdlike Guermantes he hopes will enable him to span them. Through the fairytale intertext, therefore, the boundaries between the mythical and the real shift and blur to mirror the narrator's own oscillating vision.

Saint-Loup completes the Guermantes/fairy trinity and is, moreover, the only male character in the novel to be granted this role. On the transformation noted by the narrator from Saint-Loup's initial brusqueness to his subsequent affection, we read: 'Les premiers rites d'exorcisme une fois accomplis, comme une fée hargneuse dépouille sa première apparence et se pare de grâces enchanteresses, je vis cet être dédaigneux devenir le plus aimable, le plus prévenant jeune homme que j'eusse jamais rencontré' (*JF* II 91). An initially unpromising friendship develops between the narrator and a character defined, like so many in fairytale, by duality and disguise. The image aptly follows the literal pattern of fairytale whereby the fairy godmother remains disguised while she tests the merit of the hero/heroine, only to reward him/her subsequently if found to be deserving. Saint-Loup's initial reserve is thus transformed into a willing deployment of his power to help the narrator transcend social boundaries. More implicitly, Saint-Loup's incarnation as a fairy not only plants the clue that there is more to this figure than meets the eye, but also hints at the nature of his hidden identity.[68]

This fairy trio, which comprises Mme de Guermantes, Mme de Villeparisis and Saint-Loup, offers a unifying symbol of the aristocratic Guermantes' identity. In the eyes of the young narrator, it is also a symbol of their (real or imagined) power. As the only character to be likened to a fairy who is neither a Guermantes nor an aristocrat, Mme Verdurin is, therefore, the tantalizing outsider. Yet it is she whom Proust describes as a '*véritable* fée' (my italics, *SG* III 140). Moreover, he does so in the context of an apparent imposture on her part, namely her sudden appearance in the world of the aristocracy:

> mais quand à côté d'elle [la princesse Yourbeletieff], dans son avant-scène, nous verrons, à toutes les représentations des 'Russes', siéger comme une véritable fée, ignorée jusqu'à ce jour de l'aristocratie, Mme Verdurin, nous pourrons répondre aux gens du monde qui croiront aisément Mme Verdurin fraîchement débarquée avec la troupe de Diaghilev, que cette dame avait déjà existé dans des temps différents, et passé par divers avatars dont celui-là ne différait qu'en ce qu'il était le premier qui amenait enfin, désormais assuré, et en marche d'un pas de plus en plus rapide, le succès si longtemps et si vainement attendu par la Patronne. (*SG* III 140-1)

Mme de Guermantes may be a 'fée' to the young narrator, but this fairy 'perishes' when he approaches her, for her fairy status is merely an illusion generated by the idealizing prism of the young narrator's perception. She is thus the epitome of the apparently supernatural. As Proust playfully explains: 'là où on croyait [...] rencontrer la fée Viviane on trouve le Chat botté' (*SG* III 234). From the genuinely powerful sorceress of Arthurian legend, she is transformed – following the cycle of the narrator's vision – into the protagonist of a tale based, fittingly, on the creation of an artificial façade.[69] And yet, a closer examination of the tale of Puss-in-Boots may seem to muddy the waters of this apparently clear allusion, for, in the fairytale, the guise of grandeur that Puss-in-Boots creates for his master is preserved intact. Why, then, should Proust introduce this tale in relation to the narrator's crumbling illusions surrounding Mme de Guermantes? Far from being inappropriate, however, Proust's reworking of the original source is apt and suggestive. Not only does its introduction highlight the narrator's likely mastery of Mme de Guermantes, in the form of the cat who helps him acquire status; in inverting its outcome, Proust also stresses the need to uncover the truth that lies behind appearance, to refuse the easy path of surface perception. By extension, this new rendering of *Le Chat botté* highlights the importance of the narrator's transition from passivity to activity. A passive re-enactment of the original source would ally him with the characters in the tale who are the dupe of the deceptive façade created by Puss-in-Boots. If he is to transcend the status of helpless, 'acted-upon' character and achieve that of creating agent/writer, he must unravel the misguided illusions of the character's perceptions. Only then will he be able to create the imaginative illusions of the writer's vision.

In contrast to Mme de Guermantes's deceptive fairy status, Mme Verdurin, Proust seems to be suggesting, is a true fairy, for she has the power to reinvent herself and, ultimately, to manipulate the social world to her advantage. The supreme testimony to her power is, of course, her final avatar as the princesse de Guermantes. The once 'déclassée' Odette, although never explicitly likened to a fairy, likewise presides, by *Sodome et Gomorrhe*, over a salon described as 'une salle magique' which, 'grâce à un changement à vue dans une féerie', is peopled with eminent guests (*SG* III 142). More generally, too, Proust's fascination with those capable of transmutation and renewal, according to the context in which they find themselves, is granted the same metaphorical expression: 'Chaque personne en visite chez une autre devenait différente. Sans parler des métamorphoses merveilleuses qui s'accomplissaient ainsi chez les fées, dans le salon de Mme Swann, [. . .] M. de Bréauté lui-même semblait un homme nouveau' (*SG* III 146). For Proust, it is individuals' power to remake themselves, whether on a grand scale as achieved by Mme Verdurin, or quite naturally several times a day, that represents the truly amazing, the everyday supernatural, the multifaceted plurality that can bring about a social revolution. Appropriately to Proust's vision, manifestations of social revolution are intrinsic to fairytale as a genre. Not only do these tales frequently portray marriage across the social boundaries, but Perrault himself was criticized by contemporaries for calling into question the social order by depicting a form of social mobility not acceptable to seventeenth-century French society.

If Mme Verdurin provides the fairy archetype of the everyday supernatural, the novel's characterization of Mme de Guermantes marks a transition from the apparently supernatural (in the eyes of the young narrator/protagonist) to the feigned supernatural, for this latter is the perspective of the mature narrator/protagonist and writer. Reflecting the novel's subtle slippage between the voices of each of these narrators, the two models may coincide, for even while, in the eyes of the narrator/protagonist, Mme de Guermantes continues to be endowed with the supernatural qualities of a fairy, the mature narrator/writer is already chipping away at this seemingly indestructible identity and thus also at the naivety and blindness of his younger, intradiegetical self. The homogeneity of references to Mme de Guermantes's incarnation as 'fée' in itself hints at the absence of any distinct character or identity: the narrator's idealization rarely extends beyond the single term 'fée' or its derivatives. If, as theorists such as Bettelheim imply, this establishes her as an archetype, it also suggests that she is little more than the sum of qualities dictated by the 'génie des Guermantes'.[70] Nor is she explicitly associated with any individual fairytale. To do so would be to create a set of expectations as to her actions – the intertext would assert itself – whereas Mme de Guermantes in fact does little or nothing with any power or influence she may have. Within fairytale as a genre, the fairy's most common role is to help the hero or heroine of the story to achieve the perfect love-match. This is the role implicitly played out by Mme de Villeparisis; or, at least, this is the narrator's hope, for his grandmother thwarts the possibility, denying him the fairytale's happy ending. Arguably, in the early part of the novel, Mme de Guermantes is unable to fulfil this role for the narrator, for the object of our fairytale hero's desire is the fairy herself. This deviated rendering of the fairytale structure serves from the outset to imply the impossibility of any amorous relationship between them, for such a scenario is not plausible even in the fantastical world of fairytale. Indeed, the fact that the fairy in the original tales is commonly a maternal figure casts the infatuation with Mme de Guermantes as an Oedipal desire which must be resolved.[71] Psychoanalysts, notably Bettelheim, have interpreted fairytales as a forum in which Oedipal crises are worked out:

> Fairy tales can [. . .] show the child the way through that thorniest of thickets, the oedipal period. [. . .] Through simple and direct images the fairy story helps the child to sort out his complex and ambivalent feelings, so that these begin to fall each one into a separate place, rather than being all one big muddle. (p. 74)

Only when this complex is resolved does Mme de Guermantes become a more benevolent figure, more in accordance with the conventional image of the fairy godmother:

> Mais je n'avais pas songé que ma guérison, en me donnant à l'égard de Mme de Guermantes une attitude normale, accomplirait parallèlement la même œuvre en ce qui la concernait et rendrait possible une amabilité, une amitié qui ne m'importaient plus. Jusque-là les efforts du monde entier ligués pour me rapprocher d'elle eussent expiré devant le mauvais sort que jette un amour malheureux. Des fées plus puissantes que les hommes ont décrété que, dans ces cas-là, *rien ne pourra servir jusqu'au jour où nous aurons dit sincèrement dans notre cœur la parole:*

*'Je n'aime plus.'* J'en avais voulu à Saint-Loup de ne m'avoir pas mené chez sa tante. Mais pas plus que n'importe qui, il n'était capable de briser un enchantement. (*G* II 668, my italics).

Neither a vicarious effort nor a consciously cultivated pretence can bring about a genuine transformation, only a heartfelt emotion. In this, Proust's observation mirrors the central theme of *Beauty and the Beast*, the tale which, Bettelheim argues, dramatizes most obviously the process of maturation that detaches a child's Oedipal attachment from the parent, transforming and transferring it on to the lover.[72] All these resonances suggest that Proust has consciously echoed Perrault's and others' fairytales in his novel and, in particular, the unconscious desires and the means of resolution of those desires which he detected in them.

In the wake of the narrator's 'guérison', Mme de Guermantes is metamorphosed into a 'normal' maternal figure ('une attitude normale'), advising the narrator on matters of love.[73] She also assumes the role of fairy godmother for Albertine whose mother is, like Cinderella's, dead.[74] Following the model of Cinderella's fairy godmother transforming her ward's attire, Mme de Guermantes provides advice on Albertine's clothes; but, unlike the genuine fairy godmother, she does not act directly. Cinderella/Albertine's transformation is mediated by the narrator, and Mme de Guermantes provides what limited help she does only when the narrator no longer appears to be asking anything of her. Mme de Guermantes thus emerges as an ambivalent fairy, any possible incarnation as the true 'bonne fée' of the fairytale restricted by her keen awareness of social status.[75] The indifference to social categories revealed in the original tales vanishes in the fairytale realm of the Guermantes, as the genre's utopian ideals come up against the tribalism of the European aristocracy.[76]

## THE FEIGNED SUPERNATURAL

The figure of the fairy queen occupies the space where the apparently supernatural, the everyday supernatural and the feigned supernatural merge. Mme Verdurin provides the genuine foil to the apparently undisputed fairy queen, Mme de Guermantes. She and others endowed with the power of social reinvention offer a celebratory model of the everyday supernatural. Mme de Guermantes, in contrast, represents at once the apparently supernatural to the idealizing young narrator/protagonist and the feigned supernatural for the mature narrator/writer who, by infusing his fairytale imagery with an undercurrent of caricature, debunks her elevated status. Indeed, the primary function of images of the feigned supernatural is satirical. The moment, for example, that Morel manages to secure the narrator's agreement that this latter will speak to Mme Verdurin on his behalf, 'le "respect" de Morel à mon égard s'envola comme par enchantement' (*SG* III 302). The presumption of supernatural intervention is, of course, ironic, and the image leaves neither reader nor narrator in any doubt as to the altogether human motivation and agency behind Morel's actions. Nor does the narrator come away unscathed, for images of the feigned supernatural also enable a self-ironizing perspective on the part of the mature narrator/writer who exposes the excuses of his younger intradiegetical self. In *La Prisonnière*, for instance, we read how: 'J'avais promis à Albertine que, si je ne sortais pas avec elle, je me mettrais au travail. Mais le lendemain, comme si, profitant de nos sommeils, la maison avait miraculeusement voyagé, je m'éveillais par un temps différent, sous un autre climat' (*P* III 589). The figure of the flying carpet (or house or armchair) is a powerful one for Proust which is closely bound up with his relationship to art.[77] Here though, the supernatural template – in denying any agency on the part of the narrator/protagonist – represents a denial of responsibility faced with his failure to work. As previously suggested, questions of agency and passivity are embedded in the structures of fairytale: the apparently helpless protagonist must make the transition to action if he is to overcome the obstacles before him. The supernatural forces which permeate the pages of fairytale can either help or hinder the protagonist: both good and bad fairies populate these tales. They therefore provide a potent narrative within which to play out the opposing pulls of stasis and kinesis that plague the narrator/protagonist.

## THE EVERYDAY SUPERNATURAL

In poking fun at his own capacity for procrastination, the narrator's fanciful image of a flying house also serves another purpose, for it reminds us of the quasi-magical transformation that each new day can bring. It thus encourages a freshness of vision which repoeticizes the habitual. It is this goal which lies at the heart of images of the everyday supernatural. At their least elaborate, such fairytale images recall for us the pleasures of a sound sleep, particularly for the insomniac: 'Mon sommeil et ma grasse matinée du lendemain n'étaient plus qu'un charmant conte de fées' (*G* II 391).[78] And at the more complex end of the spectrum, images of the everyday supernatural become the vehicles for an Impressionist aesthetic, as in Proust's extended meditation on the perceptions of a deaf man:

> Comme le bruit était pour lui, avant sa surdité, la forme perceptible que revêtait la cause d'un mouvement, les objets remués sans bruit semblent l'être sans cause; dépouillés de toute qualité sonore, ils montrent une activité spontanée, ils semblent

vivre; ils remuent, s'immobilisent, prennent feu d'eux-mêmes. D'eux-mêmes ils s'envolent comme les monstres ailés de la préhistoire. Dans la maison solitaire et sans voisins du sourd, le service qui, avant que l'infirmité fût complète, montrait déjà plus de réserve, se faisait silencieusement, est assuré maintenant, avec quelque chose de subreptice, par des muets, ainsi qu'il arrive pour un roi de féerie. (G II 376–7)

This same man's perception of a building collapsing is also teased out in all its experiential reality: 'moins matériel même qu'un palais de théâtre dont il n'a pourtant pas la minceur, il tombera dans l'univers magique sans que la chute de ses lourdes pierres de taille ternisse de la vulgarité d'aucun bruit la chasteté du silence' (G II 377). Proust stages the visual impression as experienced without its explanation or rationale, the effect without its cause. For the person deprived of the sense of hearing, therefore, the apparently irrational visual impression is viewed as if it were the product of magic. An unfamiliar deviation from their usual cooperation, this isolation of the senses is reminiscent of the Impressionists' separation of sensory perception from preconceived knowledge or intellect. Playing on the dual meaning of the verb 'entendre', both hearing and the too hasty impression of understanding are stripped away. Proust's is certainly not a 'surface' Impressionism;[79] but the art of observation on which the novel is based nonetheless parallels Monet's famous exhortation: 'Quand vous sortez pour peindre, pensez seulement ceci: voici un petit carré de bleu, de rose, un ovale vert, une raie jaune, et peignez-les exactement comme ils vous apparaissent.'[80] Yet the visual impression is not an end in itself for Proust; its functions are varied and, here, the estranging of the everyday challenges any presumption of effortless knowledge. By extension, if the ideal journey for Proust is not to another country or another place, but the possibility of seeing a familiar world through the eyes of another, his insights into the deaf man's perspective – as expressed through imagery of the supernatural – enable precisely such a renewal of vision with all its seeming magic.[81] As Proust explains: 'si l'habitude est une seconde nature, elle nous empêche de connaître la première dont elle n'a ni les cruautés, ni les enchantements' (SG III 151).

Proust's Impressionist aesthetic is familiar to his readers: critics have focused on the writer's stylistic Impressionism and his fictional painter Elstir's Impressionist vision.[82] But scenes of literary impressionism that are infused with imagery of fairytale and of the supernatural achieve something more, for the evocation of the world of fairytale further reminds the reader of the *pleasures* of this renewal of vision, the pleasures of a return to the credulity and pre-intellectual apprehensions of childhood which may ultimately be transformed by the adult and by the intellect into the stylized phrases of the work of art.

A variation on this 'estranging', and thus repoeticizing, effect relies on a fairytale suppression of time. For the narrator/protagonist of *Le Temps retrouvé* returning to the city after an extended period in a sanatorium, for instance, his own dislocation from Parisian society has subjectively transformed it into the palace of Sleeping Beauty. The narrator expects to find everyone lying dormant, separated from the world outside and finally to awaken with everything exactly as it was before the period of 'sleep'. In reality, he finds himself in a quite different supernatural realm, one whose social composition has undergone a kaleidoscopic reshuffling, and in which the characters have been metamorphosed into older embodiments of themselves. The ostensible absence of a natural, gradual process of ageing could find no more fitting an expression than the fairytale image:

> Le prince [de Guermantes] avait encore en recevant cet air bonhomme d'un roi de féerie que je lui avais trouvé la première fois, mais cette fois, semblant s'être soumis lui-même à l'étiquette qu'il avait imposée à ses invités, il s'était affublé d'une barbe blanche et, traînant à ses pieds qu'elles alourdissaient comme des semelles de plomb, semblait avoir assumé de figurer un des 'âges de la vie'. Ses moustaches étaient blanches aussi, comme s'il restait après elles le gel de la forêt du Petit Poucet. Elles semblaient incommoder la bouche raidie et, l'effet une fois produit, il aurait dû les enlever. (*TR* IV 499)

The metaphorical shifts within the passage – from fairytale enchantment to what appears, to the narrator, to be a deliberate and disconcerting disguise – accentuate the narrator/protagonist's disorientation on seeing this dramatically altered prince de Guermantes. The transition from this aristocrat's suitably regal status at the beginning of the passage as an imposing 'roi de féerie' to an implied association with the diminutive Tom Thumb by the end only reinforces the prince's physical degeneration.

The 'bal costumé' episode starkly demonstrates that time cannot be transcended in a physical sense, as in *Sleeping Beauty*; but from the earliest pages of the novel, there are hints that such power lies within the province of art. So absorbed does the young narrator become in his reading in *Du côté de chez Swann*, for example, that he loses track of time, a familiar experience which, in being expressed through imagery of the supernatural, serves Proust's Impressionist aesthetic:

> Quelquefois même cette heure prématurée sonnait deux coups de plus que la dernière; il y en avait donc une que je n'avais pas entendue, quelque chose qui

avait eu lieu n'avait pas eu lieu pour moi; l'intérêt de la lecture, magique comme un profond sommeil, avait donné le change à mes oreilles hallucinées et effacé la cloche d'or sur la surface azurée du silence. (S I 86–7)

The act of reading induces a separation from external reality in the narrator that is deliberately evocative of that undergone by Sleeping Beauty ('magique comme un profond sommeil'), but just as it is Sleeping Beauty's destiny eventually to awaken, so, too, can the narrator's engagement with the book he is reading be only temporary. Moreover, as we have seen, the period of 'sleep' is a passive, withdrawn one which, although necessary to development, is in itself sterile if prolonged. But passivity dominates at this stage, as implied by the 'secondhandedness' of the narrator's aesthetic endeavour – he is reading someone else's work – and by the sense of the unexplained, the not (yet) understood, which is encapsulated in the hint that magical forces are at play.

Traces of a more active and individualized aesthetic appreciation are nonetheless breaking through by *A l'ombre des jeunes filles en fleurs*. This volume signals, albeit tentatively, a more productive interplay between the work of art and the (narrator's apprehension of the) external world. The three trees which remind the narrator of the 'clochers de Martinville' generate a sense of intense happiness and of temporal boundaries wavering:

> de sorte que mon esprit ayant trébuché entre quelque année lointaine et le moment présent, les environs de Balbec vacillèrent et je me demandai si toute cette promenade n'était pas une fiction, Balbec un endroit où je n'étais jamais allé que par l'imagination, Mme de Villeparisis un personnage de roman et les trois vieux arbres la réalité qu'on retrouve en levant les yeux de dessus le livre qu'on était en train de lire et qui vous décrivait un milieu dans lequel on avait fini par se croire effectivement transporté. (*JF* II 77)[83]

The number three, as we have seen, recurs in many fairytales and taps into concepts which are embedded in the western cultural consciousness such as the Christian Trinity. With its implications of simultaneous plurality and unity, the Trinity echoes the impression of a blurring of boundaries which the narrator experiences while contemplating the 'clochers de Martinville' (S I 182). But the number three is also, for one theorist of the fairytale, the first figure of a real and reassuring plurality without the amorphousness of multiplicity.[84] These unconscious associations may, in part, explain the young narrator's sense of joy. However, the image of a quasi-supernatural transportation into the book being read – along with the confusion between past and present, external reality and fiction, which precedes it – underlines the still-underdeveloped nature of the narrator's understanding of the relationship between art and Time. Indeed, that the world of artistic creation remains mysterious and inaccessible to the narrator/protagonist for much of the novel is reinforced by the homogeneity and imaginative paucity of many of the fairytale images we find introduced in this context: a large proportion rely on little more than vaguely evocative terms such as 'enchanté' or 'enchantement'. Elstir's *Miss Sacripant*, for instance, 'me causa cette sorte particulière d'enchantement que dispensent des œuvres non seulement d'une exécution délicieuse, mais aussi d'un sujet si singulier et si séduisant que c'est à lui que nous attribuons une partie de leur charme' (*JF* II 203).[85] Despite some attempt to elucidate the nature of this 'enchantement', the extract succeeds only in coming full circle to another expression suggesting the mystification of a magical spell, 'charme'. Both 'charme' and 'enchantement' are fluid terms: supernatural in origins, they have been stripped, by a process of social dilution, of their magical meanings.[86] Characters' use of these terms in the novel may therefore acquire an unconscious duality and ambiguity, for what is intended as aesthetic praise – and, implicitly, a recognition of the transcendent power of art – may be motivated at least as much by social concerns. The ostensibly artistic Mme Verdurin, for example, may boast that Morel is able to 'enchanter' her guests with his violin (*SG* III 359), but this is as much an expression of confidence in the social success of her 'petit clan' as it is a comment on the effects of aesthetic appreciation. Likewise, Norpois – significantly, along with Swann, one of the narrator's early aesthetic (mis)guides – claims the narrator must have been 'enchanté' at La Berma's performance of the role of Phèdre (*JF* I 448). However, the fact that he also describes himself, in the same conversation, as being 'enchanté' by his visit to 'le roi Théodose' betrays not only that he perceives a veneer of aesthetic appreciation to be a necessary social accessory, but also that art possesses no 'supernatural' qualities for him (*JF* I 451). The fact that the young narrator cannot even claim to have experienced the 'enchantement' that Norpois announces seems to him to render the world of art all the more elusive.

*La Prisonnière* is, in many respects, a transitional volume in the evolution of the narrator's artistic appreciation;[87] and by the time of the events it narrates, the narrator has surpassed early aesthetic guides, such as Swann or Norpois, to become an artistic mentor himself. Indeed, Vinteuil's music provides a pivot for a comparison between Swann's and the narrator's appreciation of the supernatural qualities of art. In *Du côté de chez Swann*, Swann asks of the 'petite phrase': 'Est-ce une fée?' (*S* I 346). This tentative probing exposes not only his avoidance of the confidently independent aesthetic evaluation, but also his persistent overlaying of the uncertainties which characterize his relationship with Odette on to his response to the work of art. The narrator of *La Prisonnière*, in contrast, boldly identifies the recurrent motifs in Vinteuil's work as its 'fées familières' (*P* III 875). Moreover, the association between art and 'enchantement' that so troubled the narrator in his conversation with Norpois itself acquires a whole new sophistication in *La Prisonnière*: 'Dans la musique de Vinteuil', the narrator realizes,

> il y avait de ces visions qu'il est impossible d'exprimer et presque défendu de contempler, puisque, quand au moment de s'endormir on reçoit la caresse de leur irréel enchantement, à ce moment même, où la raison nous a déjà abandonnés, les yeux se scellent et, avant d'avoir eu le temps de connaître non seulement l'ineffable mais l'invisible, on s'endort. (*P* III 876)

'Enchantement' no longer evokes, as in earlier volumes, the frustrations of the aesthetic outsider who perceives himself as unable to understand and thus appreciate fully the work of art. It marks, rather, the narrator's newly evolved realization that art *cannot* be 'understood' in the sense of an intellectual unweaving of its component parts. To attempt to do so would be to rob it of its genuine 'magic'. While an instinctive desire to grasp the nature of, and reasons for, aesthetic pleasure persists, therefore, the realization that this is 'impossible d'exprimer [. . .] ineffable [. . .] invisible' accompanies it.

Engagement with the work of other writers can offer only a temporary and, as the fairytale imagery underlines, illusory transcendence of time. It is only in *Le Temps retrouvé* that the narrator/protagonist fully understands how such transcendence can be achieved in a permanent and productive way in the creation of his own work of art. The triggers for this revelation are the involuntary memories of the final volume of the novel. In describing the first of these – the uneven paving-stone – Proust reintroduces, but inverts, the images of enchantment which marked his earlier mystification before the work of art: 'Ceux [les doutes] qui m'assaillaient tout à l'heure au sujet de la réalité de mes dons littéraires et même de la réalité de la littérature se trouvaient levés comme par enchantement' (*TR* IV 445). In place of a distorted vision, the narrator enjoys a sudden clarity, and a clarity grounded in the supra-temporal moment. As if to highlight his freedom from his earlier perception, Proust stresses that this revelation occurs '*comme* par enchantement' (my italics), not 'par enchantement', that is, through simile rather than metaphor. A distance is thus established between the author and protagonist. The author is drawing on the figure of an enchantment as a suitable vehicle by which to convey the sudden and unforeseen nature of the revelation the narrator/protagonist has experienced. In contrast, the narrator/protagonist has been the victim of an enchantment which has perverted his vision of art and from which he has unexpectedly been freed.[88] As potential creator, this narrator/protagonist can thus distinguish himself, for the first time, from the bibliophile who opens a book 'pour s'enchanter' (*TR* IV 466). As the memories of his childhood affection for *François le Champi* make clear, he is no longer in passive thrall to existing works of art:

> Certes, la 'plume' de George Sand, pour prendre une expression de Brichot qui aimait tant dire qu'un livre était écrit 'd'une plume alerte', ne me semblait pas du tout, comme elle avait paru si longtemps à ma mère avant qu'elle modelât lentement ses goûts littéraires sur les miens, une plume magique. Mais c'était une plume que sans le vouloir j'avais électrisée comme s'amusent souvent à faire les collégiens, et voici que mille riens de Combray, et que je n'apercevais plus depuis longtemps, sautaient légèrement d'eux-mêmes et venaient à la queue leu leu se suspendre au bec aimanté, en une chaîne interminable et tremblante de souvenirs. (*TR* IV 463)

In fact, existing works of art now serve his own, acting, for instance, as triggers for his memory. No longer a homogenized 'enchantement', the existing work of art is dissected for what it can stimulate for the benefit of the narrator's own creation.

As if to reflect this, fairytale, too, becomes purely a source to be plundered by the author. The novel thus finishes with an image that subtly reintroduces previously exploited elements of the world of fairytale, but which significantly avoids any direct reference to the 'charmes', 'enchantements' or 'féeries' of the earlier narrator/character's evocations of art:

> Aussi, si elle m'était laissée assez longtemps pour accomplir mon œuvre, ne manquerais-je pas d'abord d'y décrire les hommes, cela dût-il les faire ressembler à des êtres monstrueux, comme occupant une place si considérable, à côté de celle si restreinte qui leur est réservée dans l'espace, une place au contraire prolongée sans mesure puisqu'ils touchent simultanément, comme des géants plongés dans les années à des époques, vécues par eux si distantes, entre lesquelles tant de jours sont venus se placer – dans le Temps. (*TR* IV 625)

The image of a giant with each foot in a distant (temporal) space is an evocative one in the context of the novel, for, of all the fairytales which Proust mentions, it most immediately conjures up, for the attentive reader, the seven-league boots described in *Tom Thumb* which allow the wearer simultaneously to occupy two distant spaces. Introduced at the completion of the novel, the seven-league boots, which have already been associated with involuntary memory and the creative vocation through the metaphorical significance of the car, provide a metaphorical arch which links the seven-volume span of *A la recherche*. In an image of simultaneity, they therefore convey both the distance between the narrator-as-potential-creator and the young narrator-protagonist, and the continuing necessity of this younger incarnation to the realization of the mature narrator's vocation.

This first part of the study has charted a progression from temporary stasis to an enforced realization, on the part of the narrator/protagonist, of the need to develop and, finally, to the culmination of that development in the author's creation of a metaphorical fairytale world. And yet we have seen few precise models for the narrator to emulate on this journey. Fairytale certainly presents possibilities for overcoming the obstacles fate throws in one's path and offers the encouraging message (even if the outcome of the Proustian fairytale may destabilize it) that obstacles *can* be overcome. Marina Warner argues that:

> On the whole fairy tales are not passive or active; their mood is optative – announcing what might be. Imagining the fate that lies ahead and ways of dealing with it (if adverse – as in 'Hansel and Gretel' and 'Donkeyskin'), or achieving it (if favourable – as in 'Puss in Boots'), is the stuff of Mother Goose tales. The genre is characterized by 'heroic optimism', as if to say, 'one day, we might be happy, even if it won't last.' (p. xvi)

However, the heroes and heroines of the fairytale remain on the level of archetype, the generalized embodiments of a characteristic or impulse. For the narrator/protagonist who is still unable to see beyond the everyday, unpromising heroes they depict, therefore, a more conventionally heroic ideal retains its appeal for much of his quest. It is to this that we turn in the next part of the study as we examine the legends of performance, music and text.

If, in their substance, fairytale and, as we shall see, artistic legends represent both models and counter-models for the narrator/protagonist, their various structures and conventions are also significant for the narrator/writer. Fairytale, as a genre, is 'promiscuous and omnivorous and anarchically heterogeneous, absorbing high and low elements, tragic and comic tones into its often simple, rondo-like structure of narrative'.[89] Marina Warner's description could, at least in part, apply to Proust's own text. Soriano, too, characterizes Perrault's fairytales as a synthesis of 'culture savante' and 'culture populaire' (p. xiii), highlighting, as one illustration, the blend of tones and registers which is again so typical of Proust's own aesthetic: '[Perrault] rend grotesque une situation qui pourrait être dramatique, ou parfois il affecte le ton dramatique au moment où nous avons fini par admettre que la situation est grotesque' (p. 111). The stylistic avenues opened up for Proust by fairytale are supplemented by the generic models explored in the next part of the book. These models, which include such a broad generic spectrum as puppet theatre, fable and opera, offer Proust a range of aesthetic possibilities that he may variously adopt, adapt or reject. All, however, contribute to the style and structure of the novelistic universe he chooses to create.

# II

# ARTISTIC LEGENDS: PERFORMANCE, MUSIC AND TEXT

### Introduction

From Punch and Judy to Parsifal, Tristan to talking animals, the legends that enact their familiar exploits in the pages of *A la recherche* encompass an entire generic spectrum. Not only do the tragic and the comic, the sublime and the ridiculous, high and low art rub shoulders, but the tragic is also handled in comic mode by Proust, while the comic can be invested with a dignity commonly denied it. Narratives thought familiar may thus be submitted to a deliberately allusive estrangement. This synthesis of mood and tone is intrinsic to Proust's aesthetic and philosophical vision, but what are we to make of his recourse to legend?

To think of the legendary is to conjure up images of the epic, the timeless, the heroic; in short, a distant but enduring ideal. The hero of medieval legend, for example, seems destined to embark on an arduous quest, for the Holy Grail perhaps, or, in romances of chivalry, for the esteem of the beloved. A far cry from the Combray of the child narrator or the Paris of his adolescence, the realm and, indeed, identity of the legendary hero would thus appear to symbolize, for the narrator of *A la recherche*, an alternative reality, a vicarious quest. The narrator/protagonist searches for the ideal that will transport him beyond the everyday *in* (others') art rather than, as he will ultimately discover it, *through* (his own) art. Images inspired by the legends of performance, music and text chart this progression, as the narrator is confronted (whether he realizes it or not) with a range of alternative models for emulation: the subtly distinct quests and fulfilments dramatized in Wagner's *Parsifal* and *Tristan and Isolde* vie with the morals advanced in the fables of La Fontaine or the frivolous allure of the puppet theatre. In progressing through these models, the nature of the legendary is itself subject to re-evaluation, for epic narratives appear in the most unheroic of contexts. Moreover, the gradual disclosure of the epistemological instability of legends – are they true or not? – propels the narrator towards the discovery of his own authentic truth. Of course, not all legends are epic or heroic in their dimensions. As a largely immutable western tradition that has been handed down through time, the Punch and Judy show is endowed with the status of a legend, yet the crude comedy of its eponymous couple's troubled relationship bears no relation to the mystical union of souls played out in Wagner's *Tristan and Isolde*.[1] Such disparate sources fulfill different roles within the same broader movement, however, for where Wagner's operas act as the emblematic markers of the narrator's search for an ideal, the legends occupying the farcical end of the spectrum represent the distractions from that pursuit and the alternative identity that awaits the narrator should he fail to progress. By extension, if Wagner's operas provide a measure of the self that is the narrator, the Punch and Judy show is a mechanism for enlightenment about others.

Our subject here is not, in other words, an arbitrarily eclectic spectrum of artistic legends, introduced to support or extend an isolated moment in the narrative. Each individual manipulation of a particular legend may have its own intrinsic interest. However, the fact that each of the legendary sources discussed here is clustered *in succession* throughout *A la recherche* points to a consciously contrived pattern based on the protagonist's encounter with, and subsequent progression beyond, the legendary subject: images drawn from puppet theatre, for example, predominate in *Le Côté de Guermantes*, La Fontaine's fables in *Sodome et Gomorrhe*, and evocations of Wagner's operas, above all, in *La Prisonnière*. Nor does the evidence of patterning stop here, for this clustering also charts, for the would-be writer, a progression through, and challenge to, the aesthetic hierarchy as conventionally understood. Advancing from 'low' to 'high' art, this movement culminates in aesthetic and philosophical fusion, as the accepted boundaries between these two poles blur. The narrator's 'rewriting' of Debussy's *Pelléas et Mélisande* becomes the symbol of this fusion. Legend thus charts a dual evolution: with increasing awareness as the novel progresses, the narrator/protagonist is confronted with a medley of vicarious identities and/or quests. Concurrently, the writer, who has now attained, and indeed realized, the object of his narrator's quest, has woven into the narrative a further symbolic undercurrent of generic exploration which defines his own novelistic medium: through successive transitions from puppet theatre to fable to opera, he ultimately returns to the verbal by way of a valorization of Vinteuil's 'pure', non-verbal expression. By the end of the narrative, the perspectives of narrator/protagonist and writer thus coalesce in a simultaneous release from, and celebration of, these legendary sources. Such a conclusion is not as paradoxical as it may seem. The protagonist must still find his own truth, the sole truth whose authenticity, unlike that of the truths of legend, is certain: undistorted by intellectual interpretation or conscious will, he experiences the involuntary realization of the supra-temporal moment and its significance in *Le Temps retrouvé*. But the mature protagonist and, of course, the writer also revel in the multifariousness and carnivalesque qualities of legend, notably its ability to transform, to reflect social and psychological diversity; in short, to prompt a rethinking of boundaries and hierarchies. Aesthetic, social and psychological boundaries are 'thrust down, turn[ed] over, push[ed] headfirst, transfer[red] top to bottom, and bottom to top', but these 'downward movements' described by Bakhtin are nonetheless creative and 'the end [. . .] contain[s] the potentialities of the new beginning' (p. 283).

Critical commentaries on Proust have left unexplored the role of puppet theatre and of La Fontaine's fables in the novel.[2] The coherence of Proust's exploration of Wagner in *A la recherche* and the aesthetic affinities that unite the two artists have, however, been the subjects of analysis.[3] The discussion that follows will not only offer fresh interpretations of the role of Wagner's operas within the narrator's evolution to creation; it will also uncover the complex interconnectedness, in Proust's metaphorical vision, of legends as diverse as La Fontaine's deceptively lightly cast fables and Wagner's philosophically and musically momentous inventions.

## Punch and Judy: ritual and repetition

The stars of a tradition claiming no literary value and characterized, for George Speaight, by its 'elemental appeal',[4] Punch and Judy are the undisputed 'down-and-outs' of the artistic hierarchy. Yet Proust's metaphorical handling of puppet theatre situates this hierarchy in inverse relationship to the social hierarchy, for the majority of references to 'Polichinelle', 'le guignol' or puppetry in general are introduced to metamorphose the aristocracy, appearing most frequently in *Le Côté de Guermantes* and during the 'bal costumé' episode of *Le Temps retrouvé*.[5] These aristocratic puppet-shows are not the only ones to be staged in *A la recherche*, however. The first sign for the young, infatuated narrator of Gilberte's arrival at the Champs-Elysées is the feather on her nanny's hat which he can just make out 'entre le guignol et le cirque' (*S* I 391). Although not a metaphorical reference per se, this evocation of 'le guignol' nonetheless sets the tone of anxiety and ambivalence which will typify the narrator's relationships with Gilberte, Mme de Guermantes and Albertine: not only does the structural binarism of the phrase itself embody a pendulum swing, but the traditions of neither Punch and Judy nor circus are free from pain, violence or, indeed, scenarios which, while rendered humorous through exaggeration and caricature, are rooted in sado-masochistic impulses.[6] The fact that Proust revised an early version of this passage, a version which placed Gilberte's arrival 'entre le guignol et la marchande de sucre d'orge' (I 969), highlights his awareness of the underlying significance of both circus and puppet theatre. That both of these fora of entertainment repeat a limited number of set-pieces further heralds the nature of the narrator's amorous affairs: each of his relationships is grounded in recurrent patterns of obsession and jealousy and, in each, the same dialogues are constantly replayed. To introduce 'le guignol' as one object of the narrator's gaze is, moreover, to underline the focus of his attentions at this stage: between circus and puppet show is the symbol of Gilberte's imminent arrival, between a choice of frivolous entertainments lies desire. Proust's early reference thus paves the way for the dominance of this popular spectacle as a metaphorical intertext in the social and, specifically, aristocratic domain in later volumes of the novel. Mme de Cambremer's zealous but caricatured imitation of Mme de Guermantes's style, for example, may grant her the unfortunate appearance of 'quelque pensionnaire provinciale, *montée sur fil de fer*, droite, sèche et pointue, un plumet de corbillard verticalement dressé dans les cheveux' (my italics, G II 354), but when he first attends a dinner-party at the duc and duchesse de Guermantes', the narrator also imagines himself transported into 'un théâtre de *puppazi*':

> d'autres portes s'ouvrirent par où entra la soupe fumante, comme si le dîner avait lieu dans un théâtre de *puppazi* habilement machiné et où l'arrivée tardive du jeune invité [the narrator who has been viewing the Guermantes' Elstirs] mettait, sur un signe du maître, tous les rouages en action. (G II 727)

On the surface, the analogy attests to the harmony and – as if automated – fluidity with which dinner is served. The young narrator/protagonist here shares Kleist's view of the beauty of puppet theatre, this latter identifying its grace – significantly when considered in relation to the narrator's worship of the Guermantes – as a characteristic present in its purest form only in puppets or gods.[7] Reading the narrator's perception of this aristocratic puppet-show through the filter of Kleist's essay nonetheless introduces an ironic undercurrent into the analogy, for Kleist does not initially appreciate the origins of this grace and is reliant for an explanation on the Mr C. with whom his dialogue concerning the marionette theatre takes place: Mr C. explains that it is precisely the puppets' soullessness that ensures their grace. Like Kleist at the beginning of his conversation with Mr C., the narrator/protagonist does not yet appreciate the origins of the beauty of the spectacle played out before him. He gradually becomes aware of the soullessness of their mechanical repetitions, however, and Kleist's celebratory vision mutates gradually into a perspective more akin to that of Bergson's evocation of puppetry.[8] The extract's participation in the mature narrator/writer's broader network of metaphorical references to this form of entertainment infuses it with a further double-edged, ironic flavour, for it may be the duc de Guermantes who sets this 'vaste, ingénieuse, obéissante et fastueuse horlogerie mécanique et humaine' (ibid.) in motion, but he is no less a puppet in the show being staged for the young narrator. Moreover, while the image may not imply the grotesquely unnatural appearance of the Mme de Cambremer marionette, it nevertheless reduces the dinner to just one in a series of oft-repeated set-pieces performed by a relatively limited cast of set characters. After all, the Punch and Judy show presents stock types rather than individual characterization, and, because of its historical reliance on passing trade, it contained no 'subtlety of incident' and no plot, dependent, in fact, on a succession of familiar encounters rather than any cause-and-effect sequence.[9] Just as Mme de Cambremer's slavish but ineffective emulation of Mme de Guermantes betrays a lack of independent thought and will – if she is 'montée sur fil de fer', her actions are determined by the puppeteer – so, too, do the Guermantes follow a mechanical ritual, to which an awareness of Bergson's essay on 'Le Rire' adds a subtle humour. Bergson argues that laughter occurs when the flexibility and purposefulness of human actions are replaced by seemingly mechanical forces. Repetitive speech or behaviour is a further form of mechanistic, and therefore comic, behaviour, in describing which Bergson significantly uses the image of 'le pantin à ficelles'. He comments:

> Tout le sérieux de la vie lui vient de notre liberté. Les sentiments que nous avons mûris, les passions que nous avons couvées, les actions que nous avons délibérées, arrêtées, exécutées, enfin ce qui vient de nous et ce qui est bien nôtre, voilà ce qui donne à la vie son allure quelquefois dramatique et généralement grave. Que faudrait-il pour transformer tout cela en comédie? Il faudrait se figurer que la liberté apparente recouvre un jeu de ficelles, et que nous sommes ici-bas, comme dit le poète, '. . . d'humbles marionnettes / Dont le fil est aux mains de la Nécessité'.[10]

Indeed, the positioning of the adjective 'humaine' at the conclusion of Proust's description of dinner being served advertises itself as a necessary reminder that the participants are not, in reality, puppets or machines, that this is only a mutely revelatory metaphor.

The gap between the voices of the mature narrator/writer and the young narrator/character is at its widest here, for if the former stands outside the action in order to effect an ironic debunking of these gods of the aristocratic world, the latter has stepped resolutely inside this puppet theatre, and not as a spectator, but as an 'actor'. From a distant view of the frivolous worlds of circus and 'guignol', he has first assumed the role of spectator – as symbolized by his scrutiny of Mme de Cambremer-as-puppet – finally himself to assume the role of one of its characters. His consequent deafness to all but the distractions of society, above all in *Le Côté de Guermantes*, finds its striking echo in the interplay of silence and chatter which marks his attempts to speak to his grandmother on the telephone from Doncières. On first picking up the receiver, he finds that someone else is on the line: 'quand j'amenai à moi le récepteur, ce morceau de bois se mit à parler comme Polichinelle; je le fis taire, ainsi qu'au guignol, en le remettant à sa place, mais, comme Polichinelle, dès que je le ramenais près de moi, il recommençait son bavardage' (*G* II 432–3). The unsettling ambivalence which is built into the Punch and Judy tradition – a comic, childhood entertainment dramatizing violence and threat – reasserts itself here, ultimately reaching a crescendo in the narrator's anticipation of his grandmother's inevitable death and his hurried return to Paris to be with her.[11] However, as the image suggests, while the young narrator may be fired with aspirations and resolutions when in physical or emotional proximity to his grandmother, her voice is otherwise supplanted by that of Polichinelle and his 'bavardage'. The trivial chatter with which the narrator is surrounded in society is further highlighted in an image which combines the animate and the inanimate to convey an impression of soullessness: the society that distracts the narrator from more fruitful pursuits is summed up by the talking 'morceau de bois'.

The narrator's susceptibility to the social distractions conveyed through the metaphor of puppetry is counterbalanced by a further image of deafness which, as we have seen, serves Proust's Impressionist aesthetic. In the midst of his entry into the aristocratic world of the Guermantes, the hint of an alternative to its 'bavardage' thus intrudes. As part of the network of images of the everyday supernatural explored in the first part of this book, the narrator considers how the sudden arrival of a guest must appear to a man who is deaf.[12] For him, the new arrival 'fait seulement des gestes comme dans un de ces petits théâtres de marionnettes, *si reposants pour ceux qui ont pris en dégoût le langage parlé*' (my italics, *G* II 376).[13] Viewed in conjunction with the broader metaphorical network that overlays puppet theatre and social distractions, this description hints at an awareness, even on the part of the young narrator/protagonist, that one can grow weary of social 'bavardage'. A pleasurable alternative may be experienced in the purity of sensation that is equivalent to the uncluttered, and thus renewed, perception of the visual that one would enjoy if robbed of one's sense of hearing. The young narrator has, of course, known the joy of an unadulterated contemplation of nature, but either convinced of, or fearful of confronting, what he believes to be his inability to grant that experience meaningful expression, he has yielded to the diverting babble of Polichinelle.[14] Yet the possibility of silencing Polichinelle and finding an escape from the puppet theatre the narrator has entered remains open in the form of his exposure to other artistic legends. Significantly, this will entail a shift from the textual legends of La Fontaine's fables to the music–text fusion of opera and, ultimately, to the fictional artist Vinteuil's entirely non-verbal expression. The narrator's potential alter ego, Swann, embodies the non-realization of this possibility of escape. His metaphorical association with puppet theatre as late as *Sodome et Gomorrhe* – that is, in the late stages of his illness – seems to adumbrate the now ineluctable sterility of his spiritual existence:

> Soit à cause de l'absence de ces joues qui n'étaient plus là pour le diminuer, soit que l'artériosclérose, qui est une intoxication aussi, le rougît comme eût fait l'ivrognerie ou le déformât comme eût fait la morphine, le nez de polichinelle de Swann, longtemps résorbé dans un visage agréable, semblait maintenant énorme, tuméfié, cramoisi, plutôt celui d'un vieil Hébreu que d'un curieux Valois. (*SG* III 89)

The image is an immediately visual one: Punch's nose is one of his most prominent features, exaggerated and grotesque just as Swann's has now also become. The aptness of the association is futher confirmed by the broader context for the extract, for what precedes it is Proust's description of the combination of open curiosity and silent relief on the part of the other guests, all of whom turn to stare at the shocking physical deterioration in this much altered Swann.[15] Like Punch, therefore, Swann's misfortunes are eagerly observed by all present. Yet the implications of this image extend beyond these literal resonances, for Swann's association with Punch accentuates his own failure to emerge from the rut of social 'bavardage', of repeated, barren dialogue and, but for his daughter, an unrewarding relationship. In short, it underlines his failure, fully or enduringly, to transcend the mundane.[16]

This intricate mesh of references to puppet theatre exposes the distractions which tempt the narrator/protagonist away from higher pursuits, the emptiness of society rituals and the fate that may await him should he not reject the predictable dramas played out in these familiar legends. Already, we may detect hints that the narrator/protagonist will distance himself from the willing participant in the puppet show that is his earlier self, but the closure of this metaphorical cycle is deferred until *Le Temps retrouvé* where subtle differences in the tone and style of Proust's images of puppet theatre illustrate the narrator/protagonist's evolution. However, let us not anticipate too far, for other literary legends intervene, as Proust ventures a step further in his exploration of the legends of performance, music and text, to the fables of La Fontaine.

## La Fontaine: mockery and morals

If Punch and Judy's metaphorical presence in the text sets ritual engagement with the social world in opposition to fruitful progression, then the fables of La Fontaine become signposts to indicate that the narrator/protagonist *is* developing. Indeed, his evolution towards greater insight is implied, in general terms, by the very transition from the unequivocally farcical and frivolous world of puppet theatre to a genre which is light, but not without substance.[17] The distribution of evocations of the fables of La Fontaine throughout the novel further confirms their status as markers of a 'next stage' in the narrator's vicarious (if still largely unconscious) legendary quest, for following the concentration of references to 'le guignol' in *Le Côté de Guermantes*, La Fontaine's fables predominate towards the end of this same volume and, above all, in *Sodome et Gomorrhe*. As with the 'guignol' cycle, they also re-emerge in *Le Temps retrouvé*, there acquiring new resonances and a new maturity.[18]

In contast to the imagery of puppet theatre, which is the invention of the narrator/writer, almost all the references to La Fontaine's fables are voiced by other characters, notably Odette, the Ambassadress of Turkey and, above all, M. de Cambremer. Rachel, too, recites some of La Fontaine's fables at the princesse de Guermantes's party in *Le Temps retrouvé*. When introduced by the former group of characters – and, in particular, by M. de Cambremer – La Fontaine's fables are little more than social props, consciously flagged illustrations of the speaker's (usually limited) cultural knowledge. Moreover, their handling of the tales tends to betray a lack of awareness on the part of the speaker of their more serious 'message', and, through their own words, Proust quietly lampoons these characters' foibles. Yet for the attentive reader who returns to the original source, evoked often only in title, it becomes apparent not only that these fables punctuate the narrative at significant moments in the narrator's development, but also that, in their content, they signal the very shape of that development. Like the dual goal of the fables themselves, therefore, the function of these references in Proust's narrative is at once comic on an undisguised textual level and of greater moment when we delve into the palimpsestic layers of the intertext.

One early example disrupts the pattern of distribution highlighted above. In *Du côté de chez Swann*, Odette comments, with coquettish self-denigration, on her lack of erudition in comparison with Swann: 'Je comprends que je ne peux rien faire, moi chétive, à côté de grands savants comme vous autres [. . .] Je serais comme la grenouille devant l'aréopage. Et pourtant j'aimerais tant m'instruire, savoir, être initiée' (*S* I 195). No La Fontaine fable bears the title 'La Grenouille devant l'aréopage', nor does any immediately tally with the scenario conjured up by Odette. Now, it may perhaps be entirely and ironically fitting that Odette should commit an error in citing a text which will supposedly illustrate her limited knowledge. However, the fact that M. de Cambremer also refers to 'La Grenouille devant l'aréopage' – admittedly as a (disingenuous) admission of his own ignorance – suggests the confusion may lie with Proust. And yet, not only, as we shall see, does a survey of those fables that Proust may have imperfectly recalled prove illuminating, but the introduction of the term 'aréopage' – its meaning as a prestigious assembly acquired from the Greek *Areopagus* – is itself rich in allusions.

The Areopagus, an ancient hill near the market-place in Athens, was the first site for the court of justice, as established by the city's patron goddess, Athena. It was here that murder, corruption and matters of a moral and religious nature were examined and judged. In fact, legend has it that Orestes was tried for the murder of his stepmother, Clytemnestra, and her lover, Aegisthus, by this very institution. And it was famously here, in Roman times, that Paul made a speech presenting the good news of Christian salvation to the Athenians. In a clash between Christianity and paganism, he warned that God's judgement was imminent if the Athenians did not convert, rejecting the idolatry and pantheism of their existing religious beliefs.[19] If Odette appears before Swann as before the Areopagus, therefore, the scene is set for judgement and condemnation. The privileged status of judge enjoyed by this august assembly is nonetheless turned on its head by Paul's sermon to them. In the same way, judge becomes judged in the Swann/Odette paradigm, for while Odette's 'morality' may be subject to scrutiny and open to condemnation by Swann-as-Areopagus, this judge, like the citizens of Athens and the court that represents them, is, by implication, charged with idolatry. And, indeed, it is Swann who 'worships' Odette through images, be they the Zipporah of Botticelli's *Life of Moses*, the same artist's *Madonna of the Magnificat* or Vinteuil's 'petite phrase'.[20] As for the charge of pantheism, both Swann and Odette are 'guilty' in this regard. If desire may be interpreted as a deviated form of worship, then for both, the object of worship is plural: the plurality of the objects of Odette's 'worship' multiplies, above all, in Swann's jealous imaginings, echoing the 'unknown god' of the Athenians that Paul evokes in his speech.[21] In contrast, Swann's pantheism is suggested by his simultaneous seductions – of Odette and the seamstress, for instance – and by the multiplicity of Odettes he creates in a vain attempt to ensure his continuing faithfulness to this object of worship: Odette as Zipporah, Odette as Madonna and so on. Implicitly underlining the relativism of the positions occupied by Self and Other, the roles of guilty and innocent party, judge and judged, are subtly implied to be impossible to polarize. These implications are further extended by a consideration of the possible sources, within the fables of La Fontaine, for Odette's allusion.

As a starting point, the Pléiade editors suggest 'Les Grenouilles qui demandent un Roi' as a likely source.[22] The fable presents a community of frogs who, unhappy with their democracy, request that Jupiter give them a king. He obliges by sending them 'un roi tout pacifique' who, although initially an object of fear that they hesitate to approach, is transformed into a source of disappointment: in a bathetic revelation worthy of Proust himself, we and the frogs discover that 'Celui qu'elles croyoient être un géant nouveau, [. . .] c'étoit un soliveau'.[23] They therefore ask to be relieved of this king, only to be sent a crane which devours them. The substance of the fable is thus, on the surface, a far cry from the setting for Odette's possible recourse to it. Yet the moral, which warns of the perils of dissatisfaction, chimes with, and, indeed, heralds, the paradigm swing of emotions that characterizes Swann and Odette's relationship, based on the patterns of perversity in desire compellingly examined by René Girard: possession decreases desire or, expressed differently, increases dissatisfaction. That Girard presents these patterns of behaviour in terms of unavoidable compulsion creates a parallel with the instinctive responses of the animal world. This is not, however, the only fable to place the frogs with which Odette associates herself centre-stage. That 'La Grenouille qui veut se faire aussi grosse que le Bœuf' features a frog which, heralding Odette's own self-portrayal, is described as 'la *chétive* pécore' (my italics) places this fable high on our list of possibilities (p. 3). The fable highlights the destructiveness of envy, and its moral is socially directed: 'Le monde est plein de gens qui ne sont pas plus sages: / Tout bourgeois veut bâtir comme les grands seigneurs, / Tout petit prince a des ambassadeurs; / Tout marquis veut avoir des pages' (ibid.). Like the envious frog of the fable who cannot succeed in becoming an ox, Odette will never attain the erudition of Swann. In any case, hers is not a sincere expression of envy, but merely a flirtatious brand of flattery. What is significant, though, in light of the social thrust of the moral, is that Odette's progress in society *will* defy the outcome of La Fontaine's fable. The efforts of the frog of the fable to inflate itself end in farce as it bursts: '[Elle] s'étend, et s'enfle, et se travaille / Pour égaler l'animal en grosseur; / [. . .] La chétive pécore / S'enfla si bien qu'elle creva' (ibid.). In contrast, Odette *will* be transformed into Mme de Forcheville just as Mme Verdurin will become la princesse de Guermantes. For the young narrator/protagonist seeking immutable truths, therefore, the fable represents a locus of unreliable knowledge. For the mature narrator-soon-to-be-writer, however, the fable offers not only stylistic possibilities – notably humorous devices such as bathos or farce – but also a trigger for his mature recognition of the unavailability of a single authoritative voice, of the possibility of alternative endings and, indeed, of a more sophisticated metaphorical interpretation of the outcome of the fable which has its own truth. After all, it could be argued that, despite his recognition in fairytale terms of the transformative power of characters such as Mme Verdurin, for Proust, social climbing is morally to 'burst'.

Finally, 'La Grenouille et le Rat' transforms the perpetrator of a misdeed into its victim, mirroring the inverted power dynamic that we detect in a variety of permutations in Proust's novel: the judge is judged, the torturer tortured, the jailer jailed and, indeed, the deceiver deceived. Having offered the rat a feast at its home, the frog ties the rat to its own body to help it swim there. But secretly planning to eat the rat itself, the frog subsequently tries to drown its passenger. In the midst of the ensuing struggle, a bird swoops down and devours them both. According to the moral: 'La ruse la mieux ourdie / Peut nuire à son inventeur; / Et souvent la perfidie / Retourne sur son auteur' (ibid., p. 72). Like the frog tempting the rat with new experiences and the prospect of stories to tell, Swann and, later, the narrator seem to offer the promise of expanded horizons to Odette and Albertine.[24] Yet consumption – the ideal metaphor for possession and control – is the true driving motivation, as underlined in this fable by the additional image of binding. The frog fails to realize, however, that it is bound to the rat as much as the rat is to it, and, indeed, it is the restraint this chain imposes that leads to the frog also being consumed: 'Il [le milan] fond dessus, l'enlève, et, par même moyen, / La grenouille et le lien' (ibid.). The parallels between this fable and the boomerang-style imposition of control and suffering that characterizes Swann's and, later, the narrator's relationships with women are clear. Moreover, at various points in their relationship, both Swann and Odette assume the roles of deceiver deceived. While certain of her affections – that is, before she fails to turn up at Mme Verdurin's one evening[25] – Swann is unfaithful to Odette, who is, in turn, throughout their relationship, shrouded in suspicion regarding her honesty and fidelity to him. However, what the climax of the fable illustrates is that beyond the provisional victories gained in the repeated puppet-theatre dialogues this couple enacts, all are destroyed by (suspicions of, and obsession with) deception. Where the climax of the fable presents an irreversible extinction, however, the narrator's union with Albertine is destructive only for its duration; he is not destroyed by it, and, ultimately, it becomes a source of creativity for him. An alternative ending to the literal and/or figurative deaths of Albertine and Swann is thus possible for the narrator and also, once again, for the phoenix-like Odette.[26]

Uncertainty thus surrounds which fable or fables Proust hoped to conjure up in the reader's mind through Odette's words, but it is this very uncertainty that opens up a range of interpretative pathways. It is certainly tempting to use this plurality of meaning as a template to describe a stage in the narrator's development. Together, these fables foretell the patterns of behaviour which will characterize the narrator's relationship with Albertine. We note, moreover, that while Swann is commonly identified as the narrator's double, this early image, in fact, aligns the young narrator with Odette, for she is the insincere parody of the narrator's genuine envy of, and (misguided) desire to emulate, characters such as Swann and, above all, the artist. The fables this image calls to mind illustrate literally the destructiveness of envy and, symbolically for the narrator, the fruitlessness of a journey whose goal is to imitate the identity of another person: self-deception is the ultimate example of the deceiver deceived. These fables also remind the reader of the relativism of one's position on every hierarchy, whether social, intellectual or aesthetic.[27] In other words, this early introduction of La Fontaine resonates far beyond Odette's proclamation of ignorance, representing in addition a 'moral' planted in the narrative for a narrator/protagonist who is as yet unable to appreciate its relevance. It also provides a focal point for the narrator/writer's celebration of alternative realities and rejection of monologic authority: both the peremptory moral of 'La Grenouille qui veut se faire aussi grosse que le Bœuf' and the denial of the possibility of change portrayed in the definitive ending of 'La Grenouille et le Rat' come up against a more multifaceted reality.

Our next encounter with La Fontaine in the text, which takes the form of an anecdote related by the Ambassadress of Turkey about M. de Luxembourg, marks a step forward from this early portent of the young narrator's (potential) future, for the very fact that the narrator/protagonist of *Le Côté de Guermantes* believes that the anecdote is apocryphal highlights the more questioning and increasingly cynical attitude towards his experiences in society that emerges in the course of this volume.[28] The Ambassadress relates how M. de Luxembourg, engaged to be married to a young woman whose family fortune was made in flour, was invited to dinner by his fiancée's grandfather. Luxembourg is reported to have declined (on grounds of snobbery), addressing the letter to 'M de \*\*\*, meunier'. The grandfather is said to have replied expressing his sorrow that Luxembourg should miss such an intimate gathering at which only 'le meunier, son fils et vous' would have been present (G II 827).[29] In a verbal sleight of hand, this reference to La Fontaine's 'Le Meunier, son Fils et l'Âne', of course, casts Luxembourg as an ass. On a literal, textual level, this is little more than witty repartee of the kind prized in this social environment, but if we dig deeper into the fable itself – the text that lies beneath the text – we realize that it reflects the stage the narrator himself has reached by the end of this quintessentially social volume. The fable describes a miller and his son who are taking their ass to market to be sold. In a dizzyingly comical series of repositionings, they start out by binding the ass's legs and carrying it 'comme un lustre' (p. 42); some passers-by mock them for carrying the ass when it can walk itself, so they untie it and the miller tells his son to ride it; the next passers-by criticize the son for making his father walk, so they swap places; the following group condemn the miller for sitting haughtily on the ass, so father and son exchange places again; another party they meet on the road disapprove of their riding the poor, decrepit ass at all, so the son dismounts; and the final travellers they come across mock them for walking when they have an ass to ride. The moral of the story claims that one should not try to please everyone, that one should follow one's own desires and instincts. But the narrative frame of the fable is significant, for the story of 'Le Meunier, son Fils et l'Âne' is prompted by a conversation between Racan and his guide and teacher, Malherbe, in which the former asks the latter's advice on what he should do with his life:

> Dois-je dans la province établir mon séjour? / Prendre emploi dans l'armée, ou bien charge à la cour? / Tout au monde est mêlé d'amertume et de charmes: / La guerre a ses douceurs, l'hymen a ses alarmes. / Si je suivois mon goût, je saurois où buter; / Mais j'ai les miens, la cour, le peuple à contenter. (ibid.)

The opening lines of the fable make clear that writing is Racan's desired vocation. It is also, of course, as we know, the path he will ultimately follow. But, at this stage, others divert him from realizing his vocation and even lead him to doubt its validity. The links between this fable and the narrator's own literary ambitions are evident: like Racan, he has reached a stage when a career beckons, but he is uncertain what to do and still hankers after the literary life; like his counterpart in the fable, others, notably his father, have attempted to turn him towards alternative careers in law or government; the young narrator has also been willingly drawn into the distractions of love and society, further alternatives mentioned by Racan. However, also like Racan, who shows his awareness that: 'Tout au monde est mêlé d'amertume et de charmes', the narrator has entered the demythologizing phase of his development, a stage in which he acquires a more objective perspective on what he has previously approached with awe. With its exaggeratedly compliant protagonists, the fable certainly highlights the absurdity of trying to please everyone, but the moral, in the form of Malherbe's final words of advice, does not explicitly tell Racan to follow his preferred vocation as writer. In keeping with the tenor of the fable, it is rather more open and non-prescriptive: 'Quant à vous, suivez Mars, ou l'Amour ou le prince, / Allez, venez, courez; demeurez en province; / Prenez femme, abbaye, emploi, gouvernement / Les gens en parleront, n'en doutez nullement' (p. 44). In fact, the moral of the fable seems to suggest that Racan, like the narrator, needs to enjoy a wide variety of experiences before he can fulfil his true vocation. As we shall see in the final fable evoked in the novel, 'Les Deux Pigeons', one must have adventures in order to have a story to tell. Inserted at this point in the narrative, 'Le Meunier, son Fils et l'Âne' thus traces the narrator/protagonist's growing critical perception. It also betrays his continuing, if intermittently expressed, desire to become an artist, but current inability to achieve that status. Finally, it highlights an as yet undirected and underdeveloped intuition of the necessity of an independent *apprentissage*: as the miller retorts when confronted with a passer-by's accusation that they make up a 'beau trio de baudets': '"Je suis âne, il est vrai, j'en conviens, je l'avoue; / Mais que dorénavant on me blâme, on me loue, / Qu'on dise quelque chose ou qu'on ne dise rien, / J'en veux faire à ma tête." Il le fit, et fit bien' (ibid.).

*Sodome et Gomorrhe* extends the process of demythologization initiated in *Le Côté de Guermantes* by introducing us to M. de Cambremer, the most frequent (if limited) quoter of La Fontaine. His handling of these fables also reinforces their literal status as social props that reveal more about the speakers than those speakers intend. We are told that M. de Cambremer speaks very little:

> sachant qu'il avait épousé une femme supérieure. 'Moi, indigne', disait-il à tout moment, et citait volontiers une fable de La Fontaine et une de Florian qui lui paraissaient s'appliquer à son ignorance, et, d'autre part, lui permettre, sous les formes d'une dédaigneuse flatterie, de montrer aux hommes de science qui n'étaient pas du Jockey qu'on pouvait chasser et avoir lu des fables. (*SG* III 307)[30]

As we shall see from his later references to La Fontaine, M. de Cambremer's knowledge appears to be restricted to 'L'Homme et la Couleuvre' and 'Le Chameau et les Bâtons flottants', and, indeed, the moral of the first of these fables seems a likely extract for M. de Cambremer to quote in order to express his preference for few words: 'Si quelqu'un desserre les dents, / C'est un sot. J'en conviens: mais que faut-il donc faire? / Parler de loin, ou bien se taire' (p. 215). Yet the fable betrays the presence of an unshakable arrogance beneath M. de Cambremer's expression of humility and consequent silence before his wife's (doubtful) superiority, for the moral also contains the idea that 'les grands' 'se mettent en tête / Que tout est né pour eux, quadrupèdes et gens, / Et serpens' (ibid.).[31] The irony is evident: M. de Cambremer expresses his own lack of erudition through a (highly self-conscious) show of erudition, and he does so in the form of a fable which portrays anything but humility. Indeed, to proclaim, in a socially contrived gesture, his wife's superiority over himself does not, in M. de Cambremer's eyes, render him inferior to the rest of this predominantly bourgeois gathering. Of course, these are ironies which doubtless escape the speaker who, we imagine, fails to interpret the text as a warning against man's arrogance, seeing instead in the fable its validation.

M. de Cambremer's other source of quotations from La Fontaine, 'Le Chameau et les Bâtons flottants', offers no obvious snippet which he might here have been quoting to express his lack of knowledge, but the tale nonetheless offers the perfect illustration of the stage the narrator has reached in his development. Once again, the speaker is unaware of the significance of his reference, but for the mature narrator/writer, for the reader and perhaps also, increasingly, for the narrator/protagonist, the fable illustrates the power of habit and the inevitable humanization of what one once worshipped.[32] The fable describes how the first person to see a camel ran away, the second came closer and the third put a halter on it: 'L'accoutumance aussi nous rend tout familier; / Ce qui nous paroissoit terrible et singulier / S'apprivoise avec notre vue / Quand ce vient à la continue' (p. 70). As the other image employed in the fable indicates, what seems terrifying or amazing from a distance can turn out to be quite ordinary: what looks like 'un puissant navire' becomes first a 'brûlot', then a 'nacelle', then a 'ballot' and, in reality, turns out to be nothing more than some 'bâtons flottant sur l'onde' (ibid.). If *Sodome et Gomorrhe* is the principal volume of demythologization for the narrator, then there could be no more appropriate fable than this to signpost that transition from imagination to reality. Moreover, these fables serve only to underline the growing distance between the character who invokes them and the developing narrator who hears them. They are thus a site of ironic contrasts for the narrator/writer, for the attentive reader and, increasingly, as the novel progresses, for the narrator/character himself.

Habit may equate to stasis in the context of the narrator/protagonist's development, but a lack of invention on the part of a writer may also dull the reader's encounter with his/her text. La Fontaine himself acknowledges in the Preface to the first collection that 'ces Fables étant sues de tout le monde, je ne ferais rien si je ne les rendais nouvelles par quelques traits qui en relevassent le goût'.[33] Renewing his chosen form through generic experimentation, La Fontaine created the rhymed fable. More subtly, too, his fables are infused with a new lightness of tone, an understated humour, a multi-layeredness of meaning, unexpected metaphors and an experimental blend of tones in which formal and informal language, popular speech and archaic expressions coexist.[34] In essence, La Fontaine contributed to breaking down conventional aesthetic boundaries such as the strict hierarchy of genre and tone. This extended into a refusal to confine himself to traditionally 'poetic' subjects. It is tempting to imagine, given the presence of similar features in *A la recherche*, that, on the level of stylistic innovation, La Fontaine may have shaped the narrator/writer's poetics. In generic terms, too, Proust's witty and often acerbic insights into human nature are reminiscent of the pithy snapshots of the *moraliste*. But Proust's text meanders associatively as often as it is terse and epigrammatic. Indeed, the novel oscillates between the two with studied negligence. Thus, just as La Fontaine remodels precursor texts in his retelling of simple and familiar tales of human frailty, so, too, will the narrator relate his own multifaceted story through a dynamic reworking of this and other genres which brings with it both synthesis and renewal.

La Fontaine subsequently fades out of *A la recherche*, with no reference being made to the writer or his work in either *La Prisonnière* or *Albertine disparue*. In fact, none of the legends of performance, music and text discussed in this part of the study appears in *Albertine disparue*, while it is significantly only Debussy's *Pelléas et Mélisande* and Wagner's *Parsifal* and *Tristan and Isolde* that emerge from the pages of *La Prisonnière*. We shall return to these sources shortly, but let us first consider the final evocation of La Fontaine in *Le Temps retrouvé*. It immediately differs from all that have been examined thus far, for it is neither a social quip nor conversational prop. It is, rather, a performance. Rachel is to recite Musset's *Le Souvenir* and some fables of La Fontaine at the princesse de Guermantes's party (*TR* IV 562). A few pages later, we discover that one of these fables will be 'Les Deux Pigeons' (*TR* IV 579).[35] The context is thus entirely distinct from earlier allusions to La Fontaine: previously, the significance of the fables for the narrator/protagonist's development was transparent to the narrator/writer and to the watchful reader. However, the narrator/protagonist's appreciation of their 'message' was reliant on his active consideration of the substance of fables usually evoked only by title. For the first time, here, he is a captive audience to a recitation of one of La Fontaine's fables. 'Les Deux Pigeons' is undoubtedly a suggestive fable for the narrator. It tells the story of two pigeons who love one another and are confined at home together; one of them yearns to travel, to witness new sights and enjoy new experiences; the other attempts to cloister its adventurous-spirited partner. The latter aims to persuade its home-loving companion of the merits of its journey by promising to return home and tell the story of its adventures, arguing that if it experiences nothing new, it will have nothing interesting to say: 'Quiconque ne voit guère / N'a guère à dire aussi' (p. 187). And so the adventurous pigeon leaves, suffers terrible experiences and injuries, and finally returns home half-dead. The moral makes the following exhortation: 'Amans, heureux amans, voulez-vous voyager? / Que ce soit aux rives prochaines. /

Soyez-vous l'un à l'autre un monde toujours beau, / Toujours divers, toujours nouveau; / Tenez-vous lieu de tout, comptez pour rien le reste' (p. 188). The echoes of the narrator and Albertine's relationship in this fable are unmistakable: the narrator cloistered Albertine, she yearned for freedom and finally left, but the narrator, too, was trapped and craved the experiences of travel and new encounters. But the outcome of Albertine and the narrator's story inverted that of the fable. Albertine may have left and suffered, but she died, thus destroying all possibility of the happy ending of La Fontaine's tale. Once again, therefore, reality has defied the outcome of the fable; but the literal moral, which advocates fulfilment in a loving relationship, would, in any case, have led the narrator away from his vocation, and, of course, by the time he hears the fable performed, this is a 'danger' that he has already overcome. The performance thus offers the productive reminder that adventures – including in love and the suffering it imposes – are essential if one is to have a story to tell. The fable of 'Le Meunier, son Fils et l'Âne' has already hinted at this to the young narrator, but once these adventures are complete, one must follow one's calling. To do otherwise is to risk the fate of the 'guignol', but to do so requires a new mode of perception. The moral of 'Les Deux Pigeons' contains the seeds of how this may be achieved: one must not only see things differently; one must also strive for a constant renewal of perception, for the creation of new worlds by the imagination.

Having reached the end of the path that leads to his vocation to write a novel, the narrator-soon-to-be-writer also asserts his independence from a genre characterized by its explicit didactic dimension. His will be a work which dissects, scrutinizes, exposes and mocks – often to moral ends – but which does not overtly moralize. Proust is neither unmoral nor amoral, as critics have sometimes proposed. On occasions, he subtly engages us in a rethinking of conventional moral standpoints;[36] on others, he offers astutely observed portraits of what are, clearly, to him, virtue and vice.[37] Indeed, certain of his vignettes of human shortcomings suggest the eye of a La Fontaine. But to express directly a clear-cut moral is to do the reader's work on his/her behalf. In the realms of what Proust leaves unsaid, the reader pursues his/her own mythical quest.

For all these reasons, the fable is undercut within the text itself, an effect achieved through the absurdly exaggerated avant-gardism of Rachel's performance:

> L'annonce de poésies que presque tout le monde connaissait avait fait plaisir. Mais quand on vit l'actrice, avant de commencer, chercher partout des yeux d'un air égaré, lever les mains d'un air suppliant et pousser comme un gémissement chaque mot, chacun se sentit gêné, presque choqué de cette exhibition de sentiments.

[. . .] les auditeurs furent stupéfaits en voyant cette femme, avant d'avoir émis un seul son, plier les genoux, tendre les bras, en berçant quelque être invisible, devenir cagneuse, et tout d'un coup, pour dire des vers fort connus, prendre un ton suppliant. (*TR* IV 577)

This estrangement of the familiar further underlines the narrator's self-distancing from the fable, the validity of the recitation also being undermined by the vengeful Gilberte telling a bemused Mme de Morienval that the recitation is one-quarter fabricated by Rachel, one-quarter madness, one-quarter meaningless, and the rest, La Fontaine (*TR* IV 579–80).[38] La Fontaine's appropriation and distortion by an existing artist who, although in vogue, is open to a very Proustian debunking, subtly implies the 'redundancy' of this source to a character who has now surpassed those figures, like Rachel and Swann, whose creativity is dependent on the work of another artist, and who has now learnt the lessons for which La Fontaine's fables have provided the metaphorical markers throughout the novel. For the narrator/writer in search of aesthetic models, in contrast, La Fontaine's fables have presented stylistic possibilities, not least as a rich source of animal imagery. But it is ultimately a generic form that can encompass the 'contingency or [. . .] over-bulk of reality' that the would-be writer will embrace.[39] For Malcolm Bradbury, it is the novel that reflects 'the unformed looseness of events, the shapelessness of life and of persons'. Decisive for him, too, in the search for a form appropriate to these ends, is 'the disposition of the slack prose instrument to set its own pace, catch up what it wishes, maintain endless options upon itself until the work is done' (p. 14). The outcome of the mythical quest that lies at the heart of *A la recherche* is, of course, a novel, but a whole spectrum of generic forms influences its aesthetic direction; of these, La Fontaine's fables represent just one. Having 'exhausted' their possibilities, therefore, the narrator turns to an exploration of the intergeneric in the form of opera's music-text.

## Wagner's *Parsifal* and *Tristan and Isolde*: text/music/text

Wagner's operas are layered throughout *A la recherche* to create a medley of tones and effects. They provide a mechanism to expose characters' foibles, for example, notably debunking certain figures' presumed superiority of aesthetic judgement. Thematic parallels, both explicit and implicit, also link *A la recherche* to Wagner's *Parsifal* and *Tristan and Isolde*, and while some of these resonances have been noted by critics, much remains to be said. Not only are the implied associations between characters in *A la recherche* and Wagner's works open to a potent elaboration, but ultimately *Parsifal* and *Tristan and Isolde* offer alternative models of transcendence for the mature narrator who is soon to be a writer. Representing stages in the narrator/protagonist's mythical journey, they are thus also integral to the narrator-as-future-writer's aesthetic journey, as the crucial meditations in *La Prisonnière*, above all on *Tristan and Isolde*, reveal. The attainment of these complementary journeys is characterized by synthesis: in the end, the form of transcendence the narrator seeks to achieve represents a fusion of the subtly divergent models dramatized in Wagner's *Parsifal* and *Tristan and Isolde*, while an aesthetics of synthesis, already implied in the intergeneric nature of opera itself, is further refined with reference to Debussy's *Pelléas et Mélisande*, a work cited by Proust with a frequency that surpasses evocations of *Parsifal*.

## A PROUSTIAN *PARSIFAL*

Let us begin, however, with *Parsifal*, for it is here, in *A l'ombre des jeunes filles en fleurs*, that the narrator embarks on his own Wagnerian quest. From a predominance, in the first three volumes of the novel, of intertextual analogies associating characters and situations in *A la recherche* with figures and moments in Wagner's libretto, Proust's handling of *Parsifal* gradually changes shape in the course of *A la recherche*. By *Sodome et Gomorrhe*, it is being integrated in the form of other characters' evaluations of the opera, and it finally evolves, by *La Prisonnière*, to become a vehicle to express the narrator's own independent aesthetic meditations on this and Wagner's other works. *La Prisonnière* is, in many respects, a decisive volume in the novel, but even the earliest evocations of Parsifal's quest form part of a network of allusion that paves the way for the narrator's mature approach.[40] Combining quasi-academic analysis with a passionate and sensitive engagement with Wagner's work, this evolved and autonomous appreciation stimulates the narrator's own vision of artistic creation.

The earliest intertextual association with *Parsifal* sees the young narrator waiting, in fearful expectation, to be received in Swann's house: 'Et, certes, j'eusse été moins troublé dans un antre magique que dans ce petit salon d'attente où le feu me semblait procéder à des transmutations, comme dans le laboratoire de Klingsor' (*JF* I 518). The young narrator's sense of awe, whether before the Swanns, the Guermantes or the artist, is commonly conveyed through imagery of the magical and the unknown. To cast Swann implicitly in the role of the magician, Klingsor – a figure, in Wagner's *Parsifal*, inspiring both fear and wonder – thus appears entirely apt. That Klingsor is also, as Mike Ashman proposes, a 'brilliant intellectual' further underlines the appropriateness of this metaphorical incarnation.[41] Swann is, after all, the closest approximation to an artist that the narrator has known at this stage in the novel: an aesthetically sensitive figure, his intellectual endeavours relate to the study of art. Yet Klingsor's character is defined by more than his intellect and his supernatural powers, for he is, above all, the embodiment of evil in the opera. It is he who has wounded Amfortas and he who tries to distract Parsifal from his quest for the Holy Grail. Why, then, should Swann be metaphorically linked with such a character? We may, however, recall that, in *Parsifal*, Klingsor is himself seeking the Grail – the symbol of transcendence – after being banished from the Brethren of the Knights of the Grail for his lack of purity.[42] Against this backdrop, we begin to see the bonds that link Parsifal and Klingsor, on the one hand, intertwining with those that (at least potentially) tie the narrator to Swann, on the other. Parsifal and Klingsor have embarked on the same quest, but they follow alternative paths to attain its object. In choosing the path of ruse and illusion, Klingsor's journey is misguided and, unlike Parsifal's, ultimately futile.[43] Swann is likewise the narrator's misguided alter ego, the alternative fate facing the narrator-as-Parsifal. Indeed, Klingsor's recourse to supernatural ruse and illusion finds its very earthly reflection in Swann's careful preservation of a façade behind which to conceal his personal opinion of a work of art. Our knowledge of Wagner's *Parsifal* tells us, however, that the eponymous hero will ultimately have the power to exorcize Klingsor's alternative world.[44] Within this early image, therefore, is embedded the promise that the narrator may surpass Swann, banishing the fruitless path of illusion and self-deception through the creation of an authentic new world in the work of fiction.

This power is as yet unrealized, however, and the narrator/writer's creation is only the most tentative and seemingly unaccomplishable of projects. For much of the novel, the narrator-as-Parsifal remains susceptible to the distractions of Klingsor's world. Like Parsifal wishing to emulate the 'glittering assay of men on noble horses' (p. 94), he is lured by the attractions of aristocratic society, and, like Parsifal once again, these noble figures are favoured over family: indeed, it is his ambition to join the ranks of these figures that prompts Parsifal to leave his mother, a necessary step, on the path to self-realization, as yet not unequivocally taken by the narrator.[45] On the occasion of the narrator's first attendance at a Guermantes dinner-party, M. de Guermantes introduces him to all present:

> Alors seulement je m'aperçus que venait de se produire autour de moi, de moi qui jusqu'à ce jour – sauf le stage dans le salon de Mme Swann – avais été habitué chez ma mère, à Combray et à Paris, aux façons ou protectrices ou sur la défensive

de bourgeoises rechignées qui me traitaient en enfant, un changement de décor comparable à celui qui introduit tout à coup Parsifal au milieu des filles-fleurs. Celles qui m'entouraient, entièrement décolletées (leur chair apparaissait des deux côtés d'une sinueuse branche de mimosa ou sous les larges pétales d'une rose), ne me dirent bonjour qu'en coulant vers moi de longs regards caressants comme si la timidité seule les eût empêchées de m'embrasser. Beaucoup n'en étaient pas moins fort honnêtes au point de vue des mœurs; beaucoup, non toutes, car les plus vertueuses n'avaient pas pour celles qui étaient légères cette répulsion qu'eût éprouvée ma mère. (G II 716)

The image conjures up Act 2 of *Parsifal* in which Klingsor casts a spell that makes his dark, foreboding castle vanish in favour of a garden filled with wondrous flowers and Flower Maidens. The task of these maidens is to tempt Parsifal and thus distract him from his quest for the Holy Grail. Now accepted as an equal in the Swann household, the narrator has thus replaced one 'laboratoire de Klingsor' – one source of awe and, more generally, one legendary model – with another. In an ironically overblown juxtaposition of the Holy Grail and a dinner invitation, aristocratic society is transformed, with deliberately ironic incongruity, into a goal as seemingly inaccessible and otherworldly as the object of Parsifal's quest. The effect of this hyperbolic image is, of course, to mock the young narrator's equally overblown vision of the Guermantes. The narrator is clearly identified with Parsifal here, but we must also look beyond the most conspicuous parallels. As the discussion of fairytale has shown, the narrator is frequently allied with more than one mythical figure in order to imply variously his conflicting impulses, his self-deception, the counter-productive nature of his actions; in the broadest sense, his duality.[46] Thus, the narrator also shares the role of Klingsor, for, after all, who has created the illusion that magically transforms the Guermantes' female dinner-guests into Flower Maidens, if not the narrator himself through the power of his imagination and the prism of his idealization? When viewed alongside Swann's metaphorical incarnation as Klingsor, the narrator's association with this mythical sorcerer further underlines how easily Swann's identity could be his own.

This perceptual illusion on the part of the young narrator/protagonist is enhanced by the actions of these Parisian Flower Maidens, for theirs is merely a pretence of interest in the young narrator; it is simply adherence to a set of social rituals prompted by the value apparently accorded to the narrator by the Guermantes. Proust's subtly ironic portrayal of the Flower Maidens' excesses, on the one hand, and the narrator's bemusement, on the other, exposes their displays of affection as a sham: he senses they would embrace him, a stranger, if only they dared. And yet the satirical tone of the description is tempered by the presentation of their elaborate costumes which oscillates between comic hyperbole and genuine celebration. Despite a hint of Combraysian prudishness on the part of the narrator/protagonist who is still unfamiliar with this social world, the quasi-organic synthesis of woman, nature and attire constitutes a lyrical testimony to the potentially perfect complementarity of fashion and wearer.[47]

With its quintessentially Proustian blend of tones, the image contains the seeds of the disillusion that will increasingly characterize the narrator's perception of society and, above all, the aristocracy. That the image is a mediated one – 'un changement de décor *comparable à* celui qui introduit tout à coup Parsifal au milieu des filles-fleurs' (my italics) – may be the first intimation of an unspoken and/or unacknowledged awareness, on the part of the narrator/ protagonist, that he himself has created a vision of society based on illusion. As the evening progresses, his disenchantment is granted explicit expression, as he questions whether it is for dinners such as these that so much fuss is made and that guests wear their finest clothes. The naive perplexity of the moment lived by the narrator/protagonist here combines with the causticity of hindsight enjoyed by the narrator/writer:

> Au reste ces filles-fleurs étaient à un degré étrange, faciles à être contentées par une autre personne, ou désireuses de la contenter, car plus d'une à laquelle je n'avais tenu pendant toute la soirée que deux ou trois propos dont la stupidité m'avait fait rougir, tint, avant de quitter le salon, à venir me dire, en fixant sur moi ses beaux yeux caressants, tout en redressant la guirlande d'orchidées qui contournait sa poitrine, quel plaisir intense elle avait eu à me connaître, et me parler [. . .]. Aucune de ces dames fleurs ne partit avant la princesse de Parme. (*G* II 833)

The subtle metamorphosis, in the course of the extract, from 'filles-fleurs' to the rather more matronly – and thus, arguably, improbable – seductresses implied by 'dames fleurs' marks the stripping away of the narrator's illusions. Moreover, the constant repetition, in Wagner's opera, of the inane dialogue of the 'filles-fleurs' is re-enacted in the narrator's experience of conversation with these illustrious guests. Indeed, while the purely visual image has the power to preserve their idealized aura intact, the intrusion of words, like the 'bavardage' of the society 'guignol', shatters their mythical status. As much as the aristocracy, therefore, *verbal expression* is distorted and devalued in the narrator's perception. This may, in turn, inhibit his capacity to write, for if the discourse that typifies even the most venerated of contexts is grounded in fatuous interactions, verbal expression loses its lustre. Moreover, the fact that a source of wonder – the society of the aristocracy – offers only superficial, ritual dialogue may lead the narrator to doubt that his experiences will ever merit the status of the subject of a work of art. He has yet to see that such seemingly worthless 'bavardage' can inform the work of art when couched within the insights and analysis of the writer, and, significantly, the narrator will pass through a stage when musical expression is prized above the verbal before the 'word' can be reinvested with value. Only in setting aside others' myths can the narrator write his own. Wagner's operas represent a 'halfway house' between music and speech in Proust's handling of which speech is already being debunked: the necessary repetition of motifs in a libretto finds its real-life counterpart in a simple lack of invention on the part of these 'dames fleurs'. In addition, while, in the libretto, the Flower Maidens fight over Parsifal for his love, Proust's bathetic 'opera' presents them competing for social engagements.[48] As critics such as Nattiez have suggested, pure music will mark the final stage that prepares for the narrator's own creation.[49]

The train of association by which Proust links the society of the Guermantes and Wagner's *Parsifal* also stretches out beyond these explicit evocations of the Flower Maidens. The importance ascribed to ritual by the Guermantes and their entourage, and the frequent metaphorical elevation of their parties to the level of a sacred mass, subtly ally them with the Brethren of the Knights of the Grail.[50] This suggestion is bolstered by the remarkable resemblance between the name of these gods of the faubourg Saint-Germain and that of the most prominent and, indeed, only individuated member of the Brethren, Gurnemanz. The former may, like the latter, appear to our questing heroes as a 'glittering assay', but the reality – Proust appears to imply by this association with the Brethren of the Knights of the Grail – is what Ashman calls a 'decaying society turned in on itself'.[51] And indeed, not only does the narrator increasingly perceive the sterility of this inward-looking community, but its gradual atrophy culminates in a social revolution which collapses the old hierarchies. The Brethren may be renewed when Parsifal returns the Grail to them. However, the social upheaval which engulfs the Parisian aristocracy may be interpreted as a renewal only to the extent that the apparently unshakable class hierarchy is disrupted. In reality, the old, introverted rituals are preserved. While no real renewal is achieved within the diegesis of Proust's text, however, the narrator-as-Parsifal will 'redeem' this sterile society in the work of art, the transcendent space that is the Proustian Grail. In associating the Guermantes (or the aristocracy as a whole), explicitly, with the Flower Maidens and, implicitly, with an infertile Grail Brethren, Proust thus offers deviated versions of both: a Brethren whose Grail is no more than social success and ageing Flower Maidens whose sole purpose is to secure the narrator's consent to visit them – a far cry, indeed, from the cosmic and metaphysical struggles of *Parsifal*.

Although he does not succumb to the enchantments of these 'filles-fleurs', the narrator-as-Parsifal is unable to resist Kundry. His own and others' 'redemption' in the work of art is thus delayed. Indeed, it is relegated, once again, to the realms of the potential. It is Kundry, in the opera, who banishes the 'filles-fleurs' in order herself to seduce Parsifal and tempt him from his quest. She is, therefore, the metaphorical embodiment of Albertine (or, more generally, the woman loved) on to whom the narrator's fascinated gaze shifts from the aristocratic 'filles-fleurs'.[52] And yet, a new level of complexity, undetected by previous critics, can be teased out of Proust's understanding of this ambivalent figure, for it is not only Albertine and Odette who share the features of Wagner's temptress, but also the narrator/protagonist himself. Like Kundry, he is, at the outset of the novel, under the sway of Swann-as-Klingsor and, like her, he is characterized by 'yearning'. At the beginning of Act II of *Parsifal*, Kundry pleads with Klingsor, saying: 'Yes . . . my curse. Oh! Yearning . . . yearning!' (p. 101). Although not drawn out in this part of the libretto, what she yearns for is release from her curse, for redemption. Klingsor responds with conscious ambiguity: 'Ha ha! So for the knights you're yearning?' (ibid.), insinuating a sexual motivation beneath Kundry's spiritual desire. The juxtaposition, within Kundry, of overt sexuality and a spiritual quest for redemption seems to mirror the dual pull of earthly and transcendent for the narrator. Both Kundry and the narrator are also seeking an escape from past deeds, guilt or sin.[53] However, the means they employ to effect this escape are fruitless: Kundry hopes to find redemption in the Knights of the Grail for having laughed at Christ as he was carrying the cross;[54] the narrator attempts to avoid the guilt associated with his lack of vocation and with the pain his irresolution and passivity cause his mother and grandmother in social diversions. He will realize eventually not only that the barren society of the Guermantes offers no answers, but also that transcendence of the past cannot be achieved through atonement. Moreover, if the relationship between Parsifal and Kundry is one of mutual dependency in Wagner's opera, then the narrator's dual incarnation as both Parsifal and Kundry subtly implies that the answer to his yearning lies within himself: the answer to Kundry's yearning lies with Parsifal (for he will ultimately release her from her curse), but Parsifal's awakening to awareness is also dependent on Kundry (it is her kiss which triggers his understanding). The characters in Wagner's opera – such as Klingsor, Kundry and Parsifal – thus represent the narrator's differing, and often conflicting, impulses externalized. They may also act as augurs of a path to evolution which the narrator/character has yet to comprehend.

Reflecting the scenario played out in Wagner's *Parsifal*, the narrator's focus on Albertine/Kundry is ushered in by an undifferentiated fascination with the 'jeunes filles en fleurs', for, as their collective label implies, they are granted the same metaphorical incarnation as that later attributed to the aristocratic women he meets in society.[55] The title of the second volume of Proust's novel provides a sustained reminder of this operatic link, but, otherwise, explicit evocations of Wagner's organic temptresses, in relation to the 'jeunes filles', are conspicuously absent, arguably because the narrator's fantasized vision of them as full-blown seductresses is belied by their relative innocence in reality.[56] These are not yet Flower Maidens in full blossom, soon to wither and die,[57] but merely budding Flower Maidens, burgeoning with life in contrast to their now sterile aristocratic counterparts, and not yet ready to be 'cut'. Despite the absence of explicit metaphorical links, however – the symptom, as suggested above, of the narrator's unrealized fantasy of a fully sexualized band of 'admirers' – the similarities between the Flower Maidens' first appearance in *Parsifal* and the narrator's initial vision of the 'jeunes filles' are nonetheless striking, even in terms of the language used. Just as the 'jeunes filles' initially appear as a homogeneous, even amorphous, mass, the Flower Maidens 'form [. . .] a confused, many coloured throng', the suggestion of homogeneity only reinforced by their 'shared' speech: many of the Flower Maidens' words are, for example, sung in chorus.[58]

Albertine may initially be categorized in the narrator's mind with the 'jeunes filles', but she is subsequently individuated from them, just as Kundry is distinguished from the Flower Maidens. While these latter, along with the majority of the 'jeunes filles', remain one-dimensional and fixed within a limited experiential moment, both Kundry and Albertine are rounded characters who transcend a single embodiment or experience:[59] above all, both have a past characterized by implications of 'sin' and guilt. Kundry is condemned constantly to re-enact her crime, a crime, as Borchmeyer explains, representing 'a radical reversal of the attitude which informs the metaphysical centre of *Parsifal*, namely elemental compassion for the suffering individual' (p. 18). For laughing at Christ, therefore, Kundry is unable to curtail her frequent hysterical outbursts. Albertine may not immediately be associated with a lack of compassion, although the narrator's first vision of the undifferentiated band of 'jeunes filles' highlights their adolescent cruelty, but the narrator certainly comes to fear that, like Kundry, she is forever repeating her 'crime'.[60] The narrator's suspicions are thus granted more tangible form through Albertine's implied association with Kundry. Yet this association may also – for the narrator/protagonist who is exposed to Wagner's opera and who may detect parallels between these two seductresses – be the symbol of hope that he may 'redeem' Albertine and release her from her crime. What the opera also reveals, though, and what the narrator/protagonist may be unwilling to admit, is the necessity of detaching himself from her.

Kundry's kiss is nonetheless the mechanism for Parsifal's epiphany: Amfortas's prophecy states that Parsifal will be 'Made wise through pity' (p. 87). Regardless of the pain of suspicion he endures, therefore, this metaphorical paradigm underlines the importance of the narrator's relationship with Albertine to the success of his quest. Kundry's kiss triggers an empathic association with Amfortas on Parsifal's part, for Amfortas is currently suffering because he, too, was unable to resist Kundry. The kiss also makes Parsifal realize the vacuum within himself;[61] and at this moment of revelation, Parsifal's memory is set free.[62] As Carolyn Abbate explains, Parsifal will subsequently 'take over Amfortas's office and receive his kingship'.[63] To what extent, then, does this pattern offer the narrator a model of emulation or identification?[64] Inevitably, the time frame for the narrator's experience is stretched far beyond the Wagnerian scenario in which Parsifal's rejection of Kundry and his epiphany are almost instantaneous: a brisk pace is dictated by the exigencies of Wagner's operatic medium. But the thematic parallels between the two scenarios are nonetheless unmistakable and are based on a synecdochic association between Kundry's kiss and the narrator's relationship with Albertine. The image of the kiss is, of course, endowed with potent meanings in the biblical context. Borchmeyer proposes that 'in Kundry's kiss [. . .] we find a re-enactment of Eve's seduction of Adam, and in Amfortas's fall from grace Adam's original sin' (p. 18). Kundry thus becomes the embodiment of the serpent and of temptation, a role also implicitly assigned to Albertine through their common association with Eve.[65] As with Eve's seduction of Adam, however, Kundry's kiss is a source of knowledge for Parsifal; likewise, the narrator's relationship with Albertine instructs him, at first hand, in the range of emotions which will ultimately inform the work of art he creates. In addition, the narrator's relationship with Albertine provides him with greater insight into Swann's situation with Odette and, in this sense, he, too, is 'made wise through pity'. Only now can he fully empathize with Swann/Amfortas. Adam and Eve's is not, however, the only biblical context conjured up by the image of a kiss, for it also marks Judas's betrayal of Christ. Kundry's kiss thus represents a 'warning' for the narrator: if Kundry is not only a metaphorical embodiment of Albertine, but also, in certain respects, an externalization of characteristics of the narrator himself, then Kundry's kiss becomes a symbol of the narrator's self-betrayal.[66] Thus, while his involvement with Albertine is a necessary source of enlightenment, to continue to succumb to her affections marks a failure of self-realization. Just as Kundry is necessarily rejected by Parsifal in Act II, so, too, must the narrator detach himself from Albertine.

Parsifal forcefully and unequivocally drives her away from him just moments after the kiss ('Destroyer! – Go from my side! Ever, ever be gone!'), the intervening moments being all that is required for him to experience the 'pain of loving' and the realization that to give in to her is to become like Amfortas (pp. 113–14). Amid the very Proustian images of the violence and yearning of desire, Parsifal ceases to be distracted by Kundry through his vision of the Grail, the symbol of healing and redemption. What Proust is offering us, however, is not the hyperbole of a Wagnerian opera but, rather, a picture of human realities. Its outcome may ultimately mirror that of the opera, but rather more ambivalence, hesitation and time are required before the narrator can realize the equivalent of Parsifal's vocation to find the Holy Grail and consequent 'salvation'.

Albertine may represent an essential stage in the narrator's journey towards this goal, but there, her role ends. As Abbate comments on the encounter between Parsifal and Kundry: 'Although Kundry is hardly negligible in this process [of Parsifal's metamorphosis], she is strangely neutral. Her role is to impart knowledge, thereby enabling Parsifal to achieve a transformation she could not foresee, into a mythic hero she cannot control' (p. 52).[67] The implication – if we extend our analysis to the narrator's multiple incarnations as different characters from Wagner's opera – is that if Albertine-as-Kundry cannot 'save' the narrator, the narrator-as-Kundry can. We note, however, that, in Wagner's opera, Kundry's 'salvation' is dependent on her being freed from what Ashman terms 'the psychological trap into which she has fallen (i.e. self-salvation through seduction)'.[68] Thus, if Kundry is one of a number of externalizations of the narrator's conflicting impulses, then he, too, must free himself from the psychological traps that have ensnared him, like Kundry, in repeated patterns of behaviour: notably, a belief in self-salvation through sexual relationships, through social success, and so on.

To what extent, finally, is the narrator able to 'redeem' others? In short, even if the narrator-as-Parsifal succeeds in achieving the object of his own quest, he will not have the power to 'redeem' Albertine/Kundry or Swann/Amfortas in the sense of effecting a transformation in their lives. Amfortas is Parsifal's alternative identity, just as Swann is the narrator's, for Amfortas, too, was distracted by the 'warm embraces' of a woman (p. 89).[69] In this moment of weakness, Amfortas was eternally wounded, stabbed with the Holy Spear by Klingsor: 'A wound it is that ne'er will close again' (p. 90). Characterized by images of hollowness and emptiness, he thus provides a mirror for Swann's spiritual and aesthetic sterility. Arguably, this 'wound' was self-inflicted just as the narrator's Parsifal/Klingsor duality exposes how the distractions to which he yields and the pain and emptiness they cause are also a product of the self. By extension, in Proust's rewriting of Wagner's opera, the use of dualities illustrates that characters can heal only themselves, that vicarious redemption is not possible. Just as Parsifal supplants Amfortas, therefore, so, too, will the narrator 'oust' Swann: he will both reject his identity and replace him as would-be artist, for the narrator will ultimately be fertile, where Swann, like Amfortas, was barren. The narrator cannot magically transform Swann – who is, in any case, already dead – into a fertile artist just as Parsifal cannot transform Amfortas into a fruitful king, but Amfortas is 'redeemed' through the Grail. In the same way, the narrator's work of art will accord Swann a form of redemption: not only does Swann's embodiment in the novel enable him to transcend time, but the narrator/writer's creation also represents a means of revalorizing Swann and his role in the narrator's development, without which the work of art would not exist.[70] As for Albertine, she, like Kundry, gradually realizes that the narrator cannot 'save' her (as Kundry initially believes that Parsifal can); she thus leaves in an act which marks her first step towards 'self-salvation'.

Proust's discussions of Wagner in correspondence with Reynaldo Hahn and Suzanne Lemaire as early as the 1890s provide evidence of his knowledge not only of *Parsifal* but, indeed, of all the significant works in Wagner's *œuvre*.[71] In this forum, he engaged with the philosophical and emotional content of the composer's work as much as with its aesthetic merits.[72] In subsequently writing *Parsifal* and *Tristan and Isolde* into his own masterpiece, therefore, Proust was surely reverberating the conflicts, dilemmas and resolutions dramatized by Wagner. This enabled him to crystallize his own independent aesthetic and philosophical vision through a synthesis of these and other models. The pattern of Proust's own self-definition as (future) artist – absorption, modification and/or rejection of others' evaluations – is thus written into the narrator/protagonist's experiences in *A la recherche*. As we shall now see, independent appreciation rises out of the crumbling remains of his satirical deconstruction of others' visions of Wagner.

## THE CULT OF WAGNER

Following the patterns of M. de Cambremer's appropriation of a limited selection of La Fontaine's fables, musical discernment is shown to be little more than a social prop, and no character vaunts her (albeit temperate) appreciation of Wagner more than M. de Cambremer's wife. Here, too, we detect the same duality of tone present in Proust's handling of La Fontaine. The subtle interaction of Mme de Cambremer's inflated perception of the impact of her words and the gentle irony of their narration by the writer opens up a space of comic contrasts and deflation. Other characters' evaluations of Wagner also chart the narrator's increasingly perceptive engagement, and disillusionment, with society, for confident assertions of Wagner's merits in fact provide the ironic mechanism to expose a lack of independent aesthetic judgement. Detailing the enormous popularity of Wagner in France at the time of Proust's writing, Rodrigues reveals the unthinking nature of the widespread adherence to this Wagnerian cult: 'être wagnérien suppose une série de refus et de condamnations implicites: le wagnérien voue un culte aveugle à l'Art-Religion, le wagnérien se moque de la musique qui n'est pas wagnérienne, le wagnérien considère son wagnérisme comme une ascèse' (p. 78). As for Proust's construction of Wagnerians, Rodrigues notes:

> Quant au public wagnérien, Proust est bien persuadé qu'il est majoritairement constitué de mélomanes durs d'oreille. Peu de personnages de la 'Recherche' échappent d'ailleurs à cette accusation, la mélomanie n'étant envisagée que comme un ridicule supplémentaire dans l'édifice encombré des snobismes de tous ordres. Ainsi en va-t-il des postulats wagnériens d'Oriane de Guermantes qui, au duc que Wagner 'endort immédiatement', croit faire preuve d'un goût nuancé en répondant: '*Lohengrin* est un chef d'œuvre. Même dans *Tristan* il y a çà et là une page curieuse. Et le chœur des fileuses du *Vaisseau fantôme* est une pure merveille'. (p. 85)[73]

On the surface, Mme de Cambremer's evaluations of Wagner suggest a more intricate and discerning approach than the mechanical enthusiasm betrayed by such inane evaluations as Oriane's '[c'est] une pure merveille', for she flouts the orthodoxy by arguing that Debussy's *Pelléas et Mélisande* is superior to Wagner's *Parsifal*. And yet, hers is, in reality, no less a contrived assertion of appreciation, for if Debussy is being measured against Wagner, then Mme de Cambremer's celebration of the former in no way implies, in her mind, a lack of understanding of the latter; indeed, it is as if such a bold comparison could be voiced only by the most musically sensitive. According to her, *Pelléas* is 'un petit chef-d'œuvre', and she is forever ready to launch into a spirited defence of Debussy. In this sense, she is likened to someone advocating a political cause or someone passionately defending a friend whose conduct has been questioned:

> C'était peut-être une habitude de Combray, prise auprès des sœurs de ma grand-mère qui appelaient cela: 'combattre pour la bonne cause', et qui aimaient les dîners où elles savaient, toutes les semaines, qu'elles auraient à défendre leurs dieux contre des Philistins. Telle Mme de Cambremer aimait à se 'fouetter le sang' en se 'chamaillant' sur l'art, comme d'autres sur la politique. (*SG* III 207)

Repeatedly inserted in inverted commas, her words acquire a tone of affectation and the status of oft-repeated set-pieces, indeed uninventive musical motifs.

To distract her from further deliberation and the endless pronouncements that inevitably result from it, the narrator comments to Mme de Cambremer's mother-in-law on her reportedly marvellous roses at Féterne. He then diplomatically draws Mme de Cambremer back into the conversation:

> 'C'est tout à fait *Pelléas*, lui dis-je, pour contenter son goût de modernisme, cette odeur de roses montant jusqu'aux terrasses. Elle est si forte dans la partition que, comme j'ai le hay-fever et la rose-fever, elle me faisait éternuer chaque fois que j'entendais cette scène. – Quel chef-d'œuvre que *Pelléas*! s'écria Mme de Cambremer, j'en suis férue'; et s'approchant de moi avec les gestes d'une femme sauvage qui aurait voulu me faire des agaceries, s'aidant des doigts pour piquer les notes imaginaires, elle se mit à fredonner quelque chose que je supposai être pour elle les adieux de Pelléas et continua avec une véhémente insistance comme s'il avait été d'importance que Mme de Cambremer me rappelât en ce moment cette scène, ou peut-être plutôt me montrât qu'elle se la rappelait. 'Je crois que c'est encore plus beau que *Parsifal*, ajouta-t-elle, parce que dans *Parsifal* il s'ajoute aux plus grandes beautés un certain halo de phrases mélodiques, donc caduques puisque mélodiques'. (*SG* III 208–09)

Proust's image reveals Mme de Cambremer to be as rich a source of inspiration for bodily humour as her mother-in-law.[74] Indeed, Proust's talent for teasing out the physical absurdities of people's actions is confirmed here, the comedy only enhanced by the bathetic juxtaposition of Pelléas's emotional farewell to Mélisande and Mme de Cambremer's farcically earnest whistling. As to the level of her aesthetic appreciation, its confidence belies its value, for not only is its authenticity undercut by Proust's archly hesitant clarification ('ou peut-être plutôt me montrât qu'elle se la rappelait'), but also, in its tortuously circular formulation ('un certain halo de phrases mélodiques, donc caduques puisque mélodiques'), it is so vaguely evocative as to be almost entirely meaningless.[75] As with her husband's allusions to La Fontaine, the intent and effect of the speaker's words fail to coincide. An ironic gap likewise separates the mature narrator/writer from his younger intradiegetical self, for although he confesses to mentioning *Pelléas et Mélisande* 'pour contenter son goût du modernisme', the mode of integration of the reference is heavy-handed and only superficially witty. Whether he is compromising invention for social ends or whether the social context itself is unconducive to invention, conversations such as these highlight an incompatibility, not yet fully recognized by the narrator/protagonist, between participation in the social whirl and the writing vocation. Only in *La Prisonnière*, a volume of relative withdrawal from society, does the narrator begin to engage in independent aesthetic evaluations of Wagner's work. My discussion of these evaluations follows in the footsteps of existing critical works, to which I am indebted here.[76]

### *TRISTAN AND ISOLDE*: TOWARDS AESTHETIC INDEPENDENCE

During one of Albertine's excursions without him, the narrator is able temporarily to detach his mind from her; he thus turns his attention to Vinteuil's Sonata. It reminds him initially of Combray:

> où j'avais moi-même désiré d'être un artiste. En abandonnant en fait cette ambition, avais-je renoncé à quelque chose de réel? La vie pouvait-elle me consoler de l'art, y avait-il dans l'art une réalité plus profonde où notre personnalité véritable trouve une expression que ne lui donnent pas les actions de la vie? Chaque grand artiste semble en effet si différent des autres, et nous donne tant cette sensation de l'individualité, que nous cherchons en vain dans l'existence quotidienne! (*P* III 664)

Expressing the narrator's renunciation of any hope of an artistic vocation, the extract nonetheless ends with an implied valuing of art over life. At this moment, while still considering the Sonata, and 'bien que Vinteuil fût là en train d'exprimer un rêve qui fût resté tout à fait étranger à Wagner, je ne pus m'empêcher de murmurer: "*Tristan!*"' (ibid.). The narrator therefore places the score of *Tristan and Isolde* on the piano above that of the Sonata and continues:

> Je n'avais à admirer le maître de Bayreuth aucun des scrupules de ceux à qui, comme à Nietzsche, le devoir dicte de fuir dans l'art comme dans la vie la beauté qui les tente, qui s'arrachent à *Tristan* comme ils renient *Parsifal* et, par ascétisme spirituel, de mortification en mortification parviennent, en suivant le plus sanglant des chemins de croix, à s'élever jusqu'à la pure connaissance et à l'adoration parfaite du *Postillon de Longjumeau*. Je me rendais compte de tout ce qu'a de réel l'œuvre de Wagner, en revoyant ces thèmes insistants et fugaces qui visitent un acte, ne s'éloignent que pour revenir, et parfois lointains, assoupis, presque détachés, sont à d'autres moments, tout en restant vagues, si pressants et si proches, si internes, si organiques, si viscéraux qu'on dirait la reprise moins d'un motif que d'une névralgie. (*P* III 665)

Nattiez has examined this highly significant passage in detail, arguing that it 'leads back to the theme that suggested the Wagner–Vinteuil comparison: the search for individuality. The narrator has found it not in life but in art, in music and most particularly in Wagner, because behind each work there lies the originality of a particular creative artist and because the work of art itself aims to "combin[e] diverse individualities"' (p. 13). Indeed, the narrator's doubts about art are assuaged by his contemplation of Wagner. He enumerates the qualities that link a Wagner to an Elstir to a Balzac and so on: 'Comme le spectre extériorise pour nous la composition de la lumière, l'harmonie d'un Wagner, la couleur d'un Elstir nous permettent de connaître cette essence qualitative des sensations d'un autre où l'amour pour un autre être ne nous fait pas pénétrer' (*P* III 665). The great work of art, in other words, in its subtle tones and textures, gets to the heart of things; it probes the unimportant detail to uncover the common essences of experience; it alone allows one to see through the eyes of another person; and, in this respect, it is 'superior' to life in which one's direct entanglement precludes the broader perspective.[77] The extract thus also intimates that the narrator's relationship with Albertine is an obstacle to his ever attaining such a perspective himself and so anticipates his necessary separation from her.

As if to underline this, the work of art is perceived as offering an ideal space that grants the fulfilment and 'happiness' denied in life. Rodrigues argues, drawing on the work of Vladimir Jankélévitch, that:

> 'La philosophie de la musique se réduit pour une part à une psychologie métaphorique du désir'; il n'en va pas autrement pour Proust. Sa propre expérience amoureuse s'avère un échec, la transparence des cœurs n'est qu'un leurre et l'amitié même le laisse perplexe. Aussi transpose-t-il dans la musique toutes les expériences que les relations humaines ne peuvent satisfaire. La musique de Wagner devient dès lors une métaphore possible d'un dévoilement intérieur, l'attente d'une 'félicité'.[78]

To seek such refuge in another's work, though, is surely self-deception. As the earlier discussion of the thematic parallels that tie the narrator and Parsifal has shown, redemption cannot be achieved vicariously. Philosophical and aesthetic revelations thus here coincide.

The bond between the work of artists such as Wagner, Vinteuil and Elstir can further be traced in 'la diversité':

> Là où un petit musicien prétendrait qu'il peint un écuyer, un chevalier, alors qu'il leur ferait chanter la même musique, au contraire, sous chaque dénomination, Wagner met une réalité différente, et chaque fois que paraît son écuyer, c'est une figure particulière, à la fois compliquée et simpliste, qui, avec un entrechoc de lignes joyeux et féodal, s'inscrit dans l'immensité sonore. (*P* III 665)

Every part of the work is possessed of its own individual essence, yet, as the narrator goes on to explain, this diversity is embedded within a grand design.[79] An unconscious premonition of the narrator's own work, this model of diversity within unity is achieved through the recurrent motifs, the metaphorical networks, which create and extend the artist's aesthetic vision. It is these motifs that ensure coherence between the grand design and the individual detail. The critic

Thomas Donnan has written perceptively on the musicality of *A la recherche*, identifying, in addition to the 'organic and essentially sensuous handling of language [. . .] in the dimension of words, phrases and sentence structure' , 'a metasyntactic component to Proust's style that lends a broader organic integrality to *A la recherche du temps perdu*, that of a web of motifs pervading the entire work'.[80] Of course, the narrator/protagonist does not yet realize the relevance of his observations on Wagner to his own future production; he has, he believes, abandoned his quest. And yet, the continuation of this journey, albeit on an unconscious level, is signalled by the evolution from a focus on parallels in plot and characterization to his consideration, in *La Prisonnière*, of the motifs that unite Wagner's works. As we have seen, these parallels in plot and characterization are endowed with an undercurrent of complexity that far exceeds the analogies perceived by the narrator/protagonist of the early volumes, and it is, above all, in the narrator/writer's construction that they are subtly elaborated. The development in the narrator/protagonist's approach by *La Prisonnière* – as implied by his comparing of Wagner and Vinteuil – is thus significant. It marks, moreover, a transitional site between the word/music of opera and 'pure' music. The necessity for this transition to be matched by a shift from real to fictional composer is also addressed by Nattiez who convincingly proposes that Proust

> could hardly have accorded to the work of someone else [. . .] the revelatory function he reserved for his own. Thus the work that underlay the fundamental axis of the novel – the revelation through music which leads the Narrator to his vocation as a writer – can yield its place all the more easily to a work at once absolute and imaginary, the Septet, because a new work of redemption, *A la recherche*, exists and because this new work has assimilated its message, function and content. (p. 33)

Mein concurs, adding that:

> It is precisely by writing *La Recherche* that the Proustian narrator brings about his own salvation, to a certain extent reminding us of Parsifal in the process, with the notable difference that, in the latter case, it is by the direct intervention of the composer who, by his music, completely recreated a character of legendary fame to produce a new, irreducibly individual being, paradoxically by the same token an Everyman, eminently worthy of the medieval tradition of the Mystery plays from which he springs. (p. 213)

In *La Prisonnière*, however, the narrator is still defining himself and his aesthetic with reference to the work of other artists.

The narrator pursues his meditations by arguing that a mediocre artist could never create a cycle of recurrent characters and motifs of the kind developed by Wagner and Balzac. The unity with which such cycles endow the work of art is 'ultérieure' but 'non factice' (*P* III 667). The masterpiece is dynamic, almost even organic, developing as if of its own volition and in ways that even the artist realizes only retrospectively. '[Q]uelle que soit la tristesse du poète', the narrator continues, 'elle est consolée, surpassée [. . .] par l'allégresse du fabricateur' (*P* III 667). This celebration of the work of art is only provisional. *La Prisonnière* is a volume of fluctuating viewpoints, marking out the extended period that Wagner himself could not allow between, for example, Kundry's kiss and Parsifal's rejection of her. Were it not a volume of ambivalence, the novel would lose something of its representational authenticity. Wagner, however, remains the measure for the narrator's wavering vision of art and the artist; thus, it is also through reference to this composer that the narrator expresses his doubts about art. He is, for example, troubled by what he describes as 'cette habileté vulcanienne' shared by Wagner and Elstir:

> Serait-ce elle qui donnerait chez les grands artistes l'illusion d'une originalité foncière, irréductible, en apparence reflet d'une réalité plus qu'humaine, en fait produit d'un labeur industrieux? Si l'art n'est que cela, il n'est pas plus réel que la vie, et je n'avais pas tant de regrets à avoir. Je continuais à jouer *Tristan*. Séparé de Wagner par la cloison sonore, je l'entendais exulter, m'inviter à partager sa joie, j'entendais redoubler le rire immortellement jeune et les coups de marteau de Siegfried, en qui du reste, plus merveilleusement frappées étaient ces phrases, l'habileté technique de l'ouvrier ne servait qu'à leur faire plus librement quitter la terre, oiseaux pareils non au cygne de Lohengrin mais à cette aéroplane que j'avais vu à Balbec changer son énergie en élévation, planer au-dessus des flots, et se perdre dans le ciel. (*P* III 667–8)

Here, the writer is reduced from semi-divine status to the practical world of the skilled artisan or engineer. His work may be impressive, but it is no more mysterious or mystical than any other. As Nattiez expresses it: 'However far Wagner might take us towards the absolute, his works still bear the traces of the craftsman's bench. Proust does not dare to write that they seem manufactured, but he lets it be understood' (p. 58). In apparent contradiction to his earlier assertions, the artist's labour and output are firmly rooted in the real world. Indeed, the narrator's meditation deflates the artistic vocation to a profession. Undoubtedly an expression of disenchantment, the narrator's image of the artist's 'habileté vulcanienne' also signals, more constructively, a new recognition on the narrator/protagonist's part that artistic creation is born of industry as much as of inspiration or vocation. What is more, as Vigneron highlights, 'cette conclusion désenchantée n'est qu'une étape de l'initiation esthétique du protagoniste: quelques heures plus tard il va se faire de l'art une idée plus haute'.[81] Certainly, any deflation of the work of art seems firmly set aside by the end of *La Prisonnière* when Mlle Vinteuil's lover's deciphering of Vinteuil's notebooks is equated to 'la promesse qu'il existait autre chose, réalisable par l'art sans doute, que le néant que j'avais trouvé dans tous les plaisirs et dans l'amour même, et que si ma vie me semblait si vaine, du moins n'avait-elle pas tout accompli' (*P* III 767). Indeed, the image seems to embody the hope for a rediscovery of his own vocation: as Vigneron proposes, in comparing Vinteuil's Sonata with the Septet, the narrator realizes – viscerally and intellectually – 'la réalité transcendante de l'art et l'originalité essentielle de l'artiste'.[82]

## FROM WAGNERIAN SYNTHESIS TO PROUSTIAN REDEMPTION

The scene is now set for the narrator's realization of his own vocation in *Le Temps retrouvé*, but like Parsifal, who is long prevented from returning to the Knights of the Grail by 'a fearful curse [which] led [him] astray' (p. 120), the narrator will also journey away from Paris, returning only much later, before he finally attains the object of his quest.[83] In this, he traces the patterns of withdrawal and return that lie at the heart of the mythical cycles identified by Mircea Eliade. The nature of this ultimate transcendent moment finds its echoes in both *Parsifal* and *Tristan and Isolde*, yet neither work is explicitly evoked by Proust in this context. In fact, the only references to Wagner in *Le Temps retrouvé* metaphorically connect the apocalyptic mood of wartime Paris with the Ride of the Valkyries.[84] Given their pervasive presence throughout the text, their absence at the denouement of the narrator's own spiritual journey may seem surprising. Nattiez has convincingly argued that the real artist must be cast aside in favour of the fictional creator. But there is perhaps more to it than this, for, arguably, neither of these Wagnerian quests is present explicitly in *Le Temps retrouvé* because neither offers an ideal model of transcendence for Proust. Indeed, just as Parsifal could only redeem himself, so, too, must the narrator/protagonist discover his own aesthetic-cum-philosophical vision, his own Holy Grail. Each of the models explored in this part of the study has represented a (potential) stage in the narrator's quest, and each has contributed to the development of his attitudes and aesthetics, but the narrator-soon-to-be-writer's own vision of transcendence will ultimately be based on a very Proustian synthesis. This synthesis unmistakably recalls, but also reinvents, aspects of the spiritual ideals dramatized in *Parsifal* and *Tristan and Isolde*.

Like *Parsifal*, Proust's novel can be read, in Ashman's words, as 'a basic metaphor for the acquiring of wisdom, maturity and compassion in life'.[85] Although not consistently selfless, the narrator could at no stage in his development be accused of lacking compassion, but the novel is certainly a form of *Bildungsroman*. In fact, it charts a dual progression: the narrator's path through the vagaries and illusions of childhood and adolescence to an enlightened maturity is paralleled by the concomitant realization of his artistic vocation. When the narrator finally returns to Paris and undergoes the series of revelations which lead him to his determination to create, his experiences are grounded in an impression of circularity and return. Not only does involuntary memory symbolize the ultimate return to spiritual origins, but the writer also brings closure to many of his metaphorical cycles in this volume. Images inspired by puppet theatre and evocations of the fables of La Fontaine are revived, but in altered form, reinforcing the fact that this is not a passive return to the narrator's starting point: as in the cycle of mythical return described by Eliade, the narrator has evolved. The denouement of Parsifal's quest shares the same mythical structure of return and renewal. Amfortas's wound, for example, is finally to be healed by the very weapon that inflicted it: 'So with this Spear I vanquish your enchantment: / and the wound shall be healed now / by the Spear that wounded' (p. 116). And Parsifal comments explicitly on the sense of circularity but, crucially, also, of difference. On returning to the starting point for his quest, he witnesses the same mass-like ritual performed by the Knights of the Grail – just as the narrator witnesses the same social rites enacted at the 'bal costumé' – but, as Parsifal acknowledges, 'everything seems altered' and, indeed, renewed (p. 120).[86]

Both *Parsifal* and *Tristan and Isolde* also advocate, for Ashman, a Schopenhauerian 'renunciation of selfish interest as the highest goal in life'.[87] If successful, this will bring with it a form of redemption. But this is not a miraculous redemption: neither Parsifal nor the narrator is a Christ-like figure.[88] Parsifal returns the Grail, the symbol of spiritual transcendence, to the Brethren; they are restored by its presence, for their existence is reinvested with meaning. In a similar vein, the narrator's Holy Grail, the work of art, brings renewal by granting the lives of those in it a new, because universalized, meaning. The characters in Proust's novel, although described in Time, will also transcend the individual moment, as the last words of the novel foretell:

> Aussi, si elle m'était laissée assez longtemps pour accomplir mon œuvre, ne manquerais-je pas d'abord d'y décrire les hommes, cela dût-il les faire ressembler à des êtres monstrueux, comme occupant une place si considérable, à côté de celle si restreinte qui leur est réservée dans l'espace, une place au contraire prolongée

> sans mesure puisqu'ils touchent simultanément, comme des géants plongés dans les années à des époques, vécues par eux si distantes, entre lesquelles tant de jours sont venus se placer – dans le Temps. (*TR* IV 625)

Indeed, in realizing his vocation in the creation of the work of art, the narrator will redeem not only himself and, at least within the diegesis of the text, his characters, but also Time itself. This idea is implied in strikingly similar terms in *Parsifal*: in the presence of the Grail, 'Time is one with Space' (p. 96). In this, the narrator-as-writer will enjoy a more actively transformative power than Parsifal, for he will not simply restore an existing Holy Grail but create a new one in the work of art and, through it, a supra-temporal existence for himself and his characters. In its various stages, the artist's quest thus mirrors, but ultimately transcends, that of the Wagnerian mythical hero.

With its portrayal of infidelity, forbidden love and mediated desire, *Tristan and Isolde* anticipates a number of the key themes of Proust's novel.[89] Elements of the culmination of Wagner's opera can also be detected in *A la recherche*, for, like *Parsifal*, it dramatizes a moment of ultimate transcendence in the form of a negation of the will and a rejection of earthly passions, be they social or sexual. *Tristan and Isolde* may be a monument to ideal love – a monument which portrays love in both its erotic and metaphysical forms and which dramatizes the full sweep of the lovers' emotions. However, the physical is ultimately rejected in favour of the mystical, for the text is grounded in the desire for the woman loved to share man's higher ideals. She is to act as an encouragement to man, to help him towards higher achievement through womanly compassion.[90] The opera thus represents, according to John Luke Rose, 'a search for a metaphysical solution rather than physical satisfaction'.[91]

Following Schopenhauer, Wagner presents human suffering as a result of individuation, of the *principium individuationis*. As Scruton explains:

> When the will becomes incarnate as an individual [. . .] it is as though it had opened a door into a place of torment. [. . .] Individual existence is, from the individual point of view, a mistake, yet one into which the will to live is constantly tempted by its need to show itself as Idea. The will *falls* into individuality and exists for a while trapped in a world of representation, sundered from the calm ocean of eternity that is its home. Its life as an individual [. . .] is really an expiation for original sin, which is 'the crime of existence itself'.[92]

The only escape from the suffering entailed by individuation is an intellectual renunciation, a form of self-denial: 'The intellect can overcome the will's resistance to death by showing that we have nothing to fear from death and everything to gain'.⁹³ Indeed, passing beyond the will's desire to affirm its existence as separate from the phenomenal world produces, to quote Schopenhauer, 'perfect sanctification and salvation, the phenomena of which are the state of resignation [. . .], the unshakeable peace accompanying this, and the highest joy and delight in death'.⁹⁴ The state of conscious freedom from individuation or desire is nirvana. Schopenhauer was convinced of the artist's power to perceive and express the most profound truths about the essence of being and becoming through such a negation of the will. Echoing this philosophical position, the mythical structures of *A la recherche* reveal how the narrator/protagonist ultimately frees himself from 'selfhood', from earthly desire and from the egoism of individuation in order to be able to perceive, and ultimately communicate, truth.

Despite these resonances, however, *A la recherche* does not present a faithful reflection of *Tristan and Isolde*. A potent day/night dualism runs throughout the libretto in which day signifies all that is vain, worldly and ephemeral, and night represents purity, truth and the eternal.⁹⁵ The ultimate means of embracing the night is thus naturally through death, and it is for this that Tristan and Isolde yearn. Death will unite them in a pure, ideal love of the kind that light/day/life renders impossible, and, indeed, the opera ends with the lovers' deaths. But, in this respect, it does not chime with Proust's vision. The narrator and Albertine's relationship is a travestied version of Wagner's couple. As skilfully implied in the following extract, it is a far cry from the pure and candid passion of Tristan and Isolde. The narrator is in a state of anguish because he is alone at night:

> du fond du Paris populeux et nocturne approché soudain de moi, à côté de ma bibliothèque, j'entendis tout à coup, mécanique et sublime, comme dans *Tristan* l'écharpe agitée ou le chalumeau du pâtre, le bruit de toupie du téléphone. Je m'élançai, c'était Albertine. 'Je ne vous dérange pas en vous téléphonant à une pareille heure? – Mais non . . .', dis-je, en comprimant ma joie, car ce qu'elle disait de l'heure indue était sans doute pour s'excuser de venir dans un moment, si tard, non parce qu'elle n'allait pas venir. 'Est-ce que vous venez? demandai-je d'un ton indifférent. – Mais . . . non, si vous n'avez pas absolument besoin de moi.' (SG III 128–9)⁹⁶

The symbolic acts that signal the desired union of Wagner's lovers are subtly juxtaposed to the mutual manipulation, the fluctuation between indifference and desire, that characterizes the narrator and Albertine's interaction. In its casual tragedy, too, Albertine's death shares nothing of the flavour of the sublime, shared destiny of Wagner's lovers, and, indeed, the relationship of the narrator and Albertine was long since fractured anyway. The possibility of this Wagnerian ideal is thwarted by Albertine's inability to extricate herself from the associations and suspicions of eroticism. She is unable, in other words, to acquire a metaphysical character.[97] Moreover, while the culmination of the narrator's quest may involve a Schopenhauerian rejection of the worldly and a negation of the 'selfishness' of the will, this is not an end in itself, as the denouement of *Tristan and Isolde* proposes, but, rather, a springboard, the necessary state the narrator must reach in order to be able to write. The suffering of human individuation will become the material for the work of art.

*Tristan and Isolde* offers a vision of transcendence based on a withdrawal from the external world into the inner, spiritual universe of the Self. At the end of *A la recherche*, the narrator positions himself on a corresponding course. Realizing that enlightenment lies within himself, he also acknowledges that the decision to write necessitates the death of the social self, indeed of all that light and day represent in *Tristan and Isolde*. Tristan's literal death also finds its complement in the death of the narrator's former selves. His identity has been characterized by duality, even plurality, throughout the novel: ironic tensions mark out the perceptual gap between the mature narrator/writer and the young narrator/protagonist; inner conflicts are externalized through his metaphorical incarnation as a plurality of figures from the worlds of magic, fairytale and legend. Here, these identities are surpassed in a final realization of Self.

If *Tristan and Isolde* turns inwards at its culmination, Parsifal's gaze turns outwards at the climax of the hero's quest. The Grail may be the object of a personal, spiritual quest, but Parsifal is also driven by a tangible, external goal: to retrieve the Spear and the Grail by which means he will 'cure' Amfortas, assume kingship and indirectly renew the Knights of the Grail. The work the narrator will write likewise implies ongoing engagement with the world, albeit only within the text to be written. Indeed, past realities will be endowed with new life and vigour in this text; the lives of the people the narrator has encountered will be granted a new magnitude; and the work itself will continue to engage and challenge its readers by granting access to 'cette essence qualitative des sensations d'un autre où l'amour pour un autre être ne nous fait pas pénétrer' (*P* III 665).

What Proust offers us ultimately is a philosophical fusion: at the end of *Le Temps retrouvé*, the narrator opts for withdrawal having engaged (*Tristan and Isolde*), but he also withdraws in order to engage with the work he will create and, through it, with the external world (*Parsifal*). The paths offered by neither of these legends are accepted in their entirety because his own creation necessitates a transition from a passive and/or vicarious ideal *in* art, to an active, individual ideal *through* art. None of the legends the narrator has scrutinized (whether consciously or unconsciously) as a possible model for emulation or as a refuge from his own quest can mirror precisely the independent philosophical and aesthetic position the narrator/protagonist has required the entire novel to achieve. The legends explored in this part of the study thus play no explicit role in the narrator's expression of the revelations he experiences in *Le Temps retrouvé* or in the subsequent formulation of the vocation he has realized. And yet, elements of all have directed the journey he has taken and shaped his understanding of the promise of transcendence experienced through involuntary memory and foreseen in the work of art he will create. In the course of the philosophical quest undertaken, an entire generic spectrum, ranging from the ridiculous to the sublime, has also been arrayed before us, and, like the narrator/protagonist arriving at a model of philosophical synthesis, the narrator-soon-to-be-writer has developed a doctrine of aesthetic fusion. This is a fusion of comic and tragic, high and low, which has evolved gradually with reference to such disparate sources as La Fontaine, Wagner and puppet theatre, but which is finally crystallized and expressed through Debussy's *Pelléas et Mélisande*.

## *Pelléas et Mélisande:* a model of aesthetic synthesis

*Pelléas et Mélisande* is often likened to *Tristan and Isolde* on account of its themes and 'plot', but Debussy's work is also recognized as a more 'down-to-earth', less hyperbolic version of the tale. This comparison is justified in musical terms, but also stylistically, for the libretto, based on Maeterlinck's play of the same title, is characterized by a distinctly conversational tone.[98] Although still a tragedy, therefore, it is clearly situated on a lower rung of the aesthetic hierarchy, as traditionally conceived, than Wagner's opera. Proust takes this aesthetic 'downgrading' a step further by handling the opera in comic mode. The result is an aesthetic synthesis of mood and tone which is epitomized by the narrator's meditation on the street-sellers' calls in *La Prisonnière* where Debussy's opera is superimposed on to the most mundane of contexts:

> Car l'appel qu'ils lançaient aux petites maisons voisines n'avait, à de rares exceptions près, rien d'une chanson. Il en différait autant que la déclamation – à peine colorée par des variations insensibles – de *Boris Godounov* et de *Pelléas*; mais d'autre part rappelait la psalmodie d'un prêtre au cours d'offices dont ces scènes de la rue ne sont que la contrepartie bon enfant, foraine, pourtant à demi liturgique. [. . .] Car après avoir presque 'parlé': 'Les escargots, ils sont frais, ils sont beaux', c'était avec la tristesse et le vague de Maeterlinck, musicalement transposés par Debussy, que le marchand d'escargots, dans un de ces douloureux finales par où l'auteur de *Pelléas* s'apparente à Rameau ('Si je dois être vaincue, est-ce à toi d'être mon

vainqueur?'), ajoutait avec une chantante mélancolie: 'On les vend six sous la douzaine . . .'

Il m'a toujours été difficile de comprendre pourquoi ces mots fort clairs étaient soupirés sur un ton si peu approprié, mystérieux, comme le secret qui fait que tout le monde a l'air triste dans le vieux palais où Mélisande n'a pas réussi à apporter la joie, et profond comme une pensée du vieillard Arkel qui cherche à proférer dans des mots très simples toute la sagesse et la destinée. Les notes mêmes sur lesquelles s'élève avec une douceur grandissante la voix du vieux roi d'Allemonde ou de Golaud, pour dire: 'On ne sait pas ce qu'il y a ici. Cela peut paraître étrange. Il n'y a peut-être pas d'événements inutiles', ou bien: 'Il ne faut pas s'effrayer . . . C'était un pauvre petit être mystérieux, comme tout le monde', étaient celles qui servaient au marchand d'escargots pour reprendre, en une cantilène indéfinie: 'On les vend six sous la douzaine . . .' Mais cette lamentation métaphysique n'avait pas le temps d'expirer au bord de l'infini, elle était interrompue par une vive trompette. Cette fois il ne s'agissait pas de mangeailles, les paroles du libretto étaient: 'Tond les chiens, coupe les chats, les queues et les oreilles'. (*P* III 623–5)

The narrator initially distances the street-sellers' calls from the operas of Mussorgsky and Debussy before progressing to, what is to him, a gratifyingly unforeseen realization that their manner of delivery bears some resemblance to an operatic delivery, and not of any operatic piece, but one of Mélisande's mournful arias. Yet he still identifies this sense of commonality as 'si peu approprié'. By the end of the extract, however, the narrator has accepted the similarity entirely. The unmediated metaphor, 'les paroles du libretto étaient: "Tond les chiens [. . .]"', implies that he detects no artificiality or discordance in the analogy. From an initial assertion of incongruity, based solely on a conventional assumption that opera can have nothing in common with a street-seller's chant, the narrator progressively disentangles himself from the unquestioning aesthetic judgement to pose a challenge to this strict hierarchy and to illustrate how high and low 'art' can overlap. Reminding us of Bakhtin's compelling evaluation of the street-sellers' cries in Rabelais, such apparently mundane items as 'the names of dishes, venison, wines, household objects, and kitchen utensils' are accorded their own 'intrinsic value', and the gap between the 'cris de Paris' and the work of art is further narrowed through the musicality that Bakhtin identifies in the form: 'the cries of Paris represented in themselves a noisy kitchen and a loud, abundantly served banquet; every food and dish had its own rhyme and melody' (p. 182). Thus, a seemingly humorous handling of the operatic source – the transposition of a lovers' tragedy on to an advertising pitch for some snails – comes to seem curiously apt. The influence of this realization on the writer's art is felt throughout *A la recherche* in the curious, yet fitting, blend of tones that defies the reader's expectations: literary and popular language is juxtaposed; Proust's tone and register oscillate almost imperceptibly between the comic and the tragic; sacred and profane, sublime and trivial fuse in deliberately incongruous images; and, on a more general level, characters' pompous repetition of the fashionable aesthetic judgement is humorously debunked.

## Closing the cycle: 'That's the way to do it'

We return finally to the closure of the cycle of allusions to puppet theatre, a metaphorical cycle which, in stylistic terms alone, illustrates the mature narrator/protagonist's release from the dramas repeatedly enacted by Polichinelle. Confronted with the changes in the people he meets again at the princesse de Guermantes's party after a distance of many years, the narrator's gaze turns first to M. d'Argencourt:

> C'était trop de parler d'un acteur et, débarrassé qu'il était de toute âme consciente, c'est comme une poupée trépidante, à la barbe postiche de laine blanche, que je le voyais agité, promené dans ce salon, comme dans un guignol à la fois scientifique et philosophique où il servait, comme dans une oraison funèbre ou un cours en Sorbonne, à la fois de rappel à la vanité de tout et d'exemple d'histoire naturelle. (*TR* IV 502)

This is a far cry from the amazement of the young narrator/protagonist on his first entry into the world of the Guermantes; and although this sense of awe was ironically undercut by the mature narrator/writer's multi-dimensional handling of the metaphor of puppet theatre, this visualization of M. d'Argencourt marks a new coincidence of the voices of protagonist and writer. This is no longer the perspective of the participant in the puppet theatre. It is, rather, that of the curious observer, and a more detached, indeed quasi-scientific, observer than the one who regarded the Guermantes with wonder before his entry into their world. The performances of these *mondains* whom the narrator encounters at the 'bal costumé' have not changed: as was implied in Proust's early introduction of the image of puppet theatre (*G* II 727), their incarnation as puppets suggests not only empty ritual, but also soullessness and a lack of independence, whether in aesthetic or personal judgements, style or matters of taste. These ironic tones were previously heard in the quiet voice of the narrator/writer; here, they are also perceived by the mature narrator/protagonist. His perception has developed while, despite social upheaval comparable to revolution, the social ceremonial and protocols have not. The extent of the narrator/protagonist's development is accentuated by the complexity with which he handles the metaphor of puppet theatre. In addition to the narrator's explicit articulation of the implications of M. d'Argencourt's incarnation as a puppet – he is, for example, 'débarrassé [. . .] de toute âme consciente' – other realms of knowledge and experience are drawn in besides. Tapping into both scientific and religious discourses, d'Argencourt is at once natural specimen and fitting illustration of the papal dictum, 'sic transit gloria mundi'. A seemingly improbable combination of sources, the fusion of religion and science nonetheless demonstrates the mature narrator's capacity to perceive the 'liens secrets' which unite quite disparate domains.[99] These links are, of course, fundamental to Proust's conception of metaphor.

Through metaphor, the superficial appearance of incompatibility is transcended, just as through involuntary memory, distinct time frames coalesce in a supra-temporal moment. These realizations lie at the heart of the narrator's creation. Becoming a creator entails a rejection of the sterile path of social engagement, however. On a symbolic level, the final evocation of puppet theatre in *A la recherche* achieves precisely this, for it offers a travestied version of the narrator's transcendence of time in the novelistic universe. In order to identify the people he sees with those he once knew, the narrator is obliged to consider them 'sur plusieurs plans à la fois' (*TR* IV 503). Only by looking at them with his memory as well as his eyes do they acquire depth, for they are 'des poupées baignant dans les couleurs immatérielles des années, des poupées extériorisant le Temps [. . .]' (ibid.). A reflection of their exaggerated, unnatural appearances – at least to the narrator/protagonist who is confronted with the gradual effects of time seemingly compressed into a single moment – the image of puppetry also crystallizes the narrator's own desired relationship to time, for what the guests at the party represent for the narrator (as, indeed, does he for them) is the externalization of time, not the extra-temporal moment offered by involuntary memory and its echo in the aesthetic domain, metaphor. Past and present may appear to merge if the same set-pieces are repeatedly enacted, but this passive ritual existence in fact represents a flight from challenge and change.


In exploring the legends of performance and text, we have traced a dual evolution. The mythical quest of the narrator/protagonist is paralleled by an aesthetic quest on the part of the would-be writer in search of stylistic innovation and open to generic possibilities. Challenges to accepted wisdom, to unthinking patterns of behaviour and to traditional aesthetic conventions have been essential elements in this dual endeavour, as have reminders of the necessity of change when confronted with the comforting allure of stasis. In charting these quests through to their conclusion, however, we have pushed into some dark corner those moments when the narrator *does* yield to the attractions of a retreat from challenge and change. It is to these that I turn in the final part of the book.

# III

# RITUALS AND BELIEFS

## Introduction

At every stage on the mythical journey dramatized in *A la recherche*, the narrator/protagonist is susceptible to the temptations of both passive ritual and a vicarious search for the absolute. As Proust's handling of the legends of literature and music illustrates, collective activity and the well-trodden path offer an alluring refuge from independent engagement. The fables of La Fontaine, Wagner's operas and even the familiar dramas of Polichinelle act as symbolic markers, for the reader, of a dual evolution: the various stages in the narrator/protagonist's mythical quest are complemented by the development of an aesthetic on the part of the narrator-soon-to-be-writer. The significance of these undercurrents is available to the reader willing to delve into intertexts at times only fleetingly evoked. The narrator-as-writer will also appreciate the 'message' hidden within the artistic works he has encountered and will weave this 'message' into his text. The level of awareness of the narrator/protagonist is, however, more unstable. At moments in the text, it seems likely that he is actively considering the symbolic significance of these legends for his own evolution, as, for example, when he listens to the full recitation of La Fontaine's fable of enclosure and yearning for freedom in *Le Temps retrouvé*.[1] An increased level of awareness may also be detected more generally in the later parts of the novel. But for much of the text, the role of these legends in the expression of the narrator's path to self-realization appears to be confined largely to the writer's account or the protagonist's unconscious. And yet, the narrator's flight from action and from an independent quest does not occur only on an emblematic level in the text he will ultimately write. In intradiegetical terms, too, the narrator/protagonist seeks out systems of belief and forms of ritual which offer a refuge from the challenges and necessary isolation of his journey.

Above all in moments of emotional intensity or crisis, the young narrator/protagonist resorts to the comforting illusions of power and control variously offered by spiritualism, superstition, magic, divination and astrology. Reflecting the concerns which, according to Mircea Eliade, underlie all mythical thinking, a preoccupation with what constitutes the Self, with the problematic of communication and with the compulsion to transcend time drives the narrator to embrace these rituals and beliefs.[2]

Their presence in the text fluctuates between the literal and the figurative, as apparently authentic (or at least desired) 'faith' vies with metaphorical exploitation. Indeed, the transition from the genuine pull of systems of supernatural belief to their appeal as a source of metaphor is intrinsic to the narrator's development. It is here, therefore, that a progression from magic to religion to science, of the kind described by Frazer in relation to human societies, appears to be reflected in the narrator's evolution. In fact, as we shall see, Proust offers us a more complex vision of the individual and, by extension, of society. The nineteenth century at once gave voice to Darwinism and to Mill's and Comte's belief in the capacity of the human mind to bring about orderly progression, and witnessed a spectacular rise in interest in mesmerism, phrenology, spiritualism, indeed all facets of occultism.[3] Proust similarly highlights the coexistence of magical and scientific thinking and, by extension, the persistent and pervasive presence of 'magic' in the supposedly rational, scientific world. I shall return to the nature of this 'magic' in the conclusion. For the moment, however, let us turn to the most pervasive of all the rituals and beliefs to appear in the novel and also the primary mechanism by which characters attain a (precarious) impression of power and control, namely superstition.

## Superstition and anxiety

Sir James Frazer defined superstition as the erroneous association of contiguous ideas. As summarized by Françoise Askevis-Leherpeux, superstition, for Frazer, arises from 'la généralisation erronée des deux lois fondamentales de la pensée que sont l'association d'idées par similarité et l'association d'idées par contiguïté spatiale ou temporelle'.[4] Subsequent theorists, including Bergson, may have condemned Frazer's reliance on the principle of associationism. But Frazer's conception of this phenomenon as erroneous association and 'dysfonctionnement de la pensée logique' nonetheless sounds a chord for the reader of Proust.[5] Not only do any number of the characters we encounter in *A la recherche* extract, to irrational effect, generalized truths or certainties from the superimposition of adjacent or similar circumstances, but the *terms* of Frazer's definition – based on the association or contiguity of disparate ideas – also seem, at first glance, to echo those of Proust's theory of metaphor:[6]

> On peut faire se succéder indéfiniment dans une description les objets qui figuraient dans le lieu décrit, la vérité ne commencera qu'au moment où l'écrivain prendra deux objets différents, posera leur rapport, analogue dans le monde de l'art à celui qu'est le rapport unique de la loi causale dans le monde de la science, et les enfermera dans les anneaux nécessaires d'un beau style. Même, ainsi que la vie, quand en rapprochant une qualité commune à deux sensations, il dégagera leur essence commune en les réunissant l'une et l'autre pour les soustraire aux contingences du temps, dans une métaphore. (*TR* IV 468)

However, where superstition is, in Frazer's theory, born of a deviation from logical thought, Proust's conception of metaphor stresses an 'inevitability' analogous to scientific causality. Irrational and rational are thus opposed, and the processes of superstition-creation offer an inverted image of those of metaphor-creation. Mirroring the tension between rational and irrational, science and superstition, Frazer further proposes, as we have seen, that all human societies pass through three stages: magic, religion and, ultimately, science. Applying this template to Proust's fictional universe leads to a number of conclusions. One realizes, for instance, that the first and last stages in this progression coexist: the 'truthful' creator of metaphor, who is analogous to the scientist, is the contemporary of his superstitious characters. However, one also sees that, at least on the surface, the novel embodies a chronological evolution of the kind envisaged by Frazer: from an early flirtation with superstitious acquaintances and belief, the narrator-protagonist develops towards the identity of would-be metaphor-creator or, in simple terms, artist.[7] The pages that follow explore Proust's construction of superstitious belief through his characters and simultaneously chart the narrator's progressive distancing from it.

Gustav Jahoda, in his study of *The Psychology of Superstition*, elaborates a four-part model for classifying superstitious belief. The first category of superstition, 'forming part of a cosmology or coherent world-view', is associated with various 'pagan' religions that posit the involvement in one's life of the spirits of one's forefathers or, more generally, with a traditional world-view that places strong emphasis on an ancestral past (p. 10).[8] The second is composed of 'other socially shared superstitions' which tend to be associated with good or bad luck, and includes such omens and practices as spilling salt, breaking mirrors, hanging horseshoes, touching wood and wearing charms or talismans. The third form of superstition is defined by 'occult' experiences such as visions of ghosts or forebodings of death and disaster, while the last may be termed 'personal superstitions', for it encompasses those beliefs and practices that individuals have come to adopt for themselves. An obvious example would be the belief in lucky colours or numbers.

Each of these categories has its own representative(s) in Proust's construction of superstitious belief, and all but the third – which steers us into the territory of spiritualist practices – will be discussed here.[9] Before progressing any further, however, let us answer the simple question of who, in the novel, is superstitious. The list is inclusive in terms of gender and class: Françoise is an obvious candidate, but, in addition, we find the narrator, Swann, Odette, Saint-Loup, Elstir and Mme de Guermantes all succumbing to the reassurances of superstitious belief. What differentiates them is the focus of their beliefs, for these tend to revolve around the characteristic which defines the individual in question: Françoise's centre on morality, Elstir's on art, Swann's and Saint-Loup's (and, fleetingly, the narrator's) on desire, and Mme de Guermantes's relate to social status. As for Odette, she may display the outward signs of superstitious belief, but the object of her convictions – as if to reflect her chameleon nature – remains undefined. Theorists and psychologists argue that superstitious beliefs are likely to develop in response to something disturbing, disordered or chaotic. Don Lewis notes that superstitions are linked to 'ignorance and irrational fear surrounding the great mysteries of life'.[10] Whatever Proust's superstitious characters perceive these mysteries to be, therefore, we may conclude that they have each developed their beliefs in response to a very personal, ontological malaise. Whether these characters' existence within Proust's novelistic universe is defined by class, love or art, the development in them of superstitious belief both highlights fears surrounding the questions that dominate their existence (and, thus, for them, the questions of existence) and marks an attempt to reduce uncertainty and anxiety through the adoption of superstitious practices.

Françoise embodies Jahoda's first category of superstitious belief (that is, forming part of a 'cosmology or coherent world-view'), and, at least in the anecdotal terms of the frequency with which her convictions are cited, she would appear to be the most superstitious character in the novel. She also illustrates the fine line between faith and superstition, for her superstitious codes are akin to a dogmatic, Old Testament morality:[11]

> Elle possédait à l'égard des choses qui peuvent ou ne peuvent pas se faire un code impérieux, abondant, subtil et intransigeant sur des distinctions insaisissables ou oiseuses (ce qui lui donnait l'apparence de ces lois antiques qui, à côté de prescriptions féroces comme de massacrer les enfants à la mamelle, défendent avec une délicatesse exagérée de faire bouillir le chevreau dans le lait de sa mère, ou de manger dans un animal le nerf de la cuisse). (S I 28)[12]

However, the irrational extremes of her credo are subtly marked out by Proust in his ironic opposition of 'inscriptions féroces' and 'délicatesse exagérée'. Moreover, the identification of Françoise's codes as '[des] lois antiques', along with the suggestion of an almost medieval dogma, are no accident, for it is to the Ancients and the Middle Ages that Jung attributes a mode of thought where, as explained by Jahoda, 'elaborate edifices were commonly erected on the basis of resemblances and analogies'.[13] Integral to this mode of thought, the medieval understanding of man as microcosm and universe as macrocosm appealed to Jung. The theory of an intimate link between micro- and macrocosm persisted until the scientific revolution of the seventeenth century which finally destroyed these 'harmonious and satisfying modes of thinking'.[14] The effect was a widening of the gap between Self and world which, for Jung, is both a loss and a source of malaise. Even in the industrially advanced nineteenth century, however, Françoise remains doggedly faithful to the idea of a general connection between celestial and human affairs.[15] The anachronistic nature of her convictions in this age of progress is implied by the narrator's incongruous fusion of industry and medieval fable in the passage below:

> l'on était obligé de se dire qu'il y avait en elle un passé français très ancien, noble et mal compris, comme dans ces cités manufacturières où de vieux hôtels témoignent qu'il y eut jadis une vie de cour, et où les ouvriers d'une usine de produits chimiques travaillent au milieu de délicates sculptures qui représentent le miracle de saint Théophile ou les quatre fils Aymon. (S I 28–9)

That chemical processes have ousted Saint Theophilus may imply a recognition, on Proust's part, that science is the new miracle of the modern world and, by extension, that Françoise's beliefs are obsolete, indeed that empiricism has replaced irrationality. Nonetheless, intellectual rejection does not preclude a fascination with, and attraction to, the certainties of this primitivist position. Ultimately, however, the narrator will be reluctant to accept the refusal of chance or coincidence implied by Françoise's superstitious insistence on the micro/macrocosmic relationship that binds man and universe together:[16] the crucial experiences of involuntary memory in *Le Temps retrouvé*, after all, are not divinely ordained, but grounded in chance. Furthermore, he cannot embrace the passivity of Françoise's belief system. Although she is an aggressive adherent, Françoise's convictions are unquestioning and, unlike other superstitious beliefs in the novel, they involve no superstitious practices.[17] Despite its 'shortcomings' as a doctrinal alignment, however, this belief system undoubtedly retains an aesthetic appeal, not least in its surprisingly lyrical formulation in Françoise's own speech:

Comme la vitrine d'un musée régional l'est par ces curieux ouvrages que les paysannes exécutent et passementent encore dans certaines provinces, notre appartement parisien était décoré par les paroles de Françoise inspirées d'un sentiment traditionnel et local et qui obéissaient à des règles très anciennes. (G II 363)

In the polyphony of *A la recherche*, Françoise provides another voice. This voice may be as quaintly curious as some local craft rendered obsolete by industry or technology. Nonetheless, its quasi-synaesthetic transformation – through metaphor – into a tangible object of ornamentation accentuates its potency for the narrator/protagonist, if not yet, as the reference to decoration implies, its purpose within the movement of the narrative as a whole.

Françoise is the unequivocal personification of Jahoda's first category, while the second – 'socially shared superstitions' – finds no more flamboyant a devotee than Odette. However, Mme de Guermantes, the only other superstitious woman in the novel – and, as we have seen in earlier chapters, a woman characterized by fluctuation and ambivalence – would appear to bridge the two categories. Like Odette, she wears a medallion (*G* II 834), one of the 'Christian talismans par excellence';[18] but the majority of her superstitious beliefs are dictated by a 'religion' so rigid and doctrinaire as to rival that of Françoise, namely 'la superstition des Guermantes à l'égard du vieux protocole' (*TR* IV 571). By attributing to Mme de Guermantes a deviated, social cosmology to match that of Françoise, Proust may be intimating that the former's superstitions are as anachronistic as the latter's. At the very least, the association implicitly created between the most exalted and most humble on the social hierarchy provides a prophetic hint at the pliability of social boundaries facilitated by the war in *Le Temps retrouvé*.[19] Indeed, this reference, from the final volume of the novel, is ironically situated within a passage that identifies Mme de Guermantes as an anachronism, at least in the eyes of Paris's now revolutionized high society:

> Il est vrai que, pour quelques souverains dont l'intimité lui était disputée par deux autres grandes dames, Mme de Guermantes se donnait encore la peine de les avoir à déjeuner. Mais d'une part, ils viennent rarement, connaissent des gens de peu, et la duchesse, par la superstition des Guermantes à l'égard du vieux protocole [...] faisait mettre: 'Sa Majesté a ordonné à la duchesse de Guermantes, a daigné', etc. Et les nouvelles couches, ignorantes de ces formules, en concluaient que la position de la duchesse était d'autant plus basse. (ibid.)

The same ambivalence that marked Proust's presentation of Françoise's superstitions may be detected here: those who devalue the duchesse de Guermantes are simply 'ignorantes', and, as with Françoise, her archaic formulations clearly possess their own mellifluous charm. Nonetheless, an increasingly satirical accent creeps into Proust's presentation of Mme de Guermantes and the superstitions associated with her. Towards the end of *Le Temps retrouvé*, the narrator comes to the conclusion that she is no longer witty, despite her earlier reputation as such. Yet because those who know her still expect her famously piquant remarks, they assume that even her most banal comment sparkles with wit. In this, they are likened to people who remain 'superstitieusement attachés à une marque de pâtisserie' (*TR* IV 582). The comparison, of course, punctures for the reader the inflated vision of Mme de Guermantes that the narrator/protagonist, unlike these dogged admirers, has long since left behind, for her implicit association with 'une marque de pâtisserie' is open to more than one interpretation. What is a tempting luxury for the superstitious devotee is, for the more percipient narrator, a non-essential item which – as the devotees themselves would realize if they were to replace superstition with empirical evidence – is of dubious quality anyway. It is also, of course, the now powerless counterpart to the novel's other, more potent 'pâtisserie'. The image further highlights the illogicality that so fascinated Proust in human nature, the myriad manifestations of which he scrutinizes throughout his writing. Here, in describing an illogical conviction as a superstition, Proust is identifying superstitious belief as an obstacle to truth. Aided by the ironic accent, the narrator effectively distances himself from superstitious belief as a potential means of making sense of the troubling questions of existence. What is, on the surface, no more than a humorous take on (the changing status of) a character thus acquires a whole new significance within the meta-narrative that charts the narrator's encounters with, and transcendence of, a range of belief systems.

It is, above all, Odette's early attire that places her securely within Jahoda's second category of socially shared practices:

> Sous la profusion des porte-bonheur en saphir, des trèfles à quatre feuilles d'émail, des médailles d'argent, des médaillons d'or, des amulettes de turquoise, des chaînettes de rubis, des châtaignes de topaze, il y avait dans la robe elle-même tel dessin colorié poursuivant sur un empiècement rapporté son existence antérieure, telle rangée de petits boutons de satin qui ne boutonnaient rien et ne pouvaient pas se déboutonner, une soutache cherchant à faire plaisir avec la minutie, la discrétion d'un rappel délicat, lesquels, tout autant que les bijoux, avaient l'air – n'ayant sans cela aucune justification possible – de déceler une intention, d'être un gage de tendresse, de retenir une confidence, de répondre à une superstition, de garder le souvenir d'une guérison, d'un vœu, d'un amour ou d'une philippine. (*JF* I 609–10)

On first reading a randomly eclectic array of superstitious tokens to rival the extravagant miscellany of style that is Odette's apartment, this description, in fact, reveals more about Odette than the idiosyncrasy and doubtfulness of her taste. The precious metals and gems referred to and, indeed, the very colour of these stones are steeped in a potent and – when juxtaposed as they are in Odette's attire – contradictory symbolism.[20] The fact that Proust elaborated considerably on the draft description of Odette's superstitious attire points to his awareness of the multitude of implications each emblem contains.[21] In the final version of the passage, she wears both silver medals and gold lockets, for example, yet gold is associated in superstition and in certain religious traditions with the masculine principle of the sun (that is, the yang principle in Taoist philosophy), while silver is linked to the moon, representing yin, the feminine energy of the cosmos. The balance of these two complementary principles is crucial, for, as Eliade notes, Chinese philosophy cautions that, 'any excess of *yin* activity in a particular region exasperates the feminine sexual instinct and causes "lascivious women to pervert the men"'.[22] An early hint at the danger Odette will represent for Swann, the coexistence of both masculine and feminine principles – as symbolized by gold and silver respectively – also heralds the dualities of her nature and sexual identity. That yin and yang are symbols of complementarity may be read, in more general terms, as a subtle validation of what Proust understands in terms of a dual sexual identity. However, the undoubted ascendancy in Odette of 'the feminine sexual instinct' makes her a more likely embodiment of danger than of balance. This conjecture is further confirmed by the contradictory symbolism, attached by superstition, to the various gems with which she adorns herself. While rubies are emblematic of love and passion, for instance, the sapphire represents innocence and truth. It is a giver of health and a preserver of chastity. Indeed, the colour blue denotes chaste affection in contrast to the ardour traditionally associated with red. The significance of the sapphire – truth, innocence – is also belied by the colour symbolism of the topaz, for, although the topaz represents love, affection and an aid to sweetness of disposition, it is usually yellow, a colour associated with falsity and treason. Proust insinuates the presence of these characteristics in Odette towards the end of the passage quoted, for it hints at deception ('déceler une intention'), secrecy ('retenir une confidence') and, evoking the animistic beliefs of childhood superstition, manipulation ('une soutache cherchant à faire plaisir').[23] Written into this proleptic passage, therefore, are a number of still covert revelations regarding Odette's character. It reveals the contradictions that exist within her; it hints at her superficiality and lack of purpose, as exemplified by the buttons 'qui ne boutonnaient rien'; in the absorption of past moments ('existence antérieure', 'souvenir') into the present creation that is her attire, it accentuates her existence within the present moment, in contrast to Swann's obsession with past and future; finally, the amalgam of all these qualities – her elusiveness – is implied even in the insistent use of the indefinite article to describe all that her attire seems tantalizingly, but unspecifiably, to contain ('une intention [. . .] un gage [. . .] une confidence [. . .] une guérison [. . .] un vœu'). The passage also draws on superstition to suggest, more generally, the 'insaisissable' represented by women in the novel. Recent critics, such as Ladenson, have demonstrated how female desire is the epitome of alterity for the narrator, of what cannot be represented or even visualized.[24] Taking this proposition a step further, Chaudier has argued that this failure of understanding and of representation is a threat to the creative enterprise, for it delineates the limitations of language.[25] If superstition offers a metaphorical embodiment of the 'unknowableness' of women in the novel, then, by extension, the narrator/protagonist must distance himself from superstitious belief if he is to overcome obstacles to creation.

It may seem, on occasion, that Proust endows Odette with more concrete superstitious beliefs, but these are ascribed to her, and exploited, by Swann to the extent that they acquire the quality of an irrational conviction for Swann himself. Odette's socially shared superstitions (Jahoda's second category) thus slip over into the sphere of personal superstitions for Swann (Jahoda's final category); and, indeed, all Proust's superstitious male characters embody this final category. As an illustration of the superstitious artist, Elstir offers a unique figure in the world of *A la recherche*, but the locus of superstition of other male characters is remarkably similar. Saint-Loup, for instance, consciously shows no curiosity regarding the 'jeunes filles' 'à cause d'une sorte de croyance superstitieuse que de sa propre fidélité pouvait dépendre celle de sa maîtresse' (JF II 165), while more implicitly, in connection with Swann's desire to know whether Odette is Forcheville's mistress, we find: 'Alors il voulait [. . .] le lui demander à elle-même. Il savait que, superstitieuse comme elle était, il y avait certains parjures qu'elle ne ferait pas' (S I 350), and thus he asks her to wear 'ta médaille de Notre-Dame de Laghet' (S I 357) to ensure a truthful answer.[26]

Malinowski defines magic, of which superstitious beliefs and practices comprise one element, as 'une réponse culturelle à un besoin de certitude', springing from a need to 'maîtriser l'environnement'.[27] In other words, human beings have recourse to magic when confronted with unpredictability, and the use of magic, in whatever form, has as its function to reduce uncertainty and the anxiety it provokes when situations are uncontrollable by scientific and technical knowledge alone.[28] Superstition (as a form of magic) creates the impression of control, but crucially this is no more than an illusory control. Like Freud's neurotic who compulsively touches wood or develops other ritual behaviours, Proust's jealous lovers become enslaved to obsessive practices of questioning and spying. Yet this calming of the state of anxiety through compulsive rituals can be only temporary, nor, as suggested above, does it entail the attainment of any true control or power: the loved one remains as elusive to, and independent of, the lover as the eclectic superstitious symbolism of Odette's dress has already foreshadowed.

In seeming to differentiate forms of superstitious belief according to gender, is Proust therefore challenging or confirming gender stereotypes? Conventional wisdom tends to identify women as the more superstitious gender, and this has been confirmed by studies on the subject. Askevis-Leherpeux cites a survey dating from Proust's own lifetime (1887) which concluded that women were twice as likely to be superstitious as men, and, indeed, all subsequent studies have confirmed women's greater credulity. This tendency has been explained with historical reference to women's lesser level of education and, as a result, lesser development of a scientific world-view and lesser politicization.[29] If women have had a limited influence on major events and a limited awareness of social mechanisms, then it follows that they may have a reduced sense of control over their daily lives. This lack of engagement with the political world has also been shown to influence the focus of women's superstitious belief. Thus, a 1919 study suggested that female superstition tended to focus on domestic affairs and 'la vie intime', while male superstition was more concerned with sports and work. Women, Askevis-Leherpeux argues, have thus been seen as 'chargées de magie plutôt que magiciennes à cause de leur passivité' (p. 47). We have seen in an earlier chapter how an aura of magic, generated by the implicit fairytale intertext, surrounds the mystery of womanhood for the young narrator.[30] In this sense, women, in the novel, are 'chargées de magie', but can we argue convincingly that Proust's female characters are not 'magiciennes'? Proust's male characters may be the subjects who impose the role of object of desire on the women loved, but such women nonetheless control the desire thrust upon them. Odette, Rachel and Mme de Guermantes are powerful figures, not least in terms of their role as the objects of male superstition. I shall return to this idea, after considering the other forms of Proust's challenge to the gendered construction of superstition as set out in sociological studies of this phenomenon.

Paramount among the factors that constitute this challenge is the fact that the male characters who inhabit Proust's novel are shown to be at least as superstitious as women and, in some respects, more so, above all in matters relating to 'la vie intime', the supposed preserve of women. They are also more likely, as we have seen, to develop personal superstitions, whereas female characters tend to adhere to socially shared beliefs.[31] In Proust's universe, therefore, the woman (loved) displays external signs of superstition, while men's superstitions are internal and available to us only through the narrator/writer's account. One might argue that such a construction still plays into gender stereotypes: adherence to a socially shared superstition may betoken an unquestioning, even instinctive, response, in contrast to the active experience and thought processes which generate a personal superstition. Yet, inverting this reason/instinct, male/female binarism, we can offer a counter which sets the irrationality of a conviction grounded in personal idiosyncracy in contrast to a socially shared belief based on the vestiges of a long-established and quasi-religious past. What is more, women are not, like their neurotic male counterparts, the helpless victims of superstition. If superstitious belief grants the male characters in the novel only an impression of control, their female counterparts retain a genuine power over their superstitious beliefs, their desire and, indeed, the men who desire them.

To recap, then, Proust's construction of superstition in the novel collapses established gender stereotypes in a number of respects. Firstly, he has created male characters who are at least as susceptible to the supposed reassurances of superstition as female characters in the novel. Also in contrast to prevailing wisdom, Proust presents men who turn to superstition as a means to assuage their desire to control in the context of 'la vie intime'. Proust's representation of Odette's superstitions, as embodied in her early extravagantly allusive attire, thus becomes a metaphor for the 'insaisissable' nature of the woman loved. Swann may, in turn, have recourse to superstition in a bid to 'know' her and, more broadly, to reduce epistemological uncertainty; not only is the attempt futile, but his own quasi-superstitious conviction that she is 'graspable' also highlights his greater irrationality in comparison with Odette's superficial adherence to socially shared beliefs. The power of superstition is thus shown to be illusory. Moreover, while Odette's superstitious attire may provide a series of symbols – constructed by the narrator/writer to delight the vigilant reader – of her elusiveness and of the contradictions within her, Swann is unable to perceive their significance. Even if he could decipher their symbolism, such an interpretative trail would simply lead him full circle to the conclusion that she is unknowable. Superstition does not, therefore, resolve the enigma of Odette; it is merely emblematic of it. As this carefully crafted passage reveals on a microcosmic level, however, the 'inconnaissable' as much as the 'connaissable' can become the material for a work of art. Embedded, therefore, within the construction of superstition in the novel and, indeed (as we shall see in the course of this part of the study), in other forms of ritual and belief, is the tension between the desire for closure and the refusal of closure, between the authoritative narrating voice, whose knowledge often exceeds that of the conventional first-person narrator, and the narrator/protagonist who grapples with the conundrums that face him. In attributing superstitious belief to male as much as female characters, Proust allows the narrator to discover something about the limitations of knowledge through a character with whom an acute empathy is possible, namely Swann.[32] It is also a mechanism for the author to admit to what eludes him. And, of course, in collapsing the nature/culture, superstitious/not superstitious binarism that has characterized thinking on female/male identities and beliefs, Proust further underscores the vulnerability to 'illogicality' that defines the desiring subject of whatever gender.

Despite both the narrator's empathetic relationship to Swann and the parallels between the narrator's relationship with Albertine and Swann's with Odette, neither he nor Albertine re-enacts these patterns of superstitious behaviour. The narrator's early 'flirtation' with superstitious belief in the context of his love for Gilberte might be adduced in support of a conscious distancing from such beliefs by the time of his relationship with Albertine, but this is perhaps a too hasty attribution of self-awareness to a narrator/protagonist who still has a lengthy journey to undertake.[33] Feeding into the construction of superstition which grants power to the woman loved and impotence to the desiring subject, we might argue that Swann's superstition is created and dictated by Odette: because she is superstitious, he attempts to exploit this in a bid to gain power and knowledge. Albertine, in contrast, shows no trace of superstitious belief. Why? Askevis-Leherpeux has shown how 'l'impact de la superstition apparaît moins fort chez ceux qui nient l'immortalité de l'âme, l'existence de Dieu ou d'un au-delà, que chez ceux qui adhèrent à tout ou partie des croyances' (p. 22). Odette's superstitions are entangled with an eclectic and – arguably, like her superstitious convictions – superficial religious belief. Albertine, in contrast, reveals no evidence of Christian faith or morality, defined instead by nature and the senses. Reflecting the power of the women loved in the novel, therefore, the narrator attempts, in vain, to control her by reference to the features that define her rather than through superstitious ritual: this bird is caged, she is distanced from the sea, and the narrator attempts to contain her by modelling her tastes and intellect.

This analysis began with an opposition between what Frazer defines as irrational superstition-creation and quasi-'scientific' metaphor-creation. In order to achieve the latter, the narrator/protagonist will transcend the former; that is, he will eschew the erroneous association of contiguous ideas which, understood in its widest sense, in the terms of the *Bildungsroman*, is illusion and misconception. Superstition is thus a belief system that tempts the narrator/protagonist when faced with fears and uncertainty and that, retrospectively, becomes a symbolic marker of the limitations of power and knowledge. As moments of crisis threaten to overwhelm him, other systems of belief and other rituals rise up in his path with the promise of comfort and control.

These represent distractions from his own personal, mythical quest, although they may seem to offer answers to the questions that lie at its heart. Indeed, these are the questions which, according to Eliade, lie at the heart of all mythical structures: the Self (its origins and its future), communication, time and memory. But each of these systems of ritual and belief offers an inauthentic and thus impassable route to self-realization, for each relies on unquestioning ritual and each has a collective dimension which is incompatible with the narrator's necessarily solitary journey. The narrator/protagonist will therefore negotiate an independent path through them, while the narrator-as-writer will transform them through metaphor. From the irrationality of *histoire* emerges the quasi-'scientific' *récit*.

## Spiritualism, communication and 'l'interpénétration des âmes'

Superstition, as we have seen, provides the believer with an impression of control in the face of ontological and epistemological uncertainty, be that anxieties surrounding the meaning and purpose of one's existence or the resistance of the loved one to complete knowledge or possession. Propelling the narrative beyond this flight from the 'insaisissable', images drawn from the world of spiritualism – evoking seances, mediums and ghosts[34] – signal an enforced confrontation with the illusory nature of that control, for Proust's varied appropriations of spiritualist vocabulary share a common conceptual foundation in the inaccessible and the elusive. The encounter with the elusive may lead ultimately to actual loss (in the form of death or separation) or to its metaphorical counterpart (the recognition of an irreducible alterity). Whichever the outcome, we also detect, embedded within these images of inaccessibility, the problem of communication that characterizes the medium's role and that is so crucial to the artist's endeavour.

The narrator's recourse to the world of spiritualism oscillates between the literal and the metaphorical, for spiritualism is not simply another metaphorical intertext to enrich Proust's gloriously eclectic vision. It is not just a fitting stylistic vehicle to convey an abstract idea: in *Albertine disparue*, the narrator/protagonist contemplates spiritualist practices as a literal response to the loss of Albertine.[35] I shall return to this later.

It is, however, in *Le Côté de Guermantes* that the earliest hints of a belief in the spirit world on the part of the narrator/protagonist are first sown, as anxieties concerning his grandmother's death take the form of a vivid 'premonition' of her future status as ghost.[36] Her voice on the still novel technological wonder of the telephone becomes a 'fantôme aussi impalpable que celui qui reviendrait peut-être me visiter quand ma grand-mère serait morte' (G II 434). Like mediums, the telephone operators invoke her presence (G II 435), and the narrator's terrified reaction is to hasten back to Paris to be with her and thus restore her to corporeality: 'j'avais à me délivrer au plus vite, dans ses bras, du fantôme, insoupçonné jusqu'alors et soudain évoqué par sa voix, d'une grand-mère réellement séparée de moi' (G II 438).[37] His first vision of her on returning, however, is also his first perception of her as a frail, old woman: 'Hélas, ce fantôme-là, ce fut lui que j'aperçus' (ibid.), and every 'regard habituel' directed towards her is subsequently 'une nécromancie' (G II 439).[38] Within this brief paradigm, literal and metaphorical coincide as the voices of intradiegetical narrator/protagonist and extradiegetical narrator/writer are overlaid: the literal ghost of the future that the narrator imagines symbolizes, more broadly, the apprehension with which one contemplates death and, indeed, the effects of ageing. On a metaphorical level, too, the extract hints at the tension between spiritual and material worlds which is central to spiritualist belief. It thus implicitly underscores the narrator/protagonist's attachment, at this stage, to the material rather than the spiritual, the tangible rather than the abstract. As we shall see, a conscious ambivalence as regards the narrator's ultimate resolution of this tension will persist in Proust's handling of the spiritualist intertext.

Developmental psychologists, Whiting and Child, have explained the likelihood of a development of childhood belief in parental ghosts in the following terms:

> What are the child-rearing conditions that should lead to a preoccupation with parental ghosts? . . . if a parent in caring for a child and satisfying his needs was frequently absent when he was in a state of high need – that is, hungry, cold, or suffering from some other discomfort – he would be very likely to engage in fantasies which would represent his mother or other caretaker satisfying his needs. Assuming that the mother eventually comes and feeds him or covers him up, the act should reinforce his imagined thinking and increase the probability that he will produce fantasy images of his mother when she is absent and he is in need. It is our hypothesis that this type of magical thinking underlies a preoccupation with ghosts and spirits . . .[39]

Of course, the experiences of the narrator of *A la recherche* cannot be slotted neatly into this template. Whiting and Child are clearly focusing on an earlier stage of childhood development than that reached by the narrator when expressing fears about the loss or absence of his grandmother. Their hypothesis also situates the mother at the centre of this fantasy relationship, whereas the only female ghosts to visit us in Proust's text are the narrator's grandmother and Albertine. The terms of the hypothesis nonetheless chime with the 'drame du coucher' episode and the narrator's fears concerning his mother's withholding of emotional, rather than, as Whiting and Child suggest, physical attention. Why, then, should these anxieties regarding loss be transposed, firstly, on to the grandmother and, subsequently, on to Albertine? Indeed, they turn out to be more than anxieties, for the narrator experiences actual loss through the death – the transition from material to spirit world – of both of these characters. Chaudier proposes that the fundamental 'enjeu' of *A la recherche* is for the narrator to achieve 'un détachement libérateur vis-à-vis de l'amour maternel, en recueillir les vertus sans en être dominé par la nostalgie d'une impossible possession littérale du corps de la mère' (p. 347). Without this painful release or detachment, the narrator cannot attain the status of artist.[40] Read in this light, the transferral on to other women on whom the narrator is dependent of the key concerns regarding the loss of the mother('s love) becomes a form of rehearsal for, indeed a playing-out of, the ultimate separation which he is not yet ready to experience or even articulate. The narrator must first 're-create' his grandmother and Albertine as ghosts, in his mind, if not yet in the text; he must make the transition from physical loss to an acceptance of their non-corporeality through a conscious meditation on their deaths.[41] Only when this trial performance of (acceptance of) his mother's death is complete can the narrator be released from her and effect the ultimate 'separation' from the material world that is the act of creation. This is a complex and ambiguous transition, however. The narrator's 'spiritual' creation is born of, and dependent on, experience of the material world. This, along with the difficulty of achieving complete knowledge of the Other, the elusiveness of an interpenetration of souls, reveal the extent to which spiritualism is a signifier fraught with ambivalence; indeed, an ideal marker of the elusory.

Betokening a fear and a foreboding of death in *Le Côté de Guermantes*, evocations of the spirit world become the response to the genuine loss of both grandmother and Albertine in *Sodome et Gomorrhe* and *Albertine disparue* respectively. Geoffrey Nelson defines a ghost as a spontaneously appearing spirit, that is, one whose presence is not invoked by a medium (p. 42). Drawing on this distinction, we may identify the narrator's grandmother as a ghost, appearing to the narrator without his willing it. He relates, for example, how, in an otherwise empty train compartment, 'aussitôt je vis ma grand-mère' (*SG* III 181).[42] In contrast, the narrator of the later volume considers the possibility of deliberately invoking Albertine's spirit: table-turning is mentioned twice, and references to attempted communication with the dead are, unsurprisingly, more prevalent in this volume than in any other. The contrast between the spontaneous 'materialization' of the grandmother and the prospective, wilful invocation of Albertine's spirit – that is, between an involuntary and voluntary 'resurrection' – is a potent one. Central to the culmination of the novel is the distinction between the voluntary and involuntary resurrections of memory. From this emerges the narrator's realization of the interdependence of the instinctive fruits of creative inspiration and the conscious act of the intellect which transforms them into a work of art. As yet, though, the involuntary – as represented by the appearance of the narrator's grandmother – brings not temporal transcendence, but a miring in present grief. As for the voluntary – as symbolized by spiritualist practices – it is met with scepticism by a narrator who does not yet realize its inseparability from the involuntary, and, as if to echo the narrator/protagonist's susceptibility to distraction from the effort of work, it remains untried.

Many of the metaphorical strands that underlie the spiritualist intertext have still to be teased out, but let us first examine Proust's introduction of spiritualism, on a literal level, in the context of the narrator's bereavement. Described by Vieda Skultans as an 'informal support system', spiritualism is commonly embraced as a means of coping with grief.[43] Indeed, pain, suffering and illness are central to spiritualist thought. Like the narrator of *Albertine disparue* who is tempted by this path, spiritualists and particularly mediums are often suffering from illness themselves. Yet those of an overly sensitive nature are discouraged from assuming the role of medium on the grounds that they may lack the discipline necessary to bridge the gap between material and spiritual worlds. Should they achieve this goal, they may be unable to retain control once possessed by a spirit.[44] If, as we shall see, communication between material and spirit worlds is emblematic of the artist's role, then this intertext contains within it the threat that the highly strung narrator's lack of application may prevent him from attaining the status of writer, as, indeed, may his present inability to curb his obsession with/'possession' by Albertine.

As a realistic portrait of bereavement, Proust's dissection of the narrator's reactions is compelling. An initial inability to conceptualize the reality of her death gives way, in this until now agnostic (although not irreligious) figure, to a nascent belief in, or, at least, desire to believe in, some form of life after death:[45] 'j'avais cru qu'Albertine ne partirait pas parce que je le désirais; parce que je le désirais je crus qu'elle n'était pas morte; je me mis à lire des livres sur les tables tournantes, je commençai à croire possible l'immortalité de l'âme' (*AD* IV 93). What little belief, if any, he manages to summon up is short-lived, a temporary response to the experience of loss, generated, in no small part, by the self-oriented nature of his grief: he believes Albertine cannot be dead because he wants her to be alive. Acceptance of her death is essential, however: in the literal spiritualist sense, it will allow Albertine's spirit to be released; and, in the metaphorical sense, this acceptance will free the narrator from dependency. This freedom will enable him to take the necessary step towards both literal healing and the metaphorical realignment of self in relation to mother which will lead to the final transition to the status of artist: as we have seen, the deaths of his grandmother and Albertine represent a necessary 'rehearsal' for his future independence from maternal domination.[46]

The narrative's fluctuating course subsequently veers towards an apparent acceptance of Albertine's death: 'je sentais coexister en moi la certitude qu'elle était morte, et l'espoir incessant de la voir entrer' (*AD* IV 94). And, indeed, although he continues to wish her death were a dream and to hope that when the doorbell rings it will be Albertine, returned alive and well, the narrator's doubt as to the existence of, or possibility of communicating with, the spirit world is suggested by his claim that it would be Françoise – and, by implication, not himself – who would be more likely to believe she was seeing 'un revenant' than a living Albertine (*AD* IV 103).

This is a volume of vertiginous oscillation, however, and just a few pages later, the jealousy-driven narrator is again yielding to the seductions of the seance and, specifically, the practice of table-turning. Table-turning (or tipping) refers to the manipulation of the table at which the participants sit during a seance. Although attributed to spirits, because this movement generally occurs when all the participants' hands are resting on the table, it is often disputed as the fraudulent – if not necessarily conscious – action of those present. Of all the manifestations of a spirit presence, why should Proust have repeatedly chosen table-turning as the potential medium for Albertine to reveal her presence? What immediately distinguishes this particular sign of contact with the spirit world is that it is manifested through the sense of touch, whereas other common forms of communication are auditory.[47] It seems entirely apt, therefore, that a character so defined by the body and so resistant to self-disclosure in words should represent herself through the tactile. Furthermore, the transmission of the messages communicated by the dead is, in table-turning, reliant on a number of participants. So, too, will a variety of characters engage in the narrator's search for answers from the dead Albertine: Saint-Loup, Aimé and Andrée all play a part. The potential for deception on the part of those engaged on this mission is also as real as it is among the participants in a seance.[48] Proust's choice of table-turning over other modes of communication with the spirit world thus taps into an undercurrent of allusion that both aptly conveys the narrator/protagonist's experiences of the difficulty in attaining the truth about Albertine and, more generally, provides the narrator/writer with a vehicle to express the elusiveness of complete knowledge of the Other, of 'l'interpénétration des âmes':

> Si mon regret qu'elle fût morte subissait dans ces moments-là l'influence de ma jalousie et prenait cette forme si particulière, cette influence s'étendit naturellement à mes rêves d'occultisme, d'immortalité qui n'étaient qu'un effort pour tâcher de réaliser ce que je désirais. Aussi à ces moments-là, si j'avais pu réussir à l'évoquer en faisant tourner une table, comme Bergotte croyait que c'était possible, ou à la rencontrer dans l'autre vie, comme le pensait l'abbé X\*\*\*, je ne l'aurais souhaité que pour lui répéter: 'Je sais pour la blanchisseuse [. . .]'. (AD IV 109–10)

The narrator's potential recourse to spiritualism is openly attributed to his ongoing jealousy alone. '[O]f all the emotions to be experienced in the wake of the death of a beloved other', this is, as Ingrid Wassenaar has argued, 'perhaps the most obscene and shameless, the most inexplicably promiscuous of the opportunistic degradations visited upon the suffering self, and the most in need of some kind of justification' (p. 186).[49] The desire for resolution of conflict with the now dead loved one and the persistence of destructive emotions, such as anger and jealousy, are recognized parts of the grieving process,[50] but if we read this motivation through the filter of the spiritualist intertext, the passage also illustrates that the narrator's desire for otherworldly communication is not based on the genuine values of the spiritualist, as is underlined by the surprising swoop into the rather vulgar turn of phrase, 'je sais pour la blanchisseuse'. It represents a desire for vindication, not, at least consciously, for healing, the ultimate goal of spiritualist practice.[51] In pursuing spiritualism as a literal response to his bereavement, therefore, the narrator's aims are misdirected. This insight into his underlying motivation for contemplating spiritualist practices, in combination with the attitude of scepticism implied through the subtle opposition to Bergotte, may explain why this possibility never translates into action.[52]

Moreover, the narrator seems also to realize the redundancy of a medium interposed between living and dead, for he can 'speak' to his grandmother and Albertine without such a go-between. Heralding the factors at play in the production of the future work of art, he experiences a form of communication germinated in memory and flowering in the creative imagination, as symbolically represented here by dreams:

> Mais souvent même plus clair, ce souvenir qu'Albertine était morte se combinait sans la détruire avec la sensation qu'elle était vivante. Je causais avec elle, pendant que je parlais, ma grand-mère allait et venait dans le fond de la chambre [. . .] Et sans doute une fois que j'étais réveillé cette idée d'une morte qui continue à vivre aurait dû me devenir aussi impossible à comprendre qu'elle ne l'est à l'expliquer. Mais je l'avais déjà formée tant de fois [. . .] que j'avais fini par me familiariser avec elle. (AD IV 120)

Having emerged from the vertiginous cycle of grief of *Albertine disparue*, the mature evaluations of the narrator of *Le Temps retrouvé* confirm his release from the lure of spiritualism as a genuine belief system – a release which is tacitly present, if not consciously articulated, in the penultimate volume. That the narrator is now able to refer to this Albertine 'que j'eusse reçue sans plaisir si elle m'eût été ramenée non plus de Touraine, mais de l'autre monde' (*TR* IV 284) conveys his disengagement from both the loss of Albertine and the promises of spiritualism. In addition, a shift into a metaphorical appropriation of this intertext at the 'bal costumé' offers an ironic perspective on the fruits of communication with the dead. The now old and pale Legrandin has the air of a 'revenant' about whom the narrator further explains:

> On s'étonnait de le voir si pâle, abattu, ne prononçant que de rares paroles qui avaient l'insignifiance de celles que disent les morts qu'on évoque. On se demandait quelle cause l'empêchait d'être vif, éloquent, charmant, comme on se le demande devant le 'double' insignifiant d'un homme brillant de son vivant et auquel un spirite pose pourtant des questions qui prêteraient aux développements charmeurs. Et on se disait que cette cause qui avait substitué au Legrandin coloré et rapide un pâle et songeur petit fantôme de Legrandin, c'était la vieillesse. (*TR* IV 514)

If the medium evoked here fails to draw out the scintillating character so beloved when alive, the efforts of the only other spiritualist introduced in a social context in the final volume are crowned with even less success.[53] In his attempts to identify a childhood friend, the narrator likens himself to 'un spirite essayant *en vain* d'obtenir d'une apparition une réponse qui l'identifie' (*TR* IV 523, my italics). The narrator's alignment of his failure to remember this friend's name with the medium unable to induce any profitable communication with the spirit world may also constitute a hint – only fully developed in the crucial series of involuntary memories in this volume – that the past cannot be evoked, with all the intensity and authenticity of the original experience, by a conscious effort of the will.

Abandoned as a genuine creed, spiritualism is nonetheless preserved as a source of metaphor, above all, because the questions to which spiritualism purports to offer an answer – the survival of the Self and the problem of communication – are central to the artistic enterprise.[54]

'Proof of survival' is the term used to refer to the moment in a spiritualist seance when messages are transmitted from the spirit world.[55] Indeed, spiritualism is, to quote Skultans, grounded in:

> the drive to find proof of individual survival of the personality after death, a drive which in some arose at the manifest level from intellectual curiosity, but which in

all was probably based upon a latent desire for survival. In many cases the desire to prove survival is directly the result of conscious anxieties about the survival of the unique self or the survival of the personality of friends and relations, but however it manifests itself, it is a consequence of the heightened awareness of the self that results from individualism.[56]

The narrator-as-future-writer may be less concerned with his own survival in posterity than he is with that of his characters and the transcendent truths for which they are triggers, but the spiritualist's anxieties surrounding the means of connecting the material and spiritual worlds mirror those of the narrator who is uncertain of his ability to bridge the gap between life and art. As we shall see, the narrator's meditations on the nature of artistic genius – prompted by his listening to the Vinteuil Septet in *La Prisonnière* and expressed through spiritualist vocabulary – recall so conspicuously key aspects of spiritualist thought that we may confidently argue for a conscious and informed echoing of its terms and values on Proust's part.

Skultans explains that spiritualist thought is based on the principle of a profound 'contrast between the unchanging realm of the spirit world and the change and decay of the material world' (p. 19). The spirit world exemplifies such values as love, truth and beauty, while the material world embodies pain, lust and the greed for power (ibid.). What more fitting metaphor could there be for the tension diffused throughout the text between the social/sexual world the young narrator inhabits and what he perceives to be the transcendent world of truth and beauty that is art? An innate awareness of this contrast is already present in the aesthetic meditations prompted by Vinteuil's Septet in *La Prisonnière*: the 'joie supraterrestre' the narrator experiences on listening to this piece of music contrasts with 'tout le reste de ma vie, avec le monde visible' (*P* III 765), while the music itself seems to contain 'la promesse qu'il existait autre chose, réalisable par l'art sans doute, que le néant que j'avais trouvé dans tous les plaisirs et dans l'amour même' (*P* III 767). That the narrator is tempted by spiritualist thought and practice in *Albertine disparue* thus taps into a broader, pre-existent desire for transcendence that he has intuitively, if not yet productively, associated with art. The potential for this awareness to trigger his own creativity is, however, stalled by his obsession with Albertine both before and after her death. The necessity of these experiences to his own creation may be realized in retrospect but, as we have seen, *Albertine disparue*, the volume in which spiritualism holds the greatest appeal, reveals a misdirected desire for transcendence on the narrator's part: it is mired in his continuing jealous obsession with Albertine, trapped, in other words, in the material world. As Skultans explains, the true spiritualist must be 'continuously sensitive to the eternal values and [. . .] not led astray by earthly values' (p. 19). The status of artist/medium thus remains outside the narrator's grasp. Although the artist/medium must focus on eternal, rather than earthly, values, however, this is not to suggest a rejection of the material world.[57] After all, the artist's engagement in the social and sexual spheres provides the material for the transcendent world of the work of art. The artist is the 'medium' between the two, just as the spiritualist medium affords a link between the transient and the eternal. These two spheres are thus interdependent. To bridge the gap between material and spiritual, or life and art, is not unproblematic, however, and as with the artistic enterprise, anxieties concerning communication are fundamental to spiritualist thought.[58] Mediumistic power is based on 'penetrating' the inner world of others, but concerns arise as to the possibility of conveying the precise quality of experience, of overcoming the sense of isolation when faced with pain and suffering. The artist's role may also be to experience the inner world of another: as Proust proposes in *La Prisonnière*, 'l'art [. . .] extérioris[e] dans les couleurs du spectre la composition intime de ces mondes que nous appelons les individus, et que sans l'art nous ne connaîtrions jamais' (*P* III 762). Indeed, in a clear reworking of spiritualist aims, this same extended extract evokes the capacity of music to facilitate 'la communication des âmes' (*P* III 763), to see the world, as Proust aspired to do, through the eyes of another person. Arguably, the narrator/writer of *A la recherche* achieves this goal: the insights he provides for the reader into both individual and common experiences are remarkable for their perspicacity. This quality is only enhanced by the light touch with which insights are conveyed – through an elusive metaphor, for example, or an ironic elaboration on a physical idiosyncracy. Yet the inner world of certain characters remains tantalizingly alien to the narrator/protagonist and also, to some extent, to the narrator/writer who himself leaves mysteries unsolved, not least that of the figure he hoped to understand fully through a literal recourse to spiritualism, Albertine. These ghostly metaphors thus uncover a duality that suggestively recalls the contrasting impulses at play in the recent trend in critical and psychoanalytical thinking known as hauntology:[59] the desire to unravel secrets on the part of the narrator/ protagonist is paralleled by the acceptance of 'secrecy', of an insurmountable otherness, on the part of the writer. As mentioned previously, critics have commented on the irreducible alterity of Gomorrah in the novel. In this respect, the trials of both artist and medium coincide: for both, 'la communication des âmes' is fraught with difficulty. Questions may remain unresolved but, in writing Albertine's death, the narrator/writer nonetheless replicates the role described by Skultans, of the medium helping spirits who, by virtue of having experienced a violent or untimely death, remain attached to the 'previously painful conditions to which they were bound' and thus in an ambiguous and dangerous state of transition.[60] By 'acting out the conditions of affliction' and even the spirit's death, the medium helps to release such spirits.[61] Likewise, the narrator-as-artist will become a 'medium' for his grandmother and for Albertine, re-enacting, in the text, their lives, suffering and, indeed, deaths. This will release them from their earthly conditions and allow them to achieve transcendence in the work of art. Such a re-enactment, as previously suggested, also releases the narrator from the material concerns both women represented and prepares him for the final alignment of self as artist symbolically standing beside, rather than merging with, the mother.

To what extent, then, is this transposition of the artist's role on to spiritualist practice supported by a reading of Proust? To what extent, in other words, can we claim that Proust himself perceived and exploited these resonances? The most sustained elaboration of spiritualist imagery in the novel extends the narrator's meditations on the nature of artistic creation and, specifically, Vinteuil's Sonata and Septet.[62] But the narrator/protagonist is, of course, not the only character to ascribe to Vinteuil's music this supernatural power. The 'petite phrase' from Vinteuil's Sonata has long been the national anthem of Swann and Odette's love by the time the former hears it performed again at Mme de Sainte-Euverte's soirée. Swann's conceptualization of the performance in terms of a spiritualist seance at times betrays a certain indecision: the 'petite phrase' is assigned the role of the spirit invoked and the musicians that of the medium: 'déjà la petite phrase évoquée agitait comme celui d'un médium le corps vraiment possédé d'un violoniste' (S I 346); whereas, elsewhere, he attributes a mediumistic role to Vinteuil by suggesting that Vinteuil's function is to capture a pre-existent divine being:

> Certes, humaine à ce point de vue [in the sense that it 'exist[e] réellement'], elle [the 'petite phrase'] appartenait pourtant à un ordre de créatures surnaturelles et que nous n'avons jamais vues, mais que malgré cela nous reconnaissons avec ravissement quand quelque explorateur de l'invisible arrive à en capter une, à l'amener, du monde divin où il a accès, briller quelques instants au-dessus du nôtre. (S I 345).

And while the 'petite phrase' remains consistently the 'parole ineffable' of the soul that created it (S I 346–7), from the outset, it is also indistinguishable for Swann from his love for Odette, as the sensuous physicality with which he endows it only accentuates:

> Swann la sentait présente, comme une déesse protectrice et confidente de son amour, et qui [. . .] avait revêtu le déguisement de cette apparence sonore. Et tandis qu'elle

> passait, légère, apaisante et murmurée comme un parfum, lui disant ce qu'elle avait à lui dire et dont il scrutait tous les mots, regrettant de les voir s'envoler si vite, il faisait involontairement avec ses lèvres le mouvement de baiser au passage le corps harmonieux et fuyant. (S I 342)

Although aesthetically sensitive, therefore, Swann confuses the material and spiritual worlds, for communication with the spiritual world – the metaphorical signifier for the transcendent world of art – is distorted by his overlaying on to it of material, worldly concerns. Swann's inability to release himself from the worldly is comically underlined by the comtesse de Monteriender's bathetic dissolution of the mood, ironically by means of a spiritualist reference: '"C'est prodigieux, je n'ai jamais rien vu d'aussi fort [...] depuis les tables tournantes!"' (S I 347). This elusive experience is also immediately followed by evocations of Swann's life with Odette, thus countering this potentially productive experience with stasis.

The account of Swann's experience of the 'petite phrase' in spiritualist terms is characterized by a vocabulary implying the inaccessibility and fleetingness of the essence the motif contains. It is precisely this ephemeral quality that Proust/the narrator will prize in music, for in the immediacy of its appeal to the spirit lies its power.[63] However, the narrator's experiences of Vinteuil's work in *La Prisonnière* give a subtly distinct inflection to the spiritualist imagery, combining a recognition of this essentially elusive quality with a perceptive engagement with the nature of aesthetic creation. Inasmuch as he associates the music with his love for Albertine, the narrator's experience of hearing Vinteuil's Septet in *La Prisonnière* initially parallels that of Swann.[64] However, there the similarities end, for, from the beginning of the performance, the narrator senses that there is more hidden within the music than its associations with Albertine. Consciously attempting to banish her from his mind as the embodiment of his preoccupations in the material world, he shifts his focus to the spiritual universe of the Septet: 'Et pourtant, me dis-je, quelque chose de plus mystérieux que l'amour d'Albertine semblait promis au début de cette œuvre, dans ces premiers cris d'aurore. J'essayai de chasser la pensée de mon amie pour ne plus songer qu'au musicien' (P III 758). The introduction of the spiritualist intertext here also plays with, and subverts, the various roles allotted by Swann.[65] The listener, for instance, is implicitly cast as the spirit: of the essence of Vinteuil's music – that is 'les 'éternelles investigations de Vinteuil, la question qu'il se posa sous tant de formes' (P III 760) – we are warned that 'nous pouvons en mesurer la profondeur, mais pas plus la traduire en langage humain que ne le peuvent les esprits désincarnés quand, évoqués par un médium, celui-ci les interroge sur les secrets de la mort' (ibid.). If the listeners are disincarnated spirits who, if they are to be able to answer the questions surrounding the secrets of life and death, require a medium, then it is, of course, the artist who fulfils the role of medium. This 'allocation' of roles is highly allusive, for, if the listener is a spirit who senses truth but is unable to express it, then the message that the artist-as-medium conveys to us must be grounded in the commonalities of human experience. He/she expresses what we each intuit but cannot articulate without his/her 'mediumship'. The artist is not, therefore, the 'otherworldly' being in this scenario as Swann and, indeed, the young narrator believe.[66] It is the truth that he/she is able to convey that is transcendent, and these truths are rooted in the material world of the individual listeners' experiences. It is these that provide the spark for the artist whose role it is to grant individual experience a transcendent reality in the spiritual world of the work of art; the artist thus communicates 'universalized' truths back to the listeners/readers. Proust's images subtly demonstrate how listeners/readers inhabit both the material world that inspires the musician or writer and, in a generalized, eternalized form, the spiritual, artistic world that is the result of that inspiration. As if to reflect this underlying complexity, the scope of the narrator's meditations in this part of the text extend far beyond those of Swann: while Swann's focus is limited not only to the piece he is listening to, but to the 'petite phrase' alone, the narrator engages in a much broader and richer evaluation of the nature of artistic genius.[67] Proust's handling of the spiritualist intertext to express Swann's meditations thus reveals the narrator's potential alter ego to be trapped within the present moment – that is, within the worldly preoccupations of his relationship with Odette. A failed medium, he does not progress to an understanding and articulation of the transcendent truths which spring from that present moment and, indeed, those preoccupations. This is the accomplishment reserved for the narrator of the novel who will be able to transform the mature, abstract meditations on artistic genius in *La Prisonnière* only having suffered the (second) bereavement which diverts this abstract appreciation towards a literal preoccupation with spiritualism in *Albertine disparue*.

As this exploration of spiritualist practices has shown, the role assumed by the medium is not without risks. Swann fails to surpass material preoccupations; the narrator as potential artist-medium seems equally susceptible to distraction and, because of his hypersensitivity, may be unable to control the spirit possessing him. At this end of the spectrum, spiritualism potentially rubs shoulders with the darker world of occult possession. It is to this that we now turn.

## Magic and the occult: from possession to exorcism

Encompassed within the term 'magic' figures a whole spectrum of practices and beliefs, ranging from the conjuror's sleight of hand to witches' potions, from a light-hearted expression of the pleasantly unexpected to a potentially sinister manipulation of the external world. Proust's handling of magic as a metaphorical intertext reveals a similar sweep and, indeed, the distribution of such images throughout the novel suggests a progressive transition, from a concentration of the magic of performance in the early volumes through to a predominance of the occult and black magic in later sections.

The performative magic of illusion, to take the first of these forms, is most prevalent in *A l'ombre des jeunes filles en fleurs* and *Le Côté de Guermantes* (five and six such images respectively).[68] It is here that the young narrator/ protagonist, like a conjuror's audience, is the ingenuously rapt and, by definition, passive spectator of the seemingly inexplicable wonders that surround him. Many of these relate to the artist: the admonitions, for example, which the narrator reads on the poster advertising La Berma's performance of *Phèdre* – '"Les dames ne seront pas reçues à l'orchestre en chapeau, les portes seront fermées à deux heures"' – are, for him, 'ces mots magiques' (*JF* I 436); Bergotte's assertions of the narrator's intelligence, which this latter reports to his parents, are also 'des mots magiques' (*JF* I 564); Elstir's ability to open the doors to the 'jeunes filles' for the narrator are the 'sable magique' that combines with 'la poussière des réalités' (*JF* II 220); a seascape by this same artist is a 'portrait magique' (*JF* II 255); and, on remembering a particular line from *Phèdre*, the harshness of the world disappears as if 'magiquement' (*G* II 338). However, in using the same terms in relation to a line from *Phèdre* and the words advertising its performance, to one of Elstir's paintings and his influence in introducing the narrator to the 'jeunes filles', to Bergotte's indirect influence on the narrator's parents rather than his writing, Proust highlights the narrator's inability, at this stage, to distinguish the 'moi social' of the artist from the 'moi profond', the trappings of artistic performance from the work of art itself. That these images are underdeveloped, rarely extending beyond a single word ('magique'/'magiquement'), only accentuates the narrator/protagonist's as yet unevolved understanding of art and the artist. Moreover, to choose terms reminiscent of the magic words of the theatrical magician is to imply that, like the conjuror's tricks, the narrator's understanding is based on surface impressions and illusion. Nowhere is this more starkly expressed than in the following, relatively elaborate metaphor, recounting the narrator's shock when he first meets the revered Bergotte:

> Ce nom de Bergotte me fit tressauter comme le bruit d'un revolver qu'on aurait déchargé sur moi, mais instinctivement pour faire bonne contenance je saluai; devant moi, comme ces prestidigitateurs qu'on aperçoit intacts et en redingote dans la poussière d'un coup de feu d'où s'envole une colombe, mon salut m'était rendu par un homme jeune, rude, petit, râblé et myope, à nez rouge en forme de coquille de colimaçon et à barbiche noire. J'étais mortellement triste, car ce qui venait d'être réduit en poudre, ce n'était pas seulement le langoureux vieillard dont il ne restait plus rien, c'était aussi la beauté d'une œuvre immense que j'avais pu loger dans l'organisme défaillant et sacré que j'avais, comme un temple, construit expressément pour elle, mais à laquelle aucune place n'était réservée dans le corps trapu, rempli de vaisseaux, d'os, de ganglions, du petit homme à nez camus et à barbiche noire qui était devant moi. (*JF* I 537–8)

This humorously overblown passage exposes the young narrator's (con)fusion of the man and his work. That the narrator's shock is centred on the corporeality of this artist is itself significant. While his graphically anatomical list of bodily features, both internal and external, comically reflects the young narrator's horror at being confronted, not with the ethereal figure he imagined, but a stocky little flesh-and-blood man, it also reveals how far the narrator has to travel before he will reconcile body and spirit in an act of creation. Only much later will he realize that the world is encountered and experienced by the body and that it is these experiences which will ultimately become the material for the (spiritual) work of art.[69] The identification of Bergotte as the 'prestidigitateur' in this scenario may also contain a more mature insight on the part of the narrator/writer, however, for, in the course of the novel, we witness a subtle distancing from Bergotte and his fate on the part of the narrator.[70] Given that Bergotte himself appears to reject his previous work when contemplating Vermeer's 'petit pan de mur jaune', might we not read this earlier incarnation as a conjuror or an illusionist as the proleptic hint that, when the lyrical flourishes the young narrator so admires in his work are stripped away, what is left is as insubstantial as the young narrator's imagined 'organisme défaillant et sacré'?[71]

Subsequent images from *Le Côté de Guermantes* similarly stress the narrator/protagonist's identity as passive observer. Playing on the inside/outside dialectic which is a persistent undercurrent in the novel, the narrator conceptualizes his view, from the darkened street, of soldiers playing cards in an illuminated room in terms of a magician's trick or supernatural drama:[72] the soldiers are involved in their game 'sans se douter qu'un magicien les faisait surgir de la nuit, comme dans une apparition de théâtre' (*G* II 395). The young narrator's lack of agency at this stage is intimated in the reference to the theatre which, of course, places him in the audience. It is further reflected in his relationship with Albertine in this volume, for she, too, appears suddenly in Paris without his prompting and thus as if by magic: 'Elle semblait une magicienne me présentant un miroir du temps' (*G* II 646). Her magical offering of a 'miroir du temps' at once overlays the present moment on to all their past meetings in Balbec and reveals an accelerated vision of time passed, for Albertine has also physically matured since he last saw her (*G* II 647). This moment thus seems to herald both the transcending of time through involuntary memory in *Le Temps retrouvé* and the enforced realization of time passing at the 'bal costumé'. To intertwine Albertine's arrival with these crucial moments in the final volume of the novel is to underscore the impossibility of the second without the experiences of the first. But these crucial moments in *Le Temps retrouvé* are not expressed through images of magic and illusion. The narrator must traverse the darker world of magic before he can reach that moment of epiphany and, indeed, the image above already suggests a shift away from theatrical illusion to witchcraft. As with many of the cycles of imagery in the novel, however, the mature narrator-soon-to-be-writer will articulate his distance from his earlier belief systems by means of an ironic treatment of intertexts he once used to denote genuine awe or wonder. Thus, by *La Prisonnière*, it is Morel's delight, and belief, in the infallibility of the phrase ' "pour parler affaires" ' (*P* III 562) as the introduction to requesting a loan that, in the mature narrator's wry perspective, becomes his 'formule magique' (ibid.). Similarly, in *Le Temps retrouvé*, it is the now elevated Mme Verdurin's sudden and miraculous ability to praise and welcome those she once denounced as 'bores' that becomes the stuff of magic. Hers is a 'transformation magique' (*TR* IV 308). That these images echo the early evocations of the magic of the theatre implicitly exposes the artificiality and illusion of their posturing.

The mature narrator/writer may, in this metaphorical transition from the magic of performance to sorcery and witchcraft, be rejecting the self who saw the artist as a magician and who, in resorting to such images, signalled his lack of understanding of art. Yet this does not mean that his experiences as passive and often awestruck observer are inconsequential. Events may appear to have 'happened to him' without his prompting and thus as if by magic, but, as perhaps the most important reference to sorcery and witchcraft in the novel stresses, authenticity is to be found in the involuntary, the unwilled:

> [ces réminiscences] composaient un grimoire compliqué et fleuri, leur premier caractère était que je n'étais pas libre de les choisir, qu'elles m'étaient données telles quelles. Et je sentais que ce devait être la griffe de leur authenticité. Je n'avais pas été chercher les deux pavés inégaux de la cour où j'avais buté. Mais justement la façon fortuite, inévitable, dont la sensation avait été rencontrée, contrôlait la

vérité du passé qu'elle ressuscitait, des images qu'elle déclenchait, puisque nous sentons son effort pour remonter vers la lumière, que nous sentons la joie du réel retrouvé'. (*TR* IV 457–8)

The extract identifies involuntary memory as the 'grimoire', the book of magic spells, that the narrator must decipher and ultimately 'apply' to his creation, but while the involuntary memories of *Le Temps retrouvé* are undoubtedly endowed with a greater symbolic resonance and represent a greater spur to action than the narrator's many other unwilled experiences, these latter convey no less authentic truths, at least once the narrator is able to decipher them. Indeed, they will form the foundations on which he will construct his novelistic universe.

The image of the 'grimoire' is a pivotal one. Introduced just three times in *A la recherche*, it nonetheless embraces the novel's elemental themes, namely love, art and, as we have seen, memory: Mlle Vinteuil's lover's efforts to 'débrouiller le grimoire laissé par Vinteuil' (*P* III 766) prove to be successful, while, having returned home from the Verdurins, the narrator, unlike his companion Brichot, is able to decipher the 'grimoire magique' (*P* III 834) that is the light in Albertine's room which he sees from his position in the street outside. Moreover, every image in the novel that is drawn from the worlds of sorcery and witchcraft may be slotted into one of these three thematic categories. The tea in which the madeleine is soaked is implicitly likened to a potion ('breuvage', *S* I 45); the three trees which, like the 'clochers de Martinville', seem to evoke some earlier moment are identified as an 'apparition mythique, ronde de sorcières ou de nornes' (*JF* II 78); the narrator's aesthetically mature explanation of Vinteuil's 'phrases-types' to Albertine in *La Prisonnière* makes reference not only to Dostoevsky and Hardy (*P* III 878–82), but also to the largely overlooked work, *L'Ensorcelée*, by Barbey d'Aurevilly;[73] and, in *Le Temps retrouvé*, the narrator recalls his adoration of Mme de Guermantes and accompanying dreams of penetrating 'dans le palais du sorcier ou de la fée' (*TR* IV 436).[74] Through images such as these and through the overarching emblem of the 'grimoire', Proust artfully knits together apparently disparate areas of experience, the connections between which can be perceived only in retrospect. Like the 'grimoire', the novel represents a fusion of eclectic elements which, on their own, may be mundane, but which, in combination, release a quasi-magical power. Involuntary memories may be the final, crucial ingredient that give this 'grimoire' its potency and without which knowledge and experience would not be transformed into creation, but the narrator's earlier experiences, however misguided or apparently trivial, are also essential. In uniting these elements, the narrator finally creates the elixir that ('magically') transforms individual experience into generalized truth, revealing a power of metamorphosis that far surpasses the illusionist's façade. Proust thus imbues this metaphorical source with all the potency ascribed to it by his nineteenth-century artistic precursors. Like Baudelaire and Mallarmé before him, Proustian sorcery effects not an 'imitation', but a transfiguration which 'de chaque chose extrait la quintessence'.[75]

The image of the sorcerer's 'grimoire' is thus appropriated to celebratory ends in Proust. Yet, historically, sorcery was largely the province of fraudulent and ill-intentioned practitioners.[76] As Charles Olliver explains, 'the sorcerer is an ignorant being for all his malevolence, and blindly carries out imperfect and corrupt instructions obtained by oral transition or from the many written Grimoires'.[77] Olliver's more detailed analysis may nonetheless provide an explanation for Proust's seemingly paradoxical recourse to a metaphorical intertext grounded in malevolent practices as a vehicle to express the fruitful path to creation:

> Crimes connected with Sorcery may be divided into three main types. The first type of crime is that committed by the dupes of an unhealthy curiosity or an inordinate vanity, who dream of riches or of mastering other men by means of some form of supernatural power. The second type includes all those crimes due to jealousy and envy, hate and the desire for vengeance, and crimes committed for the sake of evil. Thirdly, we find a series of crimes committed by beings who have been led away by the greed of avarice or the promptings of disordered and perverted sexual desires. The famous case of Gilles de Rais is a typical example of this last type. In such cases Sorcery proper is so mixed up with other practices, such as alchemy and Black Magic, that it is very difficult to find the line of demarcation. (p. 121)[78]

The sorcerer's crimes are threefold in focus: they are variously motivated by jealousy, a desire for power, or sexual 'deviance'. This latter will resurface when we progress into the realms of black magic, for just as sexual practices became an institutionalized part of the Black Mass, so, too, does Proust appear to associate sexual inversion with black magic through metaphor. However, jealousy and the desire for power immediately chime with the narrator's experiences in his relationship with Albertine and, as suggested by the reference to the 'grimoire' of Albertine's light in *La Prisonnière*, the narrator/protagonist revels in his privileged ability to decipher that 'grimoire', in the temporary assuagement of his jealousy, in his sense of power and control.[79] Such perspectives offer an (albeit less sinister) echo of the malevolent sorcerer. Moreover, just as the power of many sorcerers was fraudulent, having, as Olliver explains, 'no true occult aspect beyond the superstitious fear with which the sorcerer used to impress his victim', so, too, is the narrator's power definitively to master his jealousy or, indeed, Albertine.[80] As long as his 'power' remains directed towards unproductive ends, therefore, the narrator's experience will replicate that of the fraudulent sorcerer. And yet the final evocation of a 'grimoire' in the novel is quite distinct from the reference that links it to love, for, as we have seen, involuntary memory is a 'grimoire *compliqué* et *fleuri*' (*TR* IV 457, my italics). This is no longer the simple task of deciphering the light in Albertine's room. The reference to flowers also augurs growth and creation. In retaining this intertext but granting it a subtly unique emphasis, Proust highlights the narrator's evolution to a more productive harnessing of his will. The illusory, because misdirected, power of the sorcerer-lover becomes real in the hands of the would-be artist.

The line that divides sorcery from black magic is a fine one, but Olliver proposes a distinction based on the latter's focus on collective ritual in contrast to the largely individualized practices of the former. Black magic 'assume[s] a more elaborate or ceremonial form' than sorcery, its adepts 'act[ing] in accordance with a regular and well-defined system' (p. 115). Black magic may also be defined in terms of its reliance on (depraved) sexual and scatological practices and its emphasis on the principle of opposition, a principle enacted by, for example, repeating prayers backwards, reversing the cross or 'consecrating obscene or filthy objects' (ibid., p. 106).[81]

Before facing the final 'grimoire' that he will individually decipher and transmute into practice, the narrator/protagonist is, in the course of his experience, exposed to, and, indeed, engages in, a range of collective or, at least, shared rituals. The social world, for example, is governed by strict codes, adherence to which dictates one's inclusion or exclusion. Moreover, these codes – like the ritualistic basis of black magic and the Black Mass – are firmly rooted in the principle of opposition. The bourgeois Verdurins define themselves in opposition to the aristocratic Guermantes; inversely, the Guermantes find proof of their superiority in the simple fact that they are not bourgeois. Thus, just as black magic has no meaning without its opposite principle – be that God or Good – so, too, is each of these social groupings dependent on the other for meaning, despite their mutual and fervid rejection. Indeed, not only are they dependent on one another; they are also the mirror image of one another. As Proust unobtrusively lays bare as early as *Un amour de Swann*, the social rituals Swann witnesses at Mme de Sainte-Euverte's soirée are no different from those he sees paraded at the Verdurins: artificiality, displays of superior aesthetic appreciation, an insistence on informality that combines, ironically, with a set of strictly followed rituals, and an acute awareness of the judgement of others are the hallmarks of both.[82]

Sexual ritual is also fundamental to the narrator's experience, whether he assumes the role of participant or observer, and these rituals are commonly described with metaphorical reference to the world of black magic. Allusions to dark arts characterize the narrator's presentation of the scene he witnesses between Charlus and Jupien at the beginning of *Sodome et Gomorrhe*. This scene, which first reveals Charlus's homosexuality to him, evokes the 'pirouette' of these two characters, a pirouette which seems to be dictated 'comme selon les lois d'un art secret' (*SG* III 6). More explicitly, Morel's desire to seduce an innocent young woman such as Jupien's niece, then abandon her, meets with Charlus's vehement disapproval: 'Oh! Jamais', he cries. As the narrator surmises, 'soit que la présence d'un tiers l'eût refroidi [a sommelier has just come in], soit que même dans ces espèces de messes noires où il se complaisait à souiller les choses les plus saintes, il ne pût se résoudre à faire entrer des personnes pour qui il avait de l'amitié' (*SG* III 397). If we consider Charlus's penchant for the scatological in conjunction with the association here between a homosexual character and a Black Mass – with all its foundations in depravity and perversity – we might be tempted to see in Proust's chosen metaphorical intertext a condemnation of homosexuality.[83] The homosexual vicomte de Courvoisier's belief that he is the only man on earth to have such feelings and that 'ce penchant lui venait du diable' (*TR* IV 282) may be adduced in support of this view. However, not only does the sheer excess of the vicomte's misguided beliefs point to a gently ironic satire on contemporary views of homosexuality as abnormal, even among homosexuals themselves, but the evocation of Morel's 'messes noires' relates to heterosexual, not homosexual, activity. While Charlus may take particular pleasure in travestying what is pure or sacred, therefore, this 'satanic' impulse is not necessarily the product of his homosexuality. The young man's touchingly eager, but unsuccessful, attempt in Jupien's brothel to confess to some suitably 'satanique' crime, and thus impress Charlus (*TR* IV 405), further distances homosexual ritual from satanic ritual.

In intradiegetical terms, the narrator here plays the unassailable role of external observer. In contrast, the shared rituals he enacts with Albertine place him in the position of active participant. A different paradigm thus emerges, as underlined by the close and *direct* association between Albertine's suspected lesbianism and black magic. Openly summoning up the practice, common in Black Masses, of reading sacred texts backwards, we read the following in relation to Albertine's lies: 'Parfois l'écriture où je déchiffrais les mensonges d'Albertine, sans être idéographique, avait simplement besoin d'être lue à rebours' (*P* III 598). And in *Albertine disparue*, the narrator reflects on how, from the moment Albertine stopped kissing him, 'elle avait eu un air de porter le diable en terre' (*AD* IV 11). However, if Albertine is associated with black magic, it is the narrator who is 'possessed': 'J'avais pu séparer Albertine de ses complices et par là exorciser mes hallucinations' (*P* III 532). He realizes, though, that, 'Dans quelque ville que ce fût, elle n'avait pas besoin de chercher, car le mal n'était pas en Albertine seule, mais en d'autres pour qui toute occasion de plaisir est bonne' (ibid.). To link Albertine and/or lesbianism with evil and, by extension, black magic, therefore, is merely to transpose the narrator's own subjectivity on to her, composed as it is of a sense of torment, powerlessness and externality to her same-sex experiences. As the passage quoted above illustrates, however, relief from this torment – or to use Proust's metaphor, the exorcism of this demon – is only temporary, quite simply because he remains with the source of his torment. What more striking an example could we find of the (psychological and emotional) perversity – indeed the opposition, in this case, to reason – that lies at the heart of the rituals of black magic?

Permanent exorcism comes only at the end of *Albertine disparue*, significantly via a pictorial representation of exorcism, in the form of Carpaccio's *Le Patriarche di Grado exorcisant un possédé*. The choice of artist is important, for Carpaccio has previously been associated with Albertine via Fortuny's recasting of the painter's work in his fabrics. Indeed, the narrator realizes at this moment that he has before him the very painting that inspired Fortuny in creating the fabric of which Albertine's coat was made. Here, in appreciating Carpaccio's work without the mediation of Albertine, the narrator signals the end of his 'possession'. Not only is the artist no longer being considered through another art form, but the narrator's viewing of the painting prompts no jealousy, only the most fleeting moment of melancholy in recalling his past with Albertine.[84] Moreover, the painting itself is, in one crucial respect, a surprising one, for, despite its title, the viewer's eye is not drawn to the miracle – that is, the exorcism – being performed. As Jan Lauts explains:

> What captivates the eye immediately and remains indelibly impressed upon the memory is the view of Venice itself: the vista of its crowded palaces on the shores of the dark-green waters of the Grand Canal; the old wooden Rialto bridge; the maze of roof-tops and oddly shaped chimneys, silhouetted against the light sky; the Venetians reclining in their gondolas; the gaily dressed gondolieri; the youths of worldly elegance of the Compagnia della Calza and worthy patricians, whose activities fill the street on the Rialto. Only few of them pay attention to the group of white-clad brethren, who, in solemn procession, bearing candles and banners, have carried the relic and who now wait in the entrance to the Palace, while a small group of chosen brothers are allowed to witness the miracle.[85]

In drawing this painting into our view, Proust diverts our attention away from the supernatural and towards the everyday. In a rethinking of centre and margins,

Proust at once warns of the ease with which one can be distracted from key, higher concerns by the whirl of everyday life and validates the importance of those apparently trivial events that are enacted on the sidelines. Indeed, it is there that the everyday miraculous, the magical mundane takes place.[86]

This intertextual focus on the menacing world of black magic thus ends with an exorcism, an exorcism which symbolically distracts the viewer from the supernatural centre of the action. Thus, if 'la sorcellerie est la négation de la raison, le triomphe de la bêtise, du déséquilibre, et du crime',[87] the narrator's release from its spell is decisive, for it paves the way for the shift from the supernatural to the quasi-'scientific' which is analysed in the last section of this part of the book. This marks the final stage that leads to the creation of the narrator/writer's own 'sorcellerie'.

## Divination, destiny and the stars

Toute cette activité vertigineuse se fixait en une calme harmonie. Je regardais les tables rondes dont l'assemblée innombrable emplissait le restaurant, comme autant de planètes, telles que celles-ci sont figurées dans les tableaux allégoriques d'autrefois. D'ailleurs, une force d'attraction irrésistible s'exerçait entre ces astres divers et à chaque table les dîneurs n'avaient d'yeux que pour les tables où ils n'étaient pas, exception faite pour quelque riche amphitryon, lequel ayant réussi à amener un écrivain célèbre, s'évertuait à tirer de lui, grâce aux vertus de la table tournante, des propos insignifiants dont les dames s'émerveillaient. L'harmonie de ces tables astrales n'empêchait pas l'incessante révolution des servants innombrables, lesquels parce qu'au lieu d'être assis, comme les dîneurs, ils étaient debout, évoluaient dans une zone supérieure [. . .] Assises derrière un massif de fleurs, deux horribles caissières, occupées à des calculs sans fin, semblaient deux magiciennes occupées à prévoir par des calculs astrologiques les bouleversements qui pouvaient parfois se produire dans cette voûte céleste conçue selon la science du Moyen Âge.

Et je plaignais un peu tous les dîneurs parce que je sentais que pour eux les tables rondes n'étaient pas des planètes et qu'ils n'avaient pas pratiqué dans les choses un sectionnement qui nous débarrasse de leur apparence coutumière et nous permet d'apercevoir des analogies. (*JF* II 167–8)

As inexorably as a planet entering the orbit of another, the social universes represented by each table in the restaurant at Doncières are irresistibly drawn to one another, whether to snoop, to gossip, to flaunt the proofs of their social status or, indeed, to secure further proofs by their association with other planets. Thus, an image initially and aptly prompted by the purely visual similarities between this disposition of round tables and a planetary system is elaborated into an extended metaphor that plays on all the subtle nuances of the source: it exposes these social pirouettes as so intrinsic an element of 'le monde' that the participants seem not to be acting according to free will but to be driven by some larger cosmic force of which they themselves appear unaware. Indeed, it is those outside this planetary system – the waiters and the cashiers – who are granted an overarching perspective on the rituals enacted before them. Heralding the widespread attribution of divinatory powers to the servant class, the waiters 'évolu[ent] dans une zone supérieure', while the cashiers' incarnation as astrologers endows them with the privileged vision of foretellers of the 'bouleversements' these social strata may undergo. Are these 'bouleversements' imminent? Prompted, for example, by the exorbitant bill that is the chart these cashier-astrologers will draw up? Or does the term hint at a more far-reaching insight (granted ironically to those at the bottom of the current social hierarchy) into the mutability of the positions of these planets?[88] The answer remains tantalizingly elusive.

Not yet fully immersed in society himself, the young narrator/protagonist also enjoys a privileged view of the seemingly involuntary movements of these spheres. Not only that, but his conceptualization of them as planets acts as a springboard to a meditation on metaphorical vision of a kind that is rare at this point in his experience. While pitying those incapable of seeing the world as metaphor, however, the young narrator/protagonist as yet sees this quality of vision as merely an end in itself, albeit a gratifying one.

In this single extended metaphor, the themes of external influence and vision are intertwined, establishing a pattern that recurs throughout Proust's handling of images of divination, destiny and the planets. Such a conjunction of ideas may not, at first sight, seem an obvious one, but the diviner is, after all, considered to be able to see the future and to make predictions, to be endowed with a sensitivity, an ability to see beyond the material world or to interpret significant signs within it. What is this, if not a form of privileged vision? As for its relationship to the theme of external influence, the task of the diviner or, indeed, the astrologer is to decipher one's destiny, whether it be written in the stars or ordained by the gods, both of which sources imply the belief that the fate of human beings is dictated by a power outside themselves and thus beyond their responsibility or control.

This definition of the diviner may well lead the reader to expect that such a visionary becomes, in Proust's hands, a metaphor for the artist. However, this is not the case. Those endowed with divinatory powers in Proust's novelistic universe are not artists but the narrator's grandfather,[89] Françoise and, indeed, servants generally,[90] Charlus,[91] Morel, Albertine[92] and, only very belatedly, the narrator himself. If Bergotte suggests to the narrator that the artist La Berma's adoption of the poses of classical sculpture when playing the role of Phèdre 'peut être une divination' (*JF* I 550), he is nonetheless more inclined to believe that she studies these poses in museums; and while Morel is a musician, his powers of divination stretch only to his ability to detect lesbians and homosexuals, an ability shared by lesbians, who, the narrator claims, are equally sensitive to Morel's plural sexual orientation: 'Et qui eût regardé en ce moment Morel avec son air de fille au milieu de sa mâle beauté, eût compris l'obscure divination qui ne le désignait pas moins à certaines femmes qu'elles à lui' (*SG* III 396). To what, then, may we attribute this apparent rejection of divination as a metaphor for the artist?[93] A closer scrutiny of the source itself provides a clue, for within the traditions of divination lies a tension between the supernatural and the quasi-scientific. While it is generally agreed, for example, that divination incorporates a wide range of practices, all aimed, to quote Olliver, at 'the acquirement of knowledge concerning future events', it is not strictly valid to claim that it is concerned only with the future, for divination included the careful study of past and present 'and in most cases [. . .] could be more accurately defined as the interpretation of past and present events considered as clues from which prognostics can be drawn'.[94] In other words, while some adherents saw the principle underlying divination as the gods' or spirits' willingness to offer signs or warnings of their intentions in the conduct of human affairs, the alternative view held that 'from the manner or occurrence or form of one or several events the form of future events can be logically deduced'.[95] It is this tension that Proust plays on in order to elucidate the various stages in the narrator/protagonist's development, for when the narrator variously describes as a form of divination his grandfather's ability to recognize a schoolfriend's unspoken Jewish ancestry or Morel's talent for detecting a person's homosexuality, he is 'mistaking' the quasi-scientific or empirical for the supernatural. Because the narrator/protagonist sees himself as incapable of offering such insights into another character or situation, he attributes what is, in fact, based on observation and an accumulation of prior knowledge to a supernatural power. This is substantiated by the fact that divinatory powers tend to be ascribed to those who appear to have actively penetrated or, at least, understood worlds which are closed, incomprehensible or alien to the narrator, notably Judaism and its metaphorical correlative, homosexuality. Indeed, repeated references highlight the narrator's failure as a diviner, most notably as regards the enigmatic world of Gomorrah: 'J'ai dit: "Comment n'avais-je pas deviné?" Mais ne l'avais-je pas deviné dès le premier jour à Balbec? N'avais-je pas deviné en Albertine une de ces filles sous l'enveloppe charnelle desquelles palpitent plus d'êtres cachés [. . .]?' (*P* III 601). The passage quoted retrospectively imposes a power of divination on the narrator's early apprehension of Albertine, but, in reality, as we shall see, it is only in *Le Temps retrouvé* that it becomes fully developed. Significantly, this is a power based on observation and experience. It is not, as the popular conception of divination holds, a supernatural gift.

Prior to this realignment of the term, however, the narrator/protagonist and others are presented as subject to the whims of a destiny they are unable to divine or, indeed, change, and what unites almost all the references to destiny in the novel is that this is a malevolent force. References to destiny do not loom large in the early volumes of the novel: there are none in *Du côté de chez Swann*, while *A l'ombre des jeunes filles en fleurs* tends to be dominated by imagery of the stars. The relative security and thus short-sightedness of the narrator's childhood in Combray offer a valid explanation, while although the stars are understood by some as the indicators of one's destiny, the malevolence of this force is felt only from *Le Côté de Guermantes* onwards. Yet Proust's tone, when exploring the notion of destiny as a belief system or life philosophy, spans a sliding scale. It fluctuates between, at one extreme, an ironic debunking of others' apparent reliance on the principle of destiny and, on the other, a personal embracing of the principle that has the ring of self-deception. A quasi-scientific recognition that destiny can exist in the form of heredity occupies the middle ground between these two poles on the spectrum.

The narrator incisively attributes to the duc de Guermantes a sham obeisance to the powers of fortune, for example. In relation to those whom the duc and duchesse meet frequently at others' houses but do not entertain at their own, we read:

> À peine étaient-ils partis que le duc demandait aimablement des renseignements sur eux, pour avoir l'air de s'intéresser à la qualité intrinsèque des personnes qu'il ne recevait pas par la méchanceté du destin ou à cause de l'état nerveux d'Oriane pour lequel la fréquentation des femmes était mauvaise. (G II 754)

In establishing as parallel and alternative causes the hostile, supernatural forces of destiny and Oriane's entirely mundane – and altogether doubtful – nervous state, Proust ironically exposes how this world of seemingly cosmic importance (at least to the aristocrats who people it) is, in fact, governed by trivial, subjective concerns: not only is it an entirely human power that dictates the duc de Guermantes's social arrangements, but the motivation for this control is implied to be jealousy of other women rather than a supernaturally ordained plan for the harmony of the universe.

Mme de Guermantes is not the only character to be presented in these terms; indeed, the woman loved is commonly presented in *A la recherche* as a force of destiny, a controlling influence on the lover. Rachel, for example, exercises her power over Saint-Loup even when they are apart: '[elle] continuait à régir ses actes comme ces astres qui nous gouvernent par leur attraction' (G II 473).[96] And, indeed, the frequent embodiment of the women the narrator loves as heavenly bodies would seem to suggest that he is hopeful that this is where his destiny lies. Fittingly, to express the after-effects on the young narrator/protagonist of their fleeting presence on the beach at Balbec, he describes his first vision of the 'jeunes filles' as being 'comme une lumineuse comète' (JF II 149), while their initial homogeneity in his eyes is aptly conveyed through his imagining them, when sitting in a circle, as '[une] sorte de blanche et vague constellation' (JF II 180), the movements of which he tries to predict by means of an 'astronomie passionnée' (JF II 188).[97] The duchesse de Guermantes is herself associated with the stars and, whether the marker of an egalitarian social perspective or a recognition that love transcends social difference, she is granted the same metaphorical embodiment as the 'jeunes filles'. In fact, the narrator deliberately fuses her with them in his mind:

> Mais, en attendant, de temps à autre, le scintillant sourire de Mme de Guermantes, la sensation de douceur qu'il m'avait donnée, me revenaient. Et sans trop savoir ce que je faisais, je m'essayais à les placer [. . .] à côté des idées romanesques que je possédais depuis longtemps et que la froideur d'Albertine, le départ prématuré de Gisèle et, avant cela, la séparation voulue et trop prolongée d'avec Gilberte avaient libérées (l'idée par exemple d'être aimé d'une femme, d'avoir une vie en commun avec elle); puis c'était l'image de l'une ou l'autre des deux jeunes filles que j'approchais de ces idées auxquelles, aussitôt après, je tâchais d'adapter le souvenir de la duchesse. Auprès de ces idées, le souvenir de Mme de Guermantes à l'Opéra était bien peu de chose, une petite étoile à côté de la longue queue de sa comète flamboyante. (G II 359–60)

Not only does this metaphor subtly establish the extent to which all the narrator's experiences in love imitate one another, but this imagery of the stars also suggests the seeming inaccessibility of these women to the young narrator.[98] This interpretation is reinforced by the fact that the metaphorical association of the 'jeunes filles' with heavenly bodies ceases as soon as he comes to know them, and when Mme de Guermantes finally invites the narrator to dinner, he remarks how: 'je l'avais vue dévier de sa marche stellaire' (G II 672). These heavenly bodies plummet to the material world.[99] What hierarchy is implied in the quotation is thus a perceptual rather than a social one. It is the narrator's memory of Mme de Guermantes at the opera that is transformed into a small star like those that make up the constellation of 'jeunes filles'. Yet this star fades into insignificance in comparison with the blazing comet that is the metaphorical incarnation of the fantasy of a shared life which the narrator projects on to her.

However, this idealizing image subtly deconstructs itself, for if a comet's tail creates a spectacular impression, the comet itself is, in fact, a relatively small body. What is more, its tail, like the aura surrounding Mme de Guermantes, is both tenuous and transient. Tapping into the patterns of mythical thinking that permeate the novel, the comet – believed, in primitive societies, to be an omen of catastrophe or death (particularly of kings or rulers) – thus implicitly heralds the death of this imagined queen of the social hierarchy.[100]

If women only *appear* to possess the power to rule the lover's destiny, this is nonetheless balanced in other contexts by an awareness that one's fate *is* at times beyond individual control. However, this recognition is based on scientific and, specifically, medical principles, not on a genuine belief in the supernatural, despite the harnessing of its terms – and specifically those of sorcery – to convey here the sufferer's feelings of impotence faced with this sinister fate. As the narrator remarks of the dying Swann: 'Nos existences sont en réalité, par l'hérédité, aussi pleines de chiffres cabalistiques, de sorts jetés, que s'il y avait vraiment des sorcières' (G II 866). Only later will this scientific understanding of fate or destiny extend to other areas of experience where, for the moment, an understanding of destiny as a supernatural force remains appealing inasmuch as it fosters an unchallenged passivity or stasis. Indeed, the narrator will rely on the principle of heredity/destiny in order to imply an inability to control events, even when, contrary to the case of Swann's illness, this lack of power has only a doubtful basis in scientific or medical fact. Surmising that his own habit of remaining in bed during the day has been passed on to him by Tante Léonie, the narrator comments how, when we reach a certain age, the soul of the child we were and that of the souls of our dead ancestors 'viennent nous jeter à poignée leurs richesses et leurs mauvais sorts' (P III 587). The fact, however, that Léonie's defining characteristic was her hypochondria allows the mature narrator/writer implicitly to expose the young narrator/protagonist's refuge in 'mauvais sorts' as a flimsy excuse for his own lack of will.[101]

A similar flight from free will may underlie the narrator's realization that his pursuit of Gilberte, Mme de Guermantes, Mlle de Stermaria and Albertine has replicated the same emotions and the same tensions between an idealized fantasy and a disappointing reality: 'mon sort était de ne poursuivre que des fantômes, des êtres dont la réalité pour une bonne part était dans mon imagination' (SG III 401). However, implicit within this supernatural justification may also be the suggestion on Proust's part that it is an inherent dimension of human nature to repeat the same mistakes, especially within the Proustian universe, in matters of the heart: irrational compulsions assume the strength of a force of destiny that the reality of free will is at pains to overcome. As we read in the final volume of the novel, 'aimer est un mauvais sort comme ceux qu'il y a dans les contes, contre quoi on ne peut rien jusqu'à ce que l'enchantement ait cessé' (*TR* IV 284). The necessity for the narrator to be freed from amorous entanglements if he is to take responsibility for his own 'fate' and to exercise the will necessary to create is thus all the more compelling. As if to herald the narrator's own eventual realization of this necessity, *Albertine disparue* implies an awareness – previously absent from the narrator's meditations on his own will and emotions and reserved for those of other characters – that he is consciously and self-deceivingly using the principle of destiny as a crutch. Attempting to replace Albertine with Mlle de Stermaria, with all the intensity and dependency of the earlier relationship, he admits: 'Il était encore temps alors, et c'eût été pour Mlle de Stermaria que se fût exercée cette activité de l'imagination qui nous fait extraire d'une femme une telle notion de l'individuel qu'elle nous paraît unique en soi et pour nous prédestinée et nécessaire' (*AD* IV 83).

The narrator's attempts at replicating his relationship with Albertine thus prompt a new level of self-awareness. However, as argued in previous sections, of all the women to whose influence the narrator willingly succumbs, his mother lies at the furthest reach of the trajectory that ends with self-realization. Stéphane Chaudier identifies the narrator's contemplation of the mosaics in St Mark's as the defining moment for the narrator in the process of situating himself as an individual independent of his mother. Yet a final planetary image – part of a network which is intricately bound up with the notion of destiny – follows quickly on the heels of this moment of aesthetic appreciation to reconfirm the narrator's believed lack of free will and continuing dependency on his mother. Having resolved to remain in Venice alone, the narrator experiences another near miss when he rushes to the train station just in time to return to Paris with her, a decision which he describes as follows: 'Mais enfin, d'antres plus obscurs que ceux d'où s'élance la comète qu'on peut prédire – grâce à l'insoupçonnable puissance défensive de l'habitude invétérée, grâce aux réserves cachées que par une impulsion subite elle jette au dernier moment dans la mêlée –, mon action surgit enfin' (*AD* IV 233–4). The study of the mosaics may represent a moment of pure aesthetic contemplation for the narrator, unobstructed, despite her proximity, by thoughts of his mother;[102] but it does not represent a complete volte-face in the narrator, nor, of course, is it the final stage which prepares him for his own artistic creation. Many years will pass before this is achieved, and, as the extract reveals, the narrator continues to allow himself to be governed by habit and by impulse at this still-youthful stage. Nonetheless, as the progression in Proust's handling of this metaphorical intertext suggests, an evolution has occurred in the protagonist himself, for we note that the comets he once saw as inaccessible, supernatural elements – the fitting metaphorical embodiment for the women he has loved – have become 'graspable'. Through scientific study, the narrator acknowledges that they can be predicted, and it is no longer what is external to himself that seems impossible to penetrate but, rather, the internal workings of his own mind and emotions. Astrology shades suggestively into astronomy.

As if to mirror this progression, we come full circle to the power of divination that the narrator was once so conscious of lacking. In *Le Temps retrouvé*, this is a power he is now able to exercise and, as is explicitly stated, it is his previous contact with worlds which he believed he had no power to divine, notably Gomorrah, that has inculcated in him this skill:

> Au temps où je croyais ce qu'on disait, j'aurais été tenté, en entendant l'Allemagne, puis la Bulgarie, puis la Grèce protester de leurs intentions pacifiques, d'y ajouter foi. Mais, depuis que la vie avec Albertine et avec Françoise m'avait habitué à soupçonner chez elles des pensées, des projets qu'elles n'exprimaient pas, je ne laissais aucune parole, juste en apparence, de Guillaume II, de Ferdinand de Bulgarie, de Constantin de Grèce, tromper mon instinct, qui *devinait* ce que machinait chacun d'eux. (*TR* IV 350, my italics)

Divination has become not a divine gift, nor – to harness the duality of the verb 'deviner' in French – is it random guesswork; it is, rather, the result of a mental effort, and this same skill can later be brought to bear on the series of involuntary memories which, in his earlier life, the narrator had been unable (or unwilling to try) to unravel. Resolved to grasp the cause 'de cette félicité, du caractère de certitude avec lequel elle s'imposait' (*TR* IV 449), he divines it ('je la devinais', ibid.) by comparing all the experiences of involuntary memory and uncovering what they have in common. The answer is progressively teased out over the following pages.

As if to reinforce this mature stage in his development, the cycle of images relating to divination, destiny and the planets is completed by reiterative and explicitly re-evaluative evocations of earlier metaphors. We read, for example:

> C'est pendant des années que Bergotte m'avait paru un doux vieillard divin, que je m'étais senti paralysé comme par une apparition devant le chapeau gris de Swann, le manteau violet de sa femme, le mystère dont le nom de sa race entourait la duchesse de Guermantes jusque dans un salon: origines presque fabuleuses, charmante mythologie de relations devenues si banales ensuite, mais qu'elles prolongeaient dans le passé comme en plein ciel, avec un éclat pareil à celui que projette la queue étincelante d'une comète. (*TR* IV 552)

The *memory* of his earlier elevation of Mme de Guermantes to the status of heavenly body persists. However, the tail of the comet in the earlier image relating to her referred implicitly to a hoped-for future moment when he would be loved and needed by Mme de Guermantes;[103] here, in contrast, the narrator's gaze has shifted backwards, with the emphasis placed firmly on the past. What remains are memories which nonetheless retain their value (and thus their association with heavenly bodies) inasmuch as they will provide the material for the work of art.[104]

From the narrator/protagonist in the restaurant at Doncières who saw the tables as planets yielding to the laws of attraction and who sowed into his image the subtle seed that social structures could change, the novel draws to a close with a return to the same image, here aptly introduced to confirm that these structures, like the cycles of the planets, were not only far from immutable, but that they may also, in the future beyond the novel, come full circle:

> Car si dans ces périodes de vingt ans les conglomérats de coteries se défaisaient et se reformaient selon l'attraction d'astres nouveaux destinés d'ailleurs eux aussi à s'éloigner, puis à reparaître, des cristallisations puis des émiettements suivis de cristallisations nouvelles avaient lieu dans l'âme des êtres. (*TR* IV 570)

Based on an accumulation of experience, the narrator has achieved a broader perspective on society and its structures. And just as metaphors of divination, destiny and the planets allowed the mature narrator/writer to convey to the reader the naivety of the young narrator/protagonist, so, too, do they express his distance from that earlier self at the end of the novel: as we have seen, these metaphorical sources contain within them the scope for a transition from the supernatural to the quasi-scientific, from the supernatural power of divination to a means of understanding events based on observation and the interpretation of prior knowledge. In making these transitions, the narrator has disentangled the various strands of meaning implied by the concept of destiny: if, at the end of the novel, physical illness may still prevent him from creating the work he has resolved to write, he nonetheless recognizes that free will, responsibility and action lie within the power of the individual endowed with the artistic genius required to transform observation into creation.[105]

The various rituals and beliefs explored in this final part of the study intertwine with one another throughout the volumes of *A la recherche*. In moving between them, we must also move back and forth within the novel and the different moments in the narrator's experience that are played out in each volume. Each set of rituals or beliefs is nonetheless discussed as an individual paradigm, for each has its own emphasis and function within the broader context of the narrator's mythical quest. Superstitious rituals dramatize the desire for power and control, but also reveal the limitations of knowledge; spiritualist practice is not only the site of an enforced confrontation with the illusory nature of power and knowledge; it is also, in a shift from literal to metaphorical, a vehicle for the expression of the concerns surrounding communication that are central to the artist's endeavour. Overlapping with the themes embodied in Proust's handling of superstitious belief, spiritualism also enables the staging of an encounter with an insurmountable otherness. These first two systems of belief are thus linked by the lover's preoccupations with achieving complete knowledge of the object of desire; and, on a broader level, they generate an epistemological uncertainty which is extended symbolically to the artistic enterprise. It is, however, the worlds of magic and the occult that provide the nexus for the interconnection of love/desire, art and memory. And yet, the revelations acquired in each of these areas achieve the potential to be put into practice only when the narrator makes the transition from passivity to activity, from a reliance on the principle of destiny and its hampering 'mauvais sorts' to a belief in the possibility of independent engagement. This is realized through the belief in, and metaphors drawn from, the realms of divination, destiny and the planets.

Malcolm Bowie concludes his chapter on 'Self' in *Proust Among the Stars* with a reading of the narrator and Saint-Loup's contemplation of the wartime Paris sky with its constellations of fighter planes on apocalyptic missions, accompanied by sirens evocative of the 'Ride of the Valkyries'.[106] His comments both enlarge and offer a compellingly apt evaluation of the interconnections that lie at the heart of this study. They draw together the narrator's legendary models, his starry-eyed flight from action and responsibility, the processes of self-creation he undergoes and the path he follows to metaphorical and, with it, aesthetic creation. Bowie argues that 'many of the narrator's own metaphorical habits and, in particular, his star-gazing, his inventive play with the quadrivium, and his hesitation between explosion and fixity' are here transferred, in burlesque mode, to Saint-Loup. Saint-Loup is thus

> prolonging, and recasting in millennial terms, a mode of perception that Proust's narrator has displayed throughout the novel. Aerial combat produces new constellations, new displays of matter and kinetic energy, and these are in direct line of descent from the countless 'astral phenomena' that the narrator had previously recorded. (p. 28)

In a dialectic that combines, at once, opposition and dependency, the narrator distances himself from a former self and former mode of vision, while at the same time recognizing both its pivotal role in the processes of self-creation and the potency of its perpetuation in another form. To borrow Bowie's terms, therefore:

in transferring these images to Saint-Loup, Proust is [. . .] preparing the way for the 'real' apocalypse of the book and for the unimpeachable depth and seriousness of artistic perception and moral concern that the narrator, alone among its central characters, is eventually to acquire. Saint-Loup in becoming the supremely witty artist of scattered selfhood, the inventor of momentary geometrics and ever-changing optical effects, leaves the way open for the narrator, that nebulous modeller of nebulae, to become a single self at last. But the clarity and complexity that the book's earlier images of dispersal possess cannot simply be removed from the record by the last fortified version of selfhood upon which the narrator reports. On the contrary, those earlier explosions and starbursts have such imaginative authority that they may prove to be the feature of the book that we remember best and cherish most. If so, the centralised and resolved self on which the novel ends may be seen not as a redemption but as one momentary geometry among many others. (pp. 28–9)

# CONCLUSION

Since the nineteenth century, western culture, according to Eliade, has been making a 'prodigious effort of historiographic anamnesis. It [has sought] to discover, "awaken", and repossess the pasts of the most exotic and the most peripheral societies', the goal of such an enterprise being the 'discovery of our solidarity with these vanished or peripheral peoples'. The mythical quest dramatized in *A la recherche* is part of this endeavour, for in tapping into artistic sources such as the fairytale and legendary narratives that have been successively reinvented in time, place and genre, or systems of ritual and belief with their origins in primitive or distant worlds, such as superstition, spiritualism, divination or the occult, Proust is uncovering the essential syncretism, indeed synchronicity, of human characteristics and societies. Delving far beyond the mere facts and figures that define our historical past or contemporary Other, Proust is uncovering common forms of life, behaviour and culture. He is laying bare the 'exemplary models and paradigmatic events' that characterize, not an individual, but humanity as a whole.[1] In this, the mythical quest played out in the novel serves Proust's aim to universalize the particular, to endow his characters with an existence outside Time, and to communicate to his reader truths that transcend a particular moment, that are not limited by 'les contingences du Temps', but that unite, rather, disparate temporal and existential frames 'dans une métaphore' (*TR* IV 468). Indeed, Proust's conception of myth and metaphor coincide. For the narrator/protagonist of *A la recherche*, the recourse to mythical models creates a reassuring (if, at times, passively conceived) bridge between the experiences of Self and Other, while for the narrator/writer, myth offers a source of metaphor that is richly evocative of the processes of metaphor-creation itself.

Metaphor-creation is, for Proust, the cornerstone of artistic creation. It is the site of an intellectual re-creation of instinctive perception. After all, it is the artist who expresses what we all intuit but cannot articulate without his/her mediation. The artist's mediation thus combines, to quote Jahoda, 'rational, logical and scientific' processes with a style of thinking that is 'affective, poetic and mythical'.[2] In other words, aesthetic creation opens up a space where two sets of seemingly antithetical referents may coexist, subtly undermining conventional binary thinking such as that which opposes rational and irrational, male and female, Self and Other, heterosexual and homosexual, good and evil, high and low art. The collapsing of such polarities is, as we have seen in the course of this study, central to Proust's encounter with the supernatural and the mythical.

Paradoxically, however, the terms of Jahoda's opposition are borrowed from the distinction drawn by the anthropologist Lévy-Bruhl between 'civilized' and 'primitive', or logical and pre-logical, modes of thinking.[3] Lévy-Bruhl thus sees a chronological progression where Proust sees synchronicity. To return to the terms, if not the evolutionary pattern, of Frazer's argument, magical and scientific thinking coexist in the Proustian universe.

Marc Soriano, in his study of Perrault's fairytales, explains the source of his own fascination with the medium and impetus for pursuing his research into it, in the following terms:

> C'était celui du merveilleux ou plus exactement de la coexistence dans la même conscience des concepts scientifiques les plus avancés et des superstitions venues d'un passé lointain, celui de la contradiction au fond de chacun de nous entre la pensée rationnelle et la pensée magique. Ce scandale logique me semblait s'exprimer et se résumer assez bien dans le merveilleux, que le progrès de nos connaissances ne cesse de traquer et de mettre à la porte et qui revient aussitôt par la fenêtre, parfois même sans se donner la peine de chercher d'autres déguisements. (p. 7)

Some of the numerous disguises assumed by this 'scandale logique' have been examined in the present study. Fairytales, legends and metaphysical beliefs (in the power of superstitious practices, for example, or the influence of the stars) continue to captivate us even in the modern, 'rationalistic' world. Like us, the narrator/protagonist succumbs to their allure as a means of conceptualizing experience, of providing models for emulation, of generating an impression of power and control, of grappling with the limitations of knowledge and understanding by taking refuge in the idea of a more powerful and knowing figure (whether magical or simply heroic) than himself. The present study has charted how and why the narrator/protagonist progressively transcends these 'disguises' as literal sources of reassurance, not least among the (reluctantly embraced) reasons for this rejection being that collective belief and ritual – or, in general terms, the well-trodden path – represent a vicarious quest which cannot lead to authentic self-realization and truth. These richly allusive sources are, nonetheless, appropriated as a source of metaphorical expression by the narrator/writer, invested as they are with the preoccupations that lie at the heart of the mythical and aesthetic quest the novel will relate: the need to understand and create the Self; the desire for communication with the Other; and the complex interconnection of time, memory and the search for transcendence.

In a sense, such a movement does imply an evolutionary transition from magical to scientific thinking. The narrator of the novel certainly acquires a more 'rational' and, indeed, more actively engaged (rather than passively accepting) perspective on experience: he accepts that his 'destiny' is, in large measure, within his own control and that a failure to act is his responsibility alone. He also arrives at an intellectual, if still emotionally uncomfortable, acceptance of the limitations of knowledge, or, to use Segalen's terms, the impossibility of knowing the Other.[4]

In what respect, therefore, does magical thinking persist? Proust's text shows us that its power is present, above all, in the perceptual transformations wrought in an audience by the opera, play or Sonata it witnesses performed, in an observer by the painting s/he scrutinizes, or in a reader by the novel s/he digests. Like the narrator's magic lantern, art is not endowed with any genuinely supernatural power, and yet it has a seemingly 'magical' power to transform reality in the eyes of the person who engages with it. What more potent a vehicle to suggest this 'magical' power than Proust's recourse to a range of supernatural (interaesthetic) intertexts?[5]

Proust's novel, then, possesses its own mythical structure, but the very act of reading a novel itself marks, for Eliade, a form of re-enactment of the recitation of myth in traditional societies. '[T]he need to find one's way into "foreign" Universes and to follow the complications of a "story" is', argues Eliade, 'consubstantial with the human condition and hence irreducible.'[6] The reading of a novel, and, in particular, one like *A la recherche* that is rooted in an initiatory theme, feeds this plural impulse, whether for communication and empathy with the (fictional) Other or for a reassurance that obstacles may be overcome. Above all, though, it is their common power to offer an escape from Time that unites literature and myth:

> One 'escapes' from historical and personal time and is submerged in a time that is fabulous and trans-historical. The reader is confronted with a strange, imaginary time, whose rhythms vary indefinitely, for each narrative has its own time that is peculiar to it and to it alone. The novel does not have access to the primordial time of myths, but in so far as he tells a credible story, the novelist employs a time that is *seemingly historical* yet is condensed or prolonged, a time, then, that has at its command all the freedoms of imaginary worlds.[7]

The reader's engagement with the text cannot be a passive one, however, not least because the novel is a 'closed, hermetic universe that cannot be entered except by overcoming immense difficulties, like the initiatory ordeals of the archaic and traditional societies'.[8] The determined reader might negotiate this path of initiation with skill and sensitivity, but his/her task does not end at the final pages of the novel. 'Chaque lecteur', Proust reminds us, 'est quand il lit le propre lecteur de soi-même. L'ouvrage de l'écrivain n'est qu'une espèce d'instrument optique qu'il offre au lecteur afin de lui permettre de discerner ce que sans ce livre il n'eût peut-être pas vu en soi-même' (*TR* IV 489–90). The passage might identify the novel as a purveyor of insights that the reader may sense but not fully grasp without the artist's mediation, but it also delimits the epistemological boundaries of the novel, for if the text reveals to the reader a facet of his/her character that might otherwise have gone unnoticed, or opens up his/her imagination, it can do no more. Where the mythical quest of the narrator and writer of *A la recherche* ends, therefore, that of the reader begins.

# NOTES

## INTRODUCTION

1. Marcel Proust, *A la recherche du temps perdu*, Bibliothèque de la Pléiade, 4 vols (Paris: Gallimard, 1987-9). All references will be to this edition and will take the form: volume abbreviation, volume number, page number, e.g. *SG* III 246. See list of abbreviations on p. xi.
2. See below, pp. 92-101.
3. Roger Scruton, *Death-Devoted Heart: Sex and the Sacred in Wagner's* Tristan and Isolde (Oxford: Oxford University Press, 2004), p. 9.
4. See below, pp. 91-115.
5. See below, pp. 76-80. In addition to its foundation in ritual and the fantastical, the traditions of Polichinelle also contain such supernatural elements as the protagonist's confrontation with the Devil.
6. Ruth Nanda Anshen, in the editorial introduction to Mircea Eliade, *Myth and Reality*, World Perspectives Series 21, trans. Willard R. Trask (London: Allen & Unwin, 1964), p. ix.
7. Jean-Pierre Mothe, quoting from Jung's *Métamorphoses de l'âme et ses symboles*, in *Du Sang et du sexe dans les contes de Perrault*, Collection l'Œuvre et la Psyché (Paris: L'Harmattan, 1999), p. 178. My analysis draws on Freudian psychoanalysis and Jungian analytical psychology where these approaches prove illuminating in the context of the mythical quest undertaken by the narrator of *A la recherche*. However, this is not to suggest that the study is embedded in a systematically Jungian or psychoanalytical framework.
8. Following Laurence Coupe, the term 'mythography' is used of the reading of myth, the term 'mythopoeia' of the writing of myth. See his *Myth*, New Critical Idiom Series (London, NY: Routledge, 1997).
9. The following texts by Eliade are drawn on here: *The Myth of the Eternal Return: or, Cosmos and History*, Bollingen Series XLVI, trans. Willard R. Trask (Princeton, NJ: Princeton University Press, 1991 [1954]); *Images and Symbols: Studies in Religious Symbolism*, trans. Philip Mairet (Princeton, NJ: Princeton University Press, 1991); *Myths, Dreams and Mysteries* (London: Collins/Fontana, 1968);

and, above all, *Myth and Reality* (see n. 6). Other approaches to reading myth focus on: myths of 'deliverance'; myths of superhuman heroism; and fertility myths. Despite their differing emphases, none of these paradigms (creation, deliverance, heroism, fertility) is completely distinct from the others. Aspects of some, if not all, may be detected in most mythical narratives. Other approaches will therefore be introduced here where they open up fresh perspectives on Proust's handling of myth.

10  Eliade, *Myth and Reality*, p. 2.
11  Ibid., pp. 5–6.
12  Ibid., pp. 8, 11.
13  See, in particular, Part I, 'Fairytale romances', pp. 29–42.
14  La Fontaine defends the fables as follows: 'Les fables ne sont pas ce qu'elles semblent être; / Le plus simple animal nous y tient lieu de maître. / Une morale nue apporte de l'ennui: / Le conte fait passer le précepte avec lui. / En ces sortes de feintes il faut instruire et plaire; / Et conter pour conter me semble peu d'affaire': Jean de La Fontaine, *Fables*, Hachette French Classics, ed. Francis Tarver (London: Hachette, 1898), VI, I, 'Le Pâtre et le Lion', p. 102.
15  La Fontaine exposes the tragic side of human life: 'the image of man which emerges from the general picture', argues Odette de Mourgues, 'is that of a deceitful, greedy and cruel being'. However, this is combined with a concern to give aesthetic pleasure which finds its voice in a surface of delicacy and levity. As de Mourgues further notes, 'this kind of wit has the grace, the urbanity and the frivolous touch of the best Précieux wit, yet it succeeds in doing something altogether different': *La Fontaine: Fables* (London: Edward Arnold, 1960), pp. 23, 39. See Jean-Dominique Biard, *The Style of La Fontaine's Fables* (Oxford: Blackwell, 1966), for a full account of La Fontaine's style.
16  Eliade, *Myth and Reality*, p. 143.
17  See Part I, '*Les Mille et Une Nuits* proustiennes', pp. 42–55. See also Edward Said, *Orientalism: Western Conceptions of the Orient* (Harmondsworth: Penguin, 1991 [1978]), pp. 2–3, for the 'ontological and epistemological distinction made between "the Orient" and (most of the time) "the Occident"'. Critics of Said's work have subsequently mounted convincing challenges to this binarism. See, for example, Valerie Kennedy, *Edward Said: A Critical Introduction* (Oxford: Polity, 2000).
18  La Fontaine, in the Preface to the *Fables*, explains his choice of animals in terms of the fundamental similarities in nature between humankind and the animal world: 'Les propriétés des Animaux et leurs divers caractères y sont exprimés: par conséquent les nôtres aussi, puisque nous sommes l'abrégé de ce qu'il y a de bon et de mauvais dans les créatures irraisonnables. Quand Prométhée voulut former l'homme, il prit la qualité dominante de chaque Bête. De ces pièces si différentes il composa notre espèce: il fit cet ouvrage qu'on appelle le petit monde. Ainsi ces fables sont un tableau où chacun de nous se trouve dépeint': *Fables* (Paris: Gallimard, 1991), p. 28. To choose animals as the protagonists of his fables is therefore to comment on human nature. The extract also suggests that man and animals are just microcosmic parts of a unified creation.

19  See Eliade, *Myth and Reality*, pp. 111–13, pp. 152–61. Jean-Pierre Vernant explains how the ancient Greeks began to distinguish between *mythos*, a form of fantasy, and *logos*, as rational argument: 'Between the eighth and fourth centuries BC a whole series of interrelated conditions caused a multiplicity of differentiations, breaks and internal tensions within the mental universe of the Greeks which were responsible for distinguishing the domain of myth from other domains: the concept of myth peculiar to classical antiquity thus became clearly defined through the setting up of an opposition between *muthos* [sic] and *logos*, henceforth seen as separate and contrasting terms': *Myth and Society in Ancient Greece* (London: Methuen, 1982), p. 187. That is not to suggest, however, that late antiquity saw a comprehensive demythologization. Indeed, as Coupe argues, it was not until the Enlightenment that a 'systematic attempt was made to explain away mythology' (*Myth*, p. 10).

20  Although Proust does not mention Frazer or *The Golden Bough* in his work, reference is made to writers such as Auguste Comte and Turgot who influenced the development of Frazer's ideas. See Robert Ackerman, *The Myth and Ritual School: J. G. Frazer and the Cambridge Ritualists* (NY: Garland Science, 1990) for a discussion of how this theory was successively developed by Vico, Turgot and Comte. For references to Comte by Proust, see *Correspondance de Marcel Proust*, ed. P. Kolb, 21 vols (Paris: Plon, 1970–93), vols 3 (p. 385), 4 (p. 38), 14 (p. 269) and 16 (p. 182), and 'Pèlerinages ruskiniens en France', in *Contre Sainte-Beuve, précédé de Pastiches et mélanges et suivi de Essais et articles*, Bibliothèque de la Pléiade (Paris: Gallimard, 1971), p. 443. For references to Turgot, see *Jean Santeuil, précédé de Les Plaisirs et les jours*, Bibliothèque de la Pléiade (Paris: Gallimard, 1971), p. 435. Comte's positivist philosophy is thought to have influenced the formulation of Frazer's theory of a progression from magic to religion to science. Given Proust's familiarity with Comte's work and his curiosity regarding other evolutionary theories, such as those of Darwin, we might speculate that he knew something of Frazer's work. (See Emily Eells, *Proust's Cup of Tea: Homoeroticism and Victorian Culture* (Aldershot: Ashgate, 2002), pp. 94–9, for a discussion of the presence of Darwin's theories in Proust's novel, in particular, in the context of discussions of homosexuality.)

21  Sir James Frazer, *The Golden Bough*, 3rd edn, 12 vols (London: Macmillan, 1911–15), vol. 11, pp. 307–8. While Frazer admits to the concurrent appeal of religion and science, his theory definitively relegates magical thinking to an earlier developmental stage. We shall see, however, that magical thinking endures alongside rational thinking in Proust's novelistic universe. The novel therefore exposes this 'myth of mythlessness' (to use Coupe's terms, *Myth*, p. 9).

22  Eliade, *Myth and Reality*, p. 145.

23  See ibid., p. 147.

24  See Part II, pp. 81–91 for a discussion of the contrasts between M. de Cambremer's and the narrator/writer's handling of La Fontaine.

25  See pp. 89–91 for a full discussion of Rachel's recitation.

26  Eliade, *Myth and Reality*, p. 187.

27  Eliade, *Eternal Return*, p. 76.

28  Eliade, *Myth and Reality*, p. 18.
29  Eliade, *Images and Symbols*, p. 58.
30  Eliade, *Myth and Reality*, p. 140.
31  Ibid., pp. 141–2.
32  Mikhail Bakhtin, *Rabelais and his World*, trans. Hélène Iswolsky (Bloomington: Indiana University Press, 1984), p. 10. The rituals of black magic offer a further model of stasis, while those of superstition – although, on the surface, a re-enactment of mythical events aimed at re-creating and maintaining the power of what Eliade terms 'the Supernatural Beings' – are in fact exposed as gestures of impotence and self-deception. See below, pp. 119–30 and pp. 142–50.
33  See Eliade, *Myth and Reality*, pp. 75–6.
34  See Part I, 'The magical mundane', pp. 55–73, especially pp. 65–73.
35  A clear contrast between Freud's and Proust's return to origins and that inscribed in mythical ritual is that the former two are individual, whereas the latter is collective.
36  Memory and artistic creation have long been connected: for example, in Greek mythology, Mnemosyne (the personification of memory) is the mother of the Muses.
37  Eliade, *Myth and Reality*, p. 85.
38  See ibid., pp. 89–90.
39  This duality of recollection is also recorded in Eliade's discussion of the recovery of the past. He describes the 'different methods of "returning to the origin" [in] archaic and oriental' belief systems. The first is a 'rapid and direct re-establishment of the first situation' and is 'vertiginously swift or even instantaneous'; the second is a 'progressive return to the "origin" by proceeding backward through Time from the present moment to the "absolute beginning"'. This involves a 'meticulous and exhaustive recollecting of personal and historical events' (ibid., pp. 88–9).
40  Offering a further overlap between the structures of myth and of *A la recherche*, the transcendence of time is also linked, in mythical thinking, to the acquisition of wisdom. Eliade notes how '[a]ll of the images by means of which we try to express the paradoxical act of "escaping from time" are equally expressive of *the passage from ignorance to enlightenment*': *Images and Symbols*, p. 82. By way of explanation of these images, Eliade describes how variously '[t]he hero of a tale of initiation has to go "where the night and day meet together", or find the door in a wall where none can be seen, or go up to Heaven by a passage that half-opens for only an instant, or pass between two millstones in constant motion, between two rocks that may clash together at any moment, or between the jaws of a monster, etc. All these images express the necessity of *transcending the "pairs of opposites"*, of abolishing the polarity that besets the human condition, in order to reach the ultimate reality' (ibid., pp. 83–4). The resonances of Proustian involuntary memory and metaphor are clear.
41  See 'The "god who binds" and the symbolism of knots', in Eliade, *Images and Symbols*, ch. 3, pp. 92–124, for a full discussion of the various forms of this imagery in Indo-European mythologies.

42  'The Buddha's advice to Sariputra' underscores the need for wakefulness, repeatedly stressing the importance of being 'alert' and 'much awake'. See E. Conze (ed.), *Buddhist Scriptures* (Harmondsworth: Penguin, 1976), pp. 77–9. 'The legend of the Buddha Shakyamuni' also describes the Bodhisattva's realization that he must separate himself from the sensuous pleasure enjoyed in the company of women as 'The awakening' (ibid., p. 39). The subsequent section charts his 'Withdrawal from the women' (p. 40).

43  Indeed, the Bodhisattva himself is distracted from spiritual pursuits by his 'captivity' at the hands of women: 'They entertained him with soft words, tremulous calls, wanton swayings, sweet laughter, butterfly kisses, and seductive glances. Thus he became a captive of these women who were well versed in the subject of sensuous enjoyment and indefatigable in sexual pleasure. And it did not occur to him to come down from the palace to the ground' (ibid., p. 38).

44  Jean Pommier's study, *La Mystique de Marcel Proust*, offers valuable insights into the influence of mysticism in the novel by concentrating on the workings of involuntary memory and interpreting such moments as mystical experiences (Paris: Droz, 1939). In a similar vein, Barbara Bucknall devotes a final, persuasive chapter of her study to Proust's possible affinities with Eastern religions, filtering her comments through a particular focus on the religion of aestheticism in Proust: *The Religion of Art in Proust*, Illinois Studies in Language and Literature 60 (Urbana: University of Illinois Press, 1969), ch. 8, pp. 173–203. See also Milton Hindus, *The Proustian Vision* (NY: Columbia University Press, 1958), Jean Mouton, *Proust* (Bruges: Desclée de Brouwer, 1968) and Jean Seznec, *Marcel Proust et les dieux* (Oxford: Clarendon, 1962), all of whom touch on this question.

45  See, for example, Thomas Donnan, 'Proust "reprit à la musique son bien": A Study in Analogies between Wagnerian and Proustian Composition', *Stanford French Review*, 13/2–3 (1989), 159–74.

46  See Margaret Mein, 'Proust and Wagner', *Journal of European Studies*, xix (1989), 205–22, and Jean-Jacques Nattiez, *Proust as Musician*, trans. Derrick Puffett (Cambridge: Cambridge University Press, 1989).

47  See Mein, 'Proust and Wagner'.

48  Critics such as Nattiez have tended to concentrate on the role of *Tristan and Isolde* in the development of the narrator's aesthetic in *La Prisonnière* rather than on the thematic links between the two quests.

49  Pierre Albouy's perspective on the mythical structures that run through *A la recherche* – what he terms its 'code mythologique' – chimes in certain respects with my own. In his article on this subject, Albouy identifies the structure of the novel as charting '[la] perte des dieux et du merveilleux', arguing that 'le temps perdu est aussi celui de la mythologie vécue': 'Quelques images et structures mythiques dans *la Recherche du temps perdu*', *Revue d'Histoire Littéraire*, 71 (1971), 972–87 (p. 974). He also suggests that the artist's duty is to perform 'la résurrection du merveilleux' (ibid., p. 975), a task s/he can accomplish only having 'pass[é] par les illusions mythiques perdues', for example, in society or in love

(ibid., p. 977). However, Albouy's task is not to examine in detail the significance and interconnectedness of an apparently eclectic range of mythical narratives, rituals and beliefs. Indeed, in drawing out the novel's mythical and, more specifically in Albouy's argument, Orphic structure, this critic relies primarily on classical mythology, a source which lies outside the scope of the analysis that follows.

50   The words are those of Terence (Publius Terentius Afer) in *The Self-Tormentor*.
51   'C'est au moyen d'images que se manifeste la vérité. Par vérité, j'entends la vue la plus parfaite de la réalité, le coup d'œil qui épuise le détail de l'objet': Claude Vallée, *La Féerie de Marcel Proust* (Paris: Fasquelle, 1958), p. 35.
52   The phrase is found in ibid., p. 20, where we also read: 'Aux expressions usées, aux alliances conventionnelles, Proust substitue un vocabulaire intuitif. Il établit des parentés entre les choses qui, par ce moyen, se mettent à vivre, et des ressemblances créatrices.'
53   'Détruire l'Habitude est la condition même de l'impressionnisme et du merveilleux' (ibid., p. 44).
54   A comparable counterpart from the range of *literal* references to supernatural and mythical sources is the list of superstitious beliefs that define certain of Odette's actions. As the figures in brackets highlight, five separate superstitious beliefs are expressed; thus five, not one, are counted. Françoise reports: 'Il paraît qu'elle a bien confiance à des médailles [1]. Jamais elle ne partira en voyage si elle a entendu la chouette [2], ou bien comme un tic-tac d'horloge dans le mur [3], ou si elle a vu un chat à ménuit [4], ou si le bois d'un meuble, il a craqué [5]. Ah! c'est une personne très croyante!' (*S* I 409). The cumulative effect of the list is consciously to underline the extravagance and eclecticism of Odette's superstitions.
55   The young narrator's fascination with the iridescence of the asparagus prepared by Françoise seems to grant it a quasi-supernatural power of transformation. Thus, we read: 'Il me semblait que ces nuances célestes trahissaient les délicieuses créatures qui s'étaient amusées à se métamorphoser en légumes [. . .]' (*S* I 119). Through its association with the subsequent image of a fairy, Mme de Villeparisis's sudden and miraculous appearance in Balbec (at least to the young narrator hoping to elevate himself in Mlle de Stermaria's eyes) likewise assumes magical proportions: 'On peut penser que l'apparition soudaine, sous les traits d'une petite vieille, de la plus puissante des fées ne m'aurait pas causé plus de plaisir, dénué comme j'étais de tout recours pour m'approcher de Mlle de Stermaria, dans un pays où je ne connaissais personne' (*JF* II 45).
56   These terms are categorized as general magic and fairytale references. Brunet identifies a total of 564 uses of 'charme', 'charmer' and all their derivatives in the novel, while 'enchantement', 'enchanter' and their derivatives are used on 114 occasions. See Etienne Brunet, *Le Vocabulaire de Proust*, Travaux de linguistique quantitative 18, 3 vols (Geneva: Slatkine-Champion, 1983).
57   Similarly, the term 'deviner' – endowed with the dual meaning of guessing and divining – is counted only when invested, in the eyes of the uncomprehending young narrator, with the flavour of a supernatural gift. Otherwise, only references to the explicit terms 'divination', 'divinateur/-rice' and 'divinatoire' are counted.

58   See below, pp. 65–73.
59   The images of magic categorized as 'Magic and the occult' (Part III) relate, above all, to the workings of sorcery, demon possession and satanic ritual in the novel. These are prefaced in Part III by a discussion of the rather less malevolent magic of the illusionist, but the subtle intertwining which leads from one to the other – from the performative sleight of hand to the appearance of genuinely supernatural control – will become apparent in the course of the analysis. The images categorized in Part I as 'Magic and fairytale', in contrast, are characterized by a more innocuous vision. It is, however, recognized that fairytale is also, in large part, based on illusions. What is more, this identification of fairytale as a more innocuous vision of the magical is not to ignore the darker side of the genre.
60   See *P* III 664–8, and below, pp. 104–8.
61   We find the following evocation of his past perception: 'Au temps où je croyais [. . .] que les Guermantes habitaient tel palais en vertu d'un droit héréditaire, pénétrer dans le palais du sorcier ou de la fée, faire s'ouvrir devant moi les portes qui ne cèdent pas tant qu'on n'a pas prononcé la formule magique, me semblait aussi malaisé que d'obtenir un entretien du sorcier ou de la fée eux-mêmes' (*TR* IV 436).
62   The three subcategories listed here – Perrault, *1001* and General – correlate broadly, but not exclusively, to the three main subsections in Part I of the study: 'Fairytale romances', '*Les Mille et Une Nuits* proustiennes' and 'The magical mundane'.
63   See, for example, *TR* IV 312 for Brichot's continuing 'enchantment' with Mme Verdurin's – now the princesse de Guermantes's – much-changed salon; and *TR* IV 317 for Bloch's 'enchantment' on hearing a confession of cowardice. Aspects of the war are also a source of enchantment for Charlus (see *TR* IV 375, 423).
64   The narrator, trying to unravel the link between involuntary memory and the creation of the work of art, quotes Chateaubriand's *Mémoires d'Outre-Tombe*: 'Hier au soir je me promenais seul . . . je fus tiré de mes réflexions par le gazouillement d'une grive perchée sur la plus haute branche d'un bouleau. A l'instant, ce son magique fit reparaître à mes yeux le domaine paternel; j'oubliai les catastrophes dont je venais d'être le témoin, et, transporté subitement dans le passé, je revis ces campagnes où j'entendis si souvent siffler la grive' (*TR* IV 498).
65   Of the narrator's sudden, but delayed, recognition of the now-aged Rachel whose name Bloch whispers in his ear, we read: 'Ce nom magique rompit aussitôt l'enchantement qui avait donné à la maîtresse de Saint-Loup la forme inconnue de cette immonde vieille' (*TR* IV 579).
66   See below, pp. 124–9.
67   Similar peaks mark the distribution of references to divination, destiny and the planets in both *Le Côté de Guermantes* and *Le Temps retrouvé*. Constructed, as the former of these two volumes is, on an appropriately starry-eyed vision of society and, above all, of Mme de Guermantes, their predominance here is unsurprising. Their persistence in the more clear-eyed *Le Temps retrouvé* begs

further questions. And yet these upsurges are entirely consistent with the pattern of the narrator's development, as the discussion, in Part III, of the duality of meaning underlying the practice of divination – supernatural gift or the product of empirical observation? – will argue (pp. 150–60).

68 Ingrid Wassenaar investigates compellingly the processes and presentation of grief in *Albertine disparue*, highlighting, among other features, the closing of the gap between narrator/protagonist and narrator/writer which may, in part, explain this volume's status as one of (temporary) metaphorical dormancy: 'It is one of the unreadabilities of *Albertine disparue* that Marcel the protagonist and Marcel the writing narrator become, not simply pleasurably intertwined, but glutinously indistinguishable. The moment of self-directed contempt at his own inability to stand detached from the pain he is either still undergoing, or has already gone through, also stands in for its own infinite recurrence; and for the dimly perceived recognition from within the coils of personal agony that the subjective perspective mutates eventually into the detached external perspective'; *Proustian Passions: The Uses of Self-Justification for* A la recherche du temps perdu (Oxford: Oxford University Press, 2000), p. 182.

69 Other prominent features of *Albertine disparue* include the relatively few references to spiritualism (twelve) in comparison with other volumes of the novel (twenty in *Le Côté de Guermantes* and twenty-two in *Sodome et Gomorrhe*). However, as Table 4 shows, eleven out of the twelve are literal references to spiritualist practice, whereas the higher number of references in this thematic category in other parts of the novel may be attributable to the inclusion of images of ghosts, a common visual descriptor for the narrator.

70 There are 113 unmediated images in comparison with 43 mediated. The terms 'mediated' and 'unmediated' refer to the manner in which sources are introduced into the text. 'Mediated' encompasses, above all, similes introduced by expressions such as 'comme' or 'ainsi que', but also includes direct signalled quotation (whether signalled by italics or inverted commas) and all 'moderated' images or comparative statements, introduced by, for example, 'ressemblait à', 'pareil à', 'faisait penser à', etc. 'Unmediated' refers mainly to metaphor in the form of direct substitution as between tenor and vehicle. It also includes unquoted (unsignalled) quotation and metaphorical adjectives: the phrase 'le fauteuil magique' (*S* I 5), for example, constitutes an unmediated image.

71 *Swann* (4:1), *Jeunes filles* (5.5:1) and *Temps retrouvé* (6.5:1) follow this pattern of distribution. *Sodome* marks a slight departure, with a ratio of approximately 2:1. This is, in large part, attributable to the many literal evocations of Wagner, *Parsifal* and *Pelléas et Mélisande* in this volume of socially-inspired musical discussion.

72 See, for instance, *SG* III 353–4, where M. de Cambremer introduces an albeit unsophisticated image in order to set his fearsome ancestors in opposition to La Fontaine's 'bâtons flottants'. This is discussed in Part II of the study. See below, p. 186, n. 32.

73 Coupe, *Myth*, pp. 196–7. Albouy also highlights the playful and/or ironic currents that underline modern myth (see 'Quelques images', p. 987).

## I MAGIC AND FAIRYTALE

1 See, for example, *JF* II 93, where Saint-Loup is contrasted with the narrator on the grounds that the former favours only what is endowed with intellectual weight whereas the latter is able to see magic in the trivial. Saint-Loup is described as: 'Ne jugeant chaque chose qu'au poids d'intelligence qu'elle contient, ne percevant pas les enchantements d'imagination que me donnaient certaines [choses] qu'il jugeait frivoles [...]'.

2 On the death of the narrator's grandmother, for instance, his mother is described in the cemetery as an 'apparition surnaturelle' (*G* II 639); the term is also frequently introduced in relation to Mme de Guermantes. See, for example, *G* II 343 and 361.

3 Max Lüthe, *The Fairytale as Art Form and Portrait of Man*, trans. Jon Erikson (Bloomington: Indiana University Press, 1984), p. 11. Proust may not remove class divisions, as Lüthe's analysis appears to do in equating the king to mankind in general, but the Proustian fairytale nonetheless plays with class boundaries in a manner similar to Perrault's tales.

4 Combray's childhood bliss is tainted by, for example, the anxieties of the 'drame du coucher' and by Françoise's unsuspected brutality, as revealed in her slaughter of the chicken (*S* I 120), while even the joyous epiphanies of involuntary memory and the narrator's realization of their significance for his vocation are darkened by fears over his ability to bring this project to fruition.

5 See above, pp. 4–12.

6 Françoise's lack of compassion for the kitchen maid and intensity of empathy for suffering in the abstract are almost comical in their simultaneity and provide the perfect illustration of this coexistence (*S* I 121). Many other characters in the novel betray a similar coincidence of opposites: we witness, for example, Saint-Loup's generosity of spirit towards the narrator and vicious complicity in a plot to have a servant dismissed (*AD* IV 53); Charlus's blend of masculinity and femininity is well documented, but less noted are his haughty, often biblically inspired comments which combine, in the perfect example of Lüthe's 'magnificent and dirty' tension, with a taste for scatology (see, for example, *G* II 843 for Charlus's combination, in a single comment, of an implicit evocation of the terms of Mark 4: 9 – 'Que celui qui a des oreilles pour entendre, entende' – with scatological mockery of the narrator's confusion regarding styles of furniture: 'Un de ces jours vous prendrez les genoux de Mme de Villeparisis pour le lavabo, et on ne sait pas ce que vous y ferez'). Odette and Albertine also embody extremes of indifference and affection, kindness and cruelty in their treatment of Swann and the narrator respectively.

7 See Lüthe, pp. 161–2, for a summary of Jung's position.

8 Twin sisters feature in both *Riquet à la houppe* and *Petit Poucet*. Moreover, Marc Soriano, in his study of Perrault's tales, explains that, while three sisters appeared in the original version of *La Barbe-Bleue*, Perrault's version reduces the number to two, albeit not twins. See Marc Soriano, *Les Contes de Perrault*:

      *Culture savante et traditions populaires*, Collection Tel 22 (Paris: Gallimard, 1977), p. 170.
9   This is the case in Perrault's *Peau d'Âne*.
10  As if to reflect this fairytale association, Vinteuil's work is also described with reference to fairytale and other supernatural sources. See below, pp. 139–41.
11  Marina Warner, *From the Beast to the Blonde: On Fairy Tales and their Tellers* (London: Vintage, 1995), pp. xv–xvi.
12  Lüthe, p. 137. Lüthe's analysis uses the generic term of 'fairytale hero'. It should, however, be stressed that the fairytale heroine shares many of the same characteristics.
13  Ibid.
14  Mircea Eliade, 'Les Savants et les contes de fées', *Nouvelle Revue Française*, 4 (1956), 884–91 (p. 885).
15  Lüthe, p. 165.
16  See Edward J. Hughes, *Marcel Proust: A Study in the Quality of Awareness* (Cambridge: Cambridge University Press, 1983) for a discussion of the narrator's joy in sensation. As Hughes points out throughout his study, the narrator recognizes the appeal of, and actively seeks out, the immanence of pleasurable experience, as well as forms of pre-intellectual consciousness, believing that they offer an effortless escape from intellectual intricacies and self-doubt: 'sentient experience may allay intellectual scruples' (p. 93).
17  Certainly, by the end of the eighteenth century, editions of Perrault's tales aimed at children did not include the original, macabre follow-up to Sleeping Beauty's awakening and instantaneous, reciprocated love for the prince. Originally, altering in certain respects Basile's version of the tale, the prince's mother, who is 'de race Ogresse', orders her grandchildren cooked for her to eat, ogresses being partial to the flesh of young children. Even in Perrault's original version, however, the prince, though upset when his mother is devoured by the toads, vipers and snakes in the cauldron she had intended for her daughter-in-law and grandchildren, consoles himself with his beautiful wife and children. See Warner, pp. 220–2.
18  Male to female gender-crossing in imagery is a common by-product of Proust's metaphorical presentation of male homosexuality. On the Andromeda image, see my 'Andromeda's Mysterious Saviour: The Absent Hero in Proust's *A la recherche du temps perdu*', *Dalhousie French Studies*, 63 (2003), 53–8.
19  These themes of enclosure and mistrust are, of course, replayed in the narrator's relationship with Albertine. As for Proust's identification of Griselda's 'prison' as a tower, its evident phallic associations introduce a further symbolic marker of male subjugation into both Griselda's and Albertine's experience.
20  The prince-and-pauper theme, which is common to many fairytales, is also a feature of homosexual love in *A la recherche*, e.g. Charlus and Morel; Charlus and the young men in Jupien's brothel; the prince de Guermantes and Morel.
21  For a full discussion of the contemporary understanding of homosexuality as a 'disease', see Julius E. Rivers, *Proust and the Art of Love: The Aesthetics of Sexuality in the Life, Times and Art of Marcel Proust* (New York: Columbia

## Notes

22  University Press, 1980), especially ch. 4, 'The good faith of a chemist'. Ch. 5, 'Homosexuality and personality', also provides an enlightening account of how homosexuality was perceived to be a form of mental illness.

22  Drafts for this passage appear to substantiate such an interpretation, for they relate how, when the neighbour of a homosexual man, with whom he has engaged in a secret, homosexual relationship, finally marries and thus puts an end to these encounters, the man 'remonte dans sa tour *désormais* pur et triste comme Grisélidis' (my italics, III 931).

23  As Christopher Robinson claims: 'Proust's account of homosexuality [. . .] has its roots in contemporary German sexology [. . .] in that it sees homosexuals as "spiritual hermaphrodites".' See his *Scandal in the Ink: Male and Female Homosexuality in Twentieth-Century French Literature* (London: Cassell, 1995), p. 47.

24  Rivers appears to support such a reading when he writes: 'Clearly one side of Proust celebrated homosexual emotion and cultivated it as an important source of inspiration. But another side of Proust – the side conditioned by cultural and societal prejudice – shunned homosexuality as unnatural, degrading, and shameful' (p. 107).

25  See Mothe, ch. 1.

26  One medical theory common at the time Proust was writing the novel was that homosexuals were more likely to indulge in 'depraved' practices such as sadomasochism and pederasty. See Rivers, p. 160.

27  Mothe, p. 124.

28  See above, p. 22.

29  For an analysis of mediated or triangular desire, see René Girard, *Mensonge romantique et vérité romanesque* (Paris: Grasset, 1961). The rhetorical flourish of using three adjectives that peppers Mme de Cambremer's speech offers a further, humorous example of the number's magical potency. See *SG* III 473.

30  As Warner explains, Bluebeard plays a dual role: 'the patriarch whose orders must be obeyed on the one hand, and on the other the serpent who seduces by exciting curiosity and desire and so brings death' (p. 246).

31  A draft for an early evocation of the magic lantern explicitly identifies Bluebeard as one of the characters appearing on it: 'en adaptant à la lampe la lanterne magique, on projetait sur le mur en apparitions bleues, rouges et vertes l'histoire de Barbe-Bleue et de Geneviève de Brabant' (I 662). *Jean Santeuil* also grants Bluebeard an explicit appearance on the magic lantern (p. 316). In keeping with the associations surrounding this character in *A la recherche*, the final version renders his presence more elusive and thus 'forbidden'.

32  Proust's juxtaposition of the narrator's affection for his mother and guilt regarding his own crimes creates an implicit link with Bluebeard's killing of his nearest relative, his wife. This link is only enhanced if we remember the narrator's sense of responsibility, following his grandmother's death, for the pain he caused this other prominent, maternal figure. See, for example, *SG* III 155.

33  As Bruno Bettelheim explains: 'The key that opens the door to a secret room suggests associations to the male sexual organ, particularly in first intercourse

when the hymen is broken and blood gets on it': *The Uses of Enchantment: The Meaning and Importance of Fairy Tales* (London: Penguin, 1991 [1975]), pp. 300–1. Warner also relates how 'in many illustrated retellings of the story, the key looms very large indeed, a gigantic forbidden fruit, so engorged and positioned that the allusion can hardly be missed. In Gustave Doré's engraving to Perrault, Bluebeard reveals the forbidden key – of gigantic proportions – to his wife with the leer of a pornographer' (p. 244).

34 Splitter explains how 'men's fascination with the mysteries of childbirth and menstruation (and the bleeding that may accompany a virgin's first sexual relations) is an ancient and widespread cultural phenomenon': *Proust's Recherche: A Psychoanalytic Interpretation* (Boston, London: Routledge, 1981), p. 112.

35 Mothe, p. 35.

36 Charles Perrault, *Contes* (Paris: Gallimard, 1981), pp. 59–60, 62.

37 Mothe offers a more radical interpretation of this tale, seeing it as a story of sexual 'deficiency' and setting out a chain of evidence which identifies Bluebeard's secret as being his impotence: he must, therefore, test his wives to see if they can keep this secret. Mothe argues that Bluebeard, in fact, allows his wife to be unfaithful because of his impotence and, for him, she is ultimately a 'femme-alibi' (p. 16). One important element of Mothe's argument is Bluebeard's name, 'La Barbe-Bleue', for it combines the masculine image of a beard with a feminine article which, although dictated by the gender of 'barbe', is actually the article for his name. We thus find a combination of masculine and feminine elements. Given Proust's conceptualization of the homosexual as an 'homme-femme', we might read this as an attempt to conceal not one's impotence but, rather, one's homosexuality.

38 A further overlap with this fairytale emerges in the transmission of intelligence, or at least knowledge, by the narrator to Albertine, for she gradually comes to mirror the narrator's speech. Of Albertine's excessively stylized ode to ice cream in *La Prisonnière*, for example, he writes: '"Certes je ne parlerais pas comme elle, mais tout de même, sans moi elle ne parlerait pas ainsi, elle a subi profondément mon influence, elle ne peut donc pas ne pas m'aimer, elle est mon œuvre"' (*P* III 636).

39 In this, the narrator is like Bluebeard who, one might argue, is also destroyed by his attempts to deny his wives their individuality. By subjecting them to the same trial, he reduces them to a collective. This de-individualization is only reinforced by the absence of any reference to the wives' names.

40 See Akane Kawakami, 'Stereotype Formation and Sleeping Women: The Misreading of *Madame Chrysanthème*', *Forum for Modern Language Studies*, 38/3 (2002), 278–90, for a discussion of the figure of the sleeping woman in Pierre Loti's *Madame Chrysanthème* and Proust's *La Prisonnière*.

41 Warner describes an edition of Perrault's tales in English (illustrated by Walter Crane) which depicts the heroine of Bluebeard's tale against the explicit biblical backdrop of a wall painting of the temptation in the Garden of Eden (p. 244).

42 See Warner, p. 260.

43  Certain of the many versions of the tale of Sleeping Beauty include references to 'unnatural' practices, e.g. Sleeping Beauty's mother-in-law orders her grandchildren slaughtered and cooked for her to eat (see, for example, Perrault, p. 138). Other versions contain traces of a deviant sexuality: many precursors of Perrault, for instance, present Sleeping Beauty being raped in her sleep, to awaken only after giving birth to one or two of her offspring (see Jacques Barchilon and Peter Flinders, *Charles Perrault*, Twayne World Authors Series 639 (Boston: Twayne, 1981), p. 93; also Soriano, pp. 126–30). Perrault, in contrast, sanitized and moralized this and other tales in keeping with the moral criteria of his age, a project that chimes with the narrator's own imposition of a 'chaster' template of Sleeping Beauty on to Albertine. In Perrault's version, Prince Charming has only to kneel beside Sleeping Beauty in order to awaken her; the entire scenario is thus 'épuré et idéalisé' (Soriano, p. 128). Paul Delarue describes how Perrault tended to omit features which might shock 'le goût, le sens de la mesure, les préjugés ou les idées morales de l'homme de son temps par leur crudité ou leur caractère sauvage ou trop irrationnel': 'Les Contes merveilleux de Perrault et la tradition populaire', *Bulletin folklorique de l'Île-de-France*, January–March (1961), p. 199.

44  The narrator repeatedly describes his isolation from the outside world and inability to engage with it during his imprisonment with Albertine. We read, for example: 'Mais si le surcroît de joie, apporté par la vue des femmes impossibles à imaginer *a priori*, me rendait plus désirables, plus dignes d'être explorés, la rue, la ville, le monde, il me donnait par là même la soif de guérir, de sortir et, sans Albertine, d'être libre. Que de fois, au moment où la femme inconnue dont j'allais rêver passait devant la maison, tantôt à pied, tantôt avec toute la vitesse de son automobile, je souffris que mon corps ne pût suivre mon regard qui la rattrapait et, tombant sur elle comme tiré de l'embrasure de ma fenêtre par une arquebuse, arrêter la fuite du visage dans lequel m'attendait l'offre d'un bonheur qu'ainsi cloîtré je ne goûterais jamais!' (*P* III 537).

45  See Mothe, pp. 91–5. Soriano also explains how, in oral versions of the tale, Little Red Riding Hood performs a kind of 'striptease' (p. 156). After taking off each garment, she asks the wolf where she should put it. This detail is suppressed by the 'bienséant' Perrault.

46  Perrault's tale concludes with Little Red Riding Hood being devoured. Erich Fromm's psychoanalytical reading of *Little Red Riding Hood* identifies the protagonist's cape as a symbol of menstruation and thus the beginnings of womanhood; the warning not to go off the path or drop the basket as a caution against losing her virginity; the wolf as a crafty male, and the 'cannibalistic' act which is his goal as a sexual act in which male devours female. This theory is summarized in Soriano, ibid., p. 47.

47  Marie-Louise von Franz, *An Introduction to the Interpretation of Fairy Tales* (Dallas: Spring Publications, 1970), p. 1.

48  A number of critics have detected complex Freudian resonances in *A la recherche*. See, for example, Randolph Splitter, *Proust's* Recherche; Malcolm Bowie, *Freud,*

*Proust and Lacan: Theory as Fiction* (Cambridge: Cambridge University Press, 1987); and Milton Miller, *Nostalgia: A Psychoanalytic Study of Marcel Proust* (Boston: Houghton Mifflin, 1956).

49   Later, too, Warner describes how fairytales can be 'vehicles for the grimmest realism' (p. 225).

50   Victor Graham, Dominique Jullien and Jean-Yves Tadié have highlighted these thematic and structural parallels, as well as the miraculous transformations undergone by characters throughout *A la recherche*. See V. E. Graham, 'Marcel Proust and the *Mille et Une Nuits*', *Canadian Review of Comparative Literature*, Winter, vol. 1 (1974), 89–96; D. Jullien, *Proust et ses modèles: Les* Mille et Une nuits *et les* Mémoires *de Saint-Simon* (Paris: Corti, 1989); J.-Y. Tadié, *Lectures de Proust* (Paris: Armand Colin, 1971), pp. 224–8. Tadié's principal focus remains the crucial involuntary memories of *Le Temps retrouvé*, however, while the few more recent articles to have addressed the role of the Orient in the novel have tended to concentrate on the fusion of 'ailleurs' and 'ici', to borrow Jullien's model in his article 'Ailleurs ici: Les *Mille et Une Nuits* dans *A la recherche du temps perdu*', *Romanic Review*, 79 (1988), 466–75. Among the fusions discussed are the introduction of 'une subtile bouffée d'exotisme' into 'la francité' of the Guermantes and Combray, 'cette morne province si précautionneusement repliée sur elle-même'; the orientalization of Christian architecture; the role of the Orient in the portrayal of desire; and, ultimately, its appearance in the context of art: Alain Buisine, 'Marcel Proust: le côté de l'Orient', *Revue des Sciences Humaines*, 90 (1989), 123–44, (p. 124). In the final analysis, Jullien links the *Mille et Une Nuits* to the image of the magic lantern, 'le symbole du prisme de l'art qui transforme les choses' ('Ailleurs ici', p. 474). Both Jullien and Buisine extend their exploration beyond specific references to the *Mille et Une Nuits*, devoting considerable attention to more general evocations of the Orient. In this, they offer valuable overviews as well as detailed discussion. However, the sheer interconnectedness of images drawn from the *Mille et Une Nuits*, the often ironic rewritings – even subversions – of the tales, and the role of this collection, in *all* its incarnations, as a marker of, even a catalyst for, the narrator's gradual evolution towards stylistic creation have not been addressed. In order, therefore, to highlight this carefully elaborated design, explicit references to the *Mille et Une Nuits* or to specifically identifiable tales from the collection are the primary focus of attention here. Explicit references by title to the text as a whole or to individual stories within the collection number twenty-seven in total. These are broken down as follows: $S = 3$; $JF = 7$; $G = 1$; $SG = 5$; $P = 3$; $AD = 1$; $TR = 7$.

51   The tale of Ali-Baba is explicitly or identifiably referred to on at least five occasions in the novel: twice in *Swann*, once in *Jeunes Filles*, once in *Guermantes* and once in *Temps retrouvé*; the tale of Aladdin on at least three occasions: once in *Swann*, once in *Jeunes filles*, and once in *Temps retrouvé*; the tale of Sinbad on two occasions: once in *Jeunes filles* and once in *Temps retrouvé*; the tale of the Sleeper Awakened once, in *Jeunes filles*; and the tale of Zobéide once, in *Temps retrouvé*.

52 '[M]a grand-mère [...] croyait d'ailleurs que c'était de vulgaires assiettes achetées dans le pays' (*JF* II 258).

53 Charlus says: 'Naturellement tout cela n'a rien à voir avec le prestige de la princesse de Guermantes, mais, sans moi et mon Sésame, la demeure de celle-ci est inaccessible' (*G* II 853).

54 For example, when reading *François le Champi* to the child narrator, 'elle passait toutes les scènes d'amour' and, although she is 'une lectrice admirable', the narrator also describes his mother as 'une lectrice infidèle' (*S* I 41). Interestingly, Galland's translation of the *Mille et Une Nuits* also involved a considerable amount of sanitization of the origin text. The erotic, the sordid and the ugly, in particular, were edited out. For a full discussion of the differences between the Mardrus and Galland translations, the former of which Proust himself preferred, see Sylvette Larzul, *Les Traductions des 'Mille et Une Nuits': Étude des versions Galland, Trébutien et Mardrus, précédé de 'Traditions, traductions, trahisons' par Claude Bremond* (Paris: L'Harmattan, 1996).

55 Proust may not have had a specific painting featuring both 'un Sénégalais' and 'une odalisque' in mind, but it is interesting to examine those well-known paintings by the artists mentioned which do include such figures. Among the most celebrated are Ingres's *Odalisque à l'esclave* and Delacroix's *Mort de Sardanapale*. The blend of furious, unbridled sensuality and violence which characterizes the latter may arguably provide a more accurate reflection of what we are to discover about Charlus's sexual tastes than the serenity of Ingres's vision. However, even if Proust were thinking only in general terms of certain recurrent icons in orientalist painting, namely odalisques and black slaves rather than a specific pictorial meeting of the two, Charlus's implied gender-crossing is nonetheless significant.

56 The fact that the character played by the narrator in this scene, the caliph, is also in disguise has been interpreted by Tadié as a symbol of the narrator's conscious or unconscious concealment of his true identity, his 'moi profond', a phrase strongly associated by Proust with the creative self. Thus, the *Mille et Une Nuits* is again drawn in as the implicit but recurrent marker of the narrator's evolution towards creation. See Tadié, p. 225.

57 *Le Livre des Mille Nuits et Une Nuit, Traduction littérale et complète du texte arabe par le Dr J. C. Mardrus*, 16 vols (Paris: Charpentier et Fasquelle, 1899–1904), vol. 13, p. 295.

58 See Barchilon and Flinders, p. 96.

59 Hints of a deflation of the cult of technology are also present in the 'demoiselles du téléphone' passage. See *G* II 432.

60 William C. Carter, *The Proustian Quest* (NY, London: New York University Press, 1992), p. 8.

61 Ibid., p. 9.

62 Jean-Didier Urbain, '*I travel, therefore I am*: The "Nomad Mind" and the Spirit of Travel', trans. Charles Forsdick, *Studies in Travel Writing* 4 (2000), 141–64, (p. 156). Urbain further notes how 'Mobility is a physical movement, whereas travel, before it chooses a specific place, is above all an idea' (p. 155).

63 'L'Ogre qui se trouvait fort las du long chemin qu'il avait fait inutilement (car les bottes de sept lieues fatiguent fort leur homme), voulut se reposer, et par hasard il alla s'asseoir sur la roche où les petits garçons s'étaient cachés. [. . .] Le petit Poucet s'étant approché de l'Ogre lui tira doucement ses bottes, et les mit aussitôt. Les bottes étaient fort grandes et fort larges; mais comme elles étaient Fées, elles avaient le don de s'agrandir et de s'apetisser selon la jambe de celui qui les chaussait [. . .]' (Perrault, pp. 198–9).

64 See above, p. 22.

65 When M. d'Argencourt laughs at her wit, for example, she looks at him 'd'un air câlin, pour ajouter l'enchantement de la douceur à celui de l'esprit' (*G* II 526).

66 See, for instance, *G* II 343 and *G* II 361.

67 By way of explanation of the quotation, the narrator has just been suggesting that there are a limited number of human types, such that he sees people he knows embodied in others. Legrandin appears to have been transformed into a waiter, Swann's concierge into a passing stranger, and so on. The latter become imitations of the former; Mme de Villeparisis is, in contrast, the authentic original, 'la véritable'.

68 *Le nouveau petit Robert* defines 'fée' as an 'être imaginaire de forme féminine auquel la légende attribue un pouvoir surhumain et une influence sur la destinée des humains' (Paris: Le Robert, 1993).

69 *Le Chat botté* tells the story of the youngest of a miller's three sons who inherits only a cat. When threatened with being eaten by the starving son, the cat requests nothing but a knapsack, a pair of boots and a little time. The wily cat then creates a series of situations which give the king of those lands the impression that his master is a man of great wealth. The story ends with the king offering the miller's son (whom he believes to be a marquis) his daughter's hand in marriage.

70 See Bettelheim, p. 40.

71 In Perrault's *Cendrillon*, for example, the fairy godmother is the heroine's dead mother. Warner's analysis confirms that fairies often appear in fairytales *in loco matris* (p. 232).

72 See Bettelheim, p. 307. He continues, by way of explanation: 'This story suggests Beauty's oedipal attachment to her father not only by her asking him for a rose, but also by our being told in detail how her sisters went out enjoying themselves at parties and having lovers while Beauty always stayed home and told those who courted her that she was too young to marry and wanted "to stay with her father a few years longer". Since Beauty joins the Beast only out of love for her father, she wishes to have an asexual relation with it' (ibid.).

73 The narrator's own mother is presented as too 'sacred' a figure to advise on such matters. Indeed, both the narrator's mother and grandmother retain an aura of asexual purity.

74 Mothe identifies 'la carence parentale' which runs throughout Perrault's stories as the ultimate source of the 'perversion' they highlight, perversion for Mothe

meaning 'un détournement, un retournement de l'ordre moral, social et religieux, et de toutes les règles' (p. 187). The result of this 'carence parentale' is a failure to resolve the Oedipal complex which, once resolved, re-establishes order.

75 The interconnection of the fairy's actions and social considerations is already present in *Sleeping Beauty* where the evil fairy curses the heroine because she feels she has been snubbed by not being invited to the banquet organized to celebrate Beauty's birth.

76 To give but a few examples of how social barriers are transgressed in fairytale, Cinderella, the lowly kitchen maid, marries the prince, as does Donkeyskin who, although originally a princess, is forced to flee and, like Cinderella, become a kitchen maid because of her father's incestuous desire for her. See Edward J. Hughes, 'Proust and Social Spaces', in *The Cambridge Companion to Proust*, ed. Richard Bales (Cambridge: Cambridge University Press, 2001), pp. 151–67, for a discussion of Proust's subversion of this tribalism by metaphorically 'calling up colonial spaces and transforming the culture of the revered aristocratic subject into that of its traditionally denigrated Oriental counterpart' (p. 159).

77 The intricate elaboration on the experience of falling asleep and, indeed, awakening with which the novel opens is prompted by the experience of falling asleep while reading: 'Que s'il s'assoupit dans une position encore plus déplacée et divergente, par exemple après dîner dans un fauteuil, alors le bouleversement sera complet dans les mondes désorbités, le fauteuil magique le fera voyager à toute vitesse dans le temps et dans l'espace, et au moment d'ouvrir les paupières, il se croira couché quelques mois plus tôt dans une autre contrée' (*S* I 5). The seed is thus sown from this early stage that art has the power to transport one into different worlds, to open up new vistas. Mme de Guermantes's comment on Mme de Sainte-Euverte's refusal to miss a party provides the ironic counterpart, within the same metaphorical paradigm, to this aesthetic context: 'Si celle-ci [une fête] avait eu lieu à la campagne, elle serait montée sur une tapissière [*sic*] plutôt que de ne pas y être allée' (*SG* III 69).

78 The image of the pleasurable escape of sleep/reluctance to awaken also acquires a more complex undercurrent when viewed in conjunction with the metaphorical significance of the tale of *Sleeping Beauty*, discussed previously.

79 As he writes in *Le Temps retrouvé*, 'Comment la littérature de notations aurait-elle une valeur quelconque, puisque c'est *sous* de petites choses comme celles qu'elle note que la réalité est contenue [. . .] et qu'elles sont sans signification par elles-mêmes si on ne l'en dégage pas?' (*TR* IV 473, my italics). Françoise Leriche has argued against critical identifications of Proust as an Impressionist writer, convincingly proposing that the novel contains an 'art nouveau' aesthetic. See her 'Proust, An "Art Nouveau" Writer?', in Armine Kotin Mortimer and Katherine Kolb (eds), *Proust in Perspective: Visions and Revisions* (Urbana: University of Illinois Press, 2002), pp. 189–212. Luzius Keller has also pushed Proust 'au-delà de l'impressionnisme' towards Cubism. See his 'Proust au-delà de l'impressionnisme', in Sophie Bertho (ed.), *Proust et ses peintres* (Amsterdam:

Rodopi, 2000), pp. 57–70. An indication of the vitality of Proust's visual world, elements of all can, indeed, be detected in the novel.

80 Quoted in Luc Fraisse, *L'Esthétique de Marcel Proust* (Paris: SEDES, 1995), p. 39.

81 'Le seul véritable voyage, le seul bain de Jouvence, ce ne serait pas d'aller vers de nouveaux paysages, mais d'avoir d'autres yeux, de voir l'univers avec les yeux d'un autre, de cent autres, de voir les cent univers que chacun d'eux voit, que chacun d'eux est' (P III 762).

82 See, for example, J. Theodore Johnson, 'The Painter and his Art in the Works of Marcel Proust' (doctoral dissertation, University of Wisconsin, 1964); M. E. Chernowitz, *Proust and Painting* (New York: International University Press, 1945).

83 Although this description contains no explicit reference to fairytale, the image of transportation nonetheless draws it into this metaphorical web by association with the evocations of flying carpets and armchairs that elsewhere transport the narrator from one place or time to another. See above, p. 65.

84 The number one, for Lüthe, implies isolation or the individual and the number two suggests either equality or confrontation/polarity (p. 44).

85 In *Le Côté de Guermantes*, too, one of Elstir's paintings is vaguely described as follows: 'Cette fête au bord de l'eau avait quelque chose d'enchanteur' (G II 713).

86 The distribution per volume of the terms 'enchanter', 'enchantement', 'enchanteur' and their derivatives is as follows: $S = 15$; $JF = 24$; $G = 24$; $SG = 19$; $P = 14$; $AD = 3$; $TR = 15$. The pattern with 'charme', 'charmer', 'charmant' and their derivatives reveals the following: $S = 92$; $JF = 115$; $G = 126$; $SG = 82$; $P = 52$; $AD = 45$; $TR = 52$.

87 An examination of a variety of metaphorical sources identifies this volume as pivotal. On Proust's handling of Christian and mythological figures of speech in *La Prisonnière*, see my *Proust's Gods: Christian and Mythological Figures of Speech in the Works of Marcel Proust* (Oxford: Oxford University Press, 2000), pp. 58–63, 150–6.

88 See below, pp. 142–4, for the images of charms, enchantment and magic that characterize his early appreciation of the artist.

89 Warner, p. xvii.

## II ARTISTIC LEGENDS: PERFORMANCE, MUSIC AND TEXT

1 Speaight charts how Pulcinella first appeared as a character in Italian puppet theatre in 1618. Although in Italy, 'Pulcinella may have been one amongst many puppets [. . .], in France, in the early years of the seventeenth century, he assumed, for the first time in all their glory, the fantastic shapes that we know today, and was hailed Polichinelle, the chief hero of the marionette stage'. See George Speaight, *Punch and Judy: A History* (London: Studio Vista, 1970), pp. 12, 20. In other

words, despite minor variations, Polichinelle has survived for five centuries in the form in which we know him.
2. André Guyau's brief article, 'Proust et la fable', addresses the latter, but only to the extent that it highlights the limited instances in the novel where Proust appears to have created a mini-fable in the style of La Fontaine. Attention is drawn, for example, to the overt or implied morals which accompany certain anecdotes. The article does not, however, explore the role and significance of Proust's explicit handling of La Fontaine's fables. See A. Guyau, 'Proust et la fable', *Bulletin de la société des amis de Marcel Proust*, 18 (1978), 685–9.
3. Prominent among these studies are: Thomas Donnan, 'Wagnerian and Proustian composition'; Margaret Mein, 'Proust and Wagner'; Jean-Jacques Nattiez, *Proust as Musician*; and Jean-Marc Rodrigues, 'Genèse du wagnérisme proustien', *Romantisme: revue du 19ème siècle*, 17/57 (1987), 75–88. Their individual contributions are detailed in the relevant section.
4. Speaight, p. 16.
5. *Le Côté de Guermantes* contains eight puppet images, while in *Le Temps retrouvé* there are six images drawn from this source. Although 'Polichinelle' and 'Guignol' refer to two quite distinct puppet-show characters – Guignol, a character originating in Lyons, was a more sympathetic, more naturalistic, less bizarre figure than Polichinelle (see Speaight, p. 143) – 'guignol' is often used as a generic term for the Punch and Judy show, and there is little evidence that Proust distinguishes between the two in his images (for a possible exception, see below, n. 11).
6. Babies thrown out of windows, wife-beating and hangings are stock events in the Punch and Judy show, while, to give just one example from the circus, the clowns' performance is based on comic injury and misfortune.
7. Heinrich von Kleist, 'On the Marionette Theatre' (1810), trans. Idris Parry, http://southerncrossreview.org/9/kleist.htm. It is not certain whether Proust knew Kleist's essay. It nonetheless provides a suggestive interpretative template for the narrator's handling of the metaphor of puppet theatre.
8. Indeed, it is precisely by recalling a young man repeating several times his attempt to mirror the pose of a classical sculpture, a feat he had initially achieved entirely unconsciously, that Kleist comes to appreciate the validity of Mr C.'s argument: 'He [. . .] raised his foot a second time to prove it to me [the fact that his pose mirrored that of the sculpture], but the attempt [. . .] did not succeed. Confused, he raised his foot a third and fourth time; he must have raised it ten times more: in vain! He was unable to produce the same movement again. And the movements that he made had so comical an effect that I could hardly suppress my laughter'. The interaction of the voluntary and involuntary here is itself striking. For Bergson's evocation of puppetry, see Henri Bergson, *Le Rire: Essai sur la signification du comique* (Paris: Presses Universitaires de France, 1975).
9. Speaight, p. 78. Speaight identifies fourteen stock characters in the Punch and Judy show and its slight variants throughout Europe, although, of these, only a small number appear frequently in encounters with Punch, notably Judy, the Devil and the policeman (see ibid., pp. 85–92).

10   Bergson, p. 60. It is surely significant that of the seven metaphorical evocations of puppet theatre to appear in *Le Côté de Guermantes*, six are mediated images. Only one is an unmediated metaphor. The repeated choice of a mediated rather than an unmediated image serves to underline the deliberateness of the illusion and to draw attention to its artificiality.

11   Although Proust appears to make little distinction between Polichinelle and Guignol, the insistence of Polichinelle's voice here may nonetheless serve to emphasize the negative and threatening aspects of the puppet show.

12   See above, pp. 65–6.

13   Proust here seems to have in mind a silent form of puppet theatre. However, puppet theatre, in its various forms, is characterized not only by movement, but also by sound. Bil Baird explains: 'Equally important to the illusion [as movement] is sound. A very great part of the puppet is the music he works to, or the voice he emits. And his voice can be as much an evocation as his movements. Aside from the hundreds of word languages that people use, a puppet can speak with sighs, roars, coughs; through buzzers, poundings on the floor, bells on the ankles of the operators, and the sounds of instruments': *The Art of the Puppet* (New York: Macmillan, 1965), p. 14. If not silent, therefore, puppet theatre can certainly be non-verbal. In any case, the significance of Proust's image and intention, based on an opposition of bavardage and silence (or the non-verbal), remains.

14   An early example is his non-verbalized outburst of unmitigated joy when contemplating the effects of sun and rain on the natural world while on a childhood walk near Monjouvain: '"Zut, zut, zut, zut"' (*S* I 153).

15   'Et c'est avec une stupéfaction presque désobligeante, où il entrait de la curiosité indiscrète, de la cruauté, un retour à la fois quiet et soucieux sur soi-même (mélange à la fois de *suave mari magno* et de *memento quia pulvis*, eût dit Robert), que tous les regards s'attachèrent à ce visage [. . .]' (*SG* III 89).

16   This is not to suggest that Swann experiences no moments of transcendent insight. On listening to Vinteuil's Sonata, at both Mme Verdurin's and Mme de Sainte-Euverte's, he experiences the promise of an existence beyond everyday reality; he senses that art has the power to overcome time but, crucially, he never takes the final step of becoming a creator himself. His appreciation of Vinteuil's music, itself hopelessly intertwined with his feelings for Odette, thus marks out his spiritual high-point as a vicariously created one. See *S* I 205–8 and *S* I 339–47.

17   It should be noted that, at certain periods in its history, Guignol has been seen as a socially engaged character. Given that some of the plots dealt with social injustices against the poor, he was viewed in the late nineteenth century as 'a champion of the urban working class, sharing its fate and its ambition': Hendryk Jurkowski, *A History of European Puppetry: From its Origins to the End of the 19th Century* (Lewiston, Queenston, Lampeter: Edwin Mellen, 1996), p. 314. However, by the time Proust was writing, puppet theatre had come to be seen as a children's, rather than an adults', entertainment (ibid., p. 320). As discussed in the introduction, La Fontaine's fables, in contrast, have a more serious

function, for their aim is dual: they must not only 'plaire', but also 'instruire'. See above, p. 5.

18 Victor Graham makes only a fleeting reference to La Fontaine's fables in *The Imagery of Proust*, Language and Style Series 2 (Oxford: Blackwell, 1966), p. 154. Like other critics, he has neglected their role as metaphorical signposts to the narrator's development.

19 Reimer Faber, 'The Apostle and the Poet: Paul and Aratus', *Clarion*, 42/13 (1993), http://spindleworks.com/library/rfaber/aratus.htm.

20 See my *Proust's Gods*, pp. 116–19, for a discussion of the ironies implicit in Swann's association of Odette with the figures in these paintings.

21 'Then Paul stood in the midst of Mars' hill, and said, Ye men of Athens, I perceive that in all things ye are too superstitious. For as I passed by, and beheld your devotions, I found an altar with this inscription, TO THE UNKNOWN GOD. Whom therefore ye ignorantly worship, him declare I unto you' (Acts 17: 22–3, King James version).

22 See 'Notes et variantes', III 1518. This suggestion is made in relation to M. de Cambremer's use of the fable when, in the context of a discussion of etymologies with the 'clan Verdurin', he says: 'Vous parlez de grenouilles. Moi, en me trouvant au milieu de personnes si savantes, je me fais l'effet de la grenouille devant l'aréopage' (*SG* III 317).

23 *Fables*, Hachette edition, p. 47. All references are to this edition unless otherwise stated.

24 'Elle allégua pourtant les délices du bain, / La curiosité, le plaisir du voyage, / Cent raretés à voir le long du marécage: / Un jour il conteroit à ses petits-enfans / Les beautés de ces lieux, les mœurs des habitans, / Et le gouvernement de la chose publique / Aquatique' (p. 71). The theme of having experiences that one can subsequently narrate re-emerges in 'Les Deux Pigeons'. See below, pp. 89–90.

25 See *S* I 224–8.

26 One might argue, for example, that Swann's literal death is preceded by a figurative one.

27 La Fontaine's 'Le Lièvre et les Grenouilles' is another possible source here. It recounts how the hare is astonished to find that the frogs are afraid of him, having just been considering how fear inhibits him. The moral explains: 'Il n'est, je le vois bien, si poltron sur la terre, / Qui ne puisse trouver un plus poltron que soi' (p. 34).

28 The increasing importance, within the development of the novel, of the Ambassadress of Turkey's role as a symbolic trigger for the narrator's growing social cynicism and, ultimately, the narrator/writer's generic experimentation is underlined by the fact that she represents a relatively late addition to the manuscript, only appearing, as Alison Finch discusses, 'between the first and third Gallimard galleys'. See Alison Winton [Finch], *Proust's Additions: The Making of* A la recherche du temps perdu, 2 vols (Cambridge: Cambridge University Press, 1977), p. 258. Finch notes how, 'given her scandal-mongering

tendencies in slightly later additions, she is now dangerous to listen to, being always mistaken and in the habit of telling tales "qui semblent sortir d'un livre, non à cause de leur sérieux, mais de leur invraisemblance" (II 534c); she not only reintroduces the slander about M. de Luxembourg but insists that the duc de Guermantes is an invert [. . .]; and she reappears in an addition to *Le Temps retrouvé* as a paradigm of all who are most prone to accept rumour, and most forgetful of what has once been affirmed (III 971–72a, p. 971). The scandal just mentioned about M. de Luxembourg, and the young man himself, are, too, entirely new in the novel: the whole "épidémie" of malicious stories about him (II533–34a), and Marcel's protests, appear only as insertions on the third Gallimard galleys, and although the last of them assures us that: "J'étais intimement persuadé que toutes les histoires relatives à M. de Luxembourg étaient pareillement fausses [. . .]. La suite montrera que c'était moi qui avais raison" (II 537–40a), the reader never learns what this "suite" is' (ibid., pp. 258–9). This chimes with the general pattern, noted by Finch, whereby late additions to the drafts of the novel intensified the presence of ambiguity and uncertainty.

29  This is not the only La Fontaine fable to be referred to by the Ambassadress. Of her failed desire to appear to be an intimate of the lofty friends and family of the Guermantes, we read how 'L'ambassadrice était obligée d'avouer que son *exemple était tiré d'animaux plus petits*' (G II 824, my italics). The italicized phrase opens La Fontaine's 'La Colombe et la Fourmi' which shares its moral with the preceding 'Le Lion et le Rat': 'Il faut, autant qu'on peut, obliger tout le monde: / On a souvent besoin d'un plus petit que soi' (p. 31). Both tales show how the tide may turn in such a way that the great must rely on the small. The reference, appearing in a conversation with the Guermantes, may therefore be interpreted as a subtle herald of the shifts in the social hierarchy that occur in the novel. In *La Prisonnière*, Brichot quotes the same phrase in unworldly self-deprecation beside the baron de Charlus. See *P* III 833.

30  We note that animals link the dual focus of his activities: hunting and reading La Fontaine's fables.

31  The fable exposes man's arrogance and lack of appreciation of the benefits he enjoys. This is symbolized, in the narrative, by his ingratitude towards the cow, the ox and the tree, despite the food and shelter they provide. When forced to confront the reality of his ingratitude by a snake he has caught, the man kills it.

32  M. de Cambremer does, though, seem sufficiently familiar with this tale to use it appositely in a metaphorical context. For example, when giving a lesson in his family history to the Verdurins and wishing to depict his ancestors as fearsome warriors, he claims that '[ils] n'avaient rien des bâtons flottants du bon La Fontaine' (*SG* III 353–4). The repetition of the falsely intimate '[le] bon La Fontaine', also used in *SG* III 316–17, nonetheless betrays his too eager desire to appear familiar with the world of literature.

33  *Fables*, Gallimard edition, p. 26.

34  For a discussion of these features, see Biard, in particular chapter 2, 'The Style of the Fables – Richness, Vigour and Freedom' (pp. 35–78) and chapter 4, 'Humour' (pp. 93–126).

35 Other artists are associated with La Fontaine's Fables in the *Esquisses*. Bergotte, for example, quotes from 'Le Jardinier et son Seigneur' (see I 1391–2), and an early version of the young narrator's desire to see La Berma's performance of the role of Phèdre notes that the actress will also be reciting La Fontaine's 'Les Animaux malades de la peste' (I 1002). That neither fable, in its substance, offers a symbolic marker for the narrator may explain their omission from the final version. However, the presence of the former fable in a novel much admired by Proust, *La Chartreuse de Parme*, may point to Stendhal's influence on Proust's introduction of La Fontaine's work more generally. Significantly, 'Le Jardinier et son Seigneur' is introduced by the character Gina in order to try to dissuade Prince Ernest-Ranuce V from acting on the accusations of Rassi in the matter of his father's death. La Fontaine's fable, which Gina asks the princess to read aloud to both her and the prince, is marked out, in other words, as a possible model for imitation. See Stendhal, *La Chartreuse de Parme*, in *Romans et nouvelles*, Bibliothèque de la Pléiade (Paris: Gallimard, 1952), p. 425.

36 Proust's ambivalent, but nonetheless sympathetic, portrait of homosexuality offers one such example. See above, pp. 30–1. See also Malcolm Bowie's rethinking of the moral architecture of *A la recherche* in *Proust Among the Stars* (London: HarperCollins, 1998). Bowie argues that 'Proust's narrator, while being at times a disinterested spectator at the scene of moral action, and at others an empty space in which his fellow characters acquire, deploy and transform their individualities, is also a moral activist in his own right. He is a *moraliste* in the manner of La Rochefoucauld and La Bruyère; an unsystematic moral philosopher in the manner of Victor Cousin (1792–1867); a *moralisateur* at moments in the manner of Molière's Tartuffe or Alceste. He is not only a moral theorist but one who monitors the language of theory and brings to the words in which moral judgements are expressed a tireless philological curiosity' (p. 176). And yet, the novel is 'seldom detained by Proust's critics for further questioning on moral matters. The narrator is an introspective psychologist of unusual virtuosity; an art critic; a cultural, scientific and political commentator, and a historian of manners' (p. 177).

37 The selflessness of the narrator's grandmother offers a clear picture of virtue, while, to give just one example, the duc and duchesse de Guermantes' unfeeling reaction to Swann's revelation regarding his terminal illness requires no overt comment from the writer for us to appreciate that the scene is, nonetheless, an indictment of vice. See G II 882–4.

38 It could be argued that Rachel's performance seems absurd only in the eyes of an audience as yet unable to appreciate it and that Proust is implicitly encouraging a freshness of vision here by portraying an innovative artist defamiliarizing the familiar. The idea that it takes time for the genius of certain artists to be recognized is a recurrent theme in the novel, including in the context of Rachel's performance, where Proust humorously exposes people's uncertainty as to how to react: 'Tel, en écoutant l'actrice, chacun attendait, la tête baissée et l'œil investigateur, que d'autres prissent l'initiative de rire ou de critiquer, ou de pleurer ou d'applaudir' (*TR* IV 577). However, in the final analysis, it would seem that

Rachel is not placed in the category of misunderstood genius. Not only does the narrator realize that, throughout her performance, Rachel's attention is divided – she is constantly trying to catch his eye – but he also concludes that 'le temps qui passe n'amène pas forcément le progrès dans les arts [. . .] la Berma était, comme on dit, à cent piques au-dessus de Rachel, et le temps, en la mettant en vedette en même temps qu'Elstir, avait surfait une médiocrité et consacré un génie' (*TR* IV 580–1).

39  Malcolm Bradbury, *Possibilities: Essays on the State of the Novel* (Oxford: Oxford University Press, 1973), p. 4.

40  Margaret Mein highlights the broad correspondence between the narrator's and Parsifal's endeavours: 'It is possible to see in both *Parsifal* and *La Recherche* a progression towards perfect redemption, whether achieved by faith or art' (p. 212).

41  Mike Ashman, 'A Very Human Epic', in *Parsifal*, Opera Guide Series 34 (London: John Calder; NY: Riverrun, 1986), p. 14. All references to the libretto are from this edition.

42  Gurnemanz explains how: 'you know that here no other / save pure in heart, as brother / may enter; to those who work the will of Heaven / the Grail's most wondrous might is given. / So, it was to him, of whom you ask, denied, / Klingsor, though eagerly and long he tried. [. . .] Unable to kill the sinful, raging lust within him, / his hand upon himself he turned / to gain the Grail for which he yearned, / and by its guardian he with scorn was spurned' (ibid., pp. 90–1).

43  As discussed below, in Act 2 of the opera, Klingsor conjures up a beautiful garden peopled with flower maidens in an attempt to distract Parsifal from his goal.

44  See Dieter Borchmeyer in ibid., p. 20.

45  The necessity for the narrator to detach himself from maternal influence is discussed in more detail in the final part of this book. See the discussion of 'Spiritualism' and 'Magic and the occult'.

46  Certain critics have seen *Parsifal* as a fairytale-type narrative. Holloway describes it as a kind of 'super-charged fairy-tale. Klingsor, Amfortas and Parsifal – they are like the three wishes where only the third, restoring the *status quo antes*, gets it right; or the three sons, where only the youngest is wily (in this case dumb) enough to avoid his elders' mistakes and win the girl (in this case the Grail)': Robin Holloway, 'Experiencing Music and Imagery in *Parsifal*', in *Parsifal*, p. 41. We might add to this that Parsifal is, like the fairytale hero, a character removed from the world. We discover, for example, that his mother tried to isolate him from the harsh realities of weapons and warfare: 'To save her son from dying /as his father perished, far from arms / and people, as simple fool she raised him' (ibid., p. 94); and yet Parsifal feels compelled to separate himself from home and family and embark on adventures.

47  See the description of the princesse de Guermantes in the 'baignoire' episode, *G* II 340–1, for further examples.

48  The fact that, in Wagner's opera, the Flower Maidens are banished, chimes with the process of disillusionment charted in *Le Côté de Guermantes*. See *Parsifal*, p. 110.

⁴⁹ This is discussed below, p. 106.
⁵⁰ See, for example, G II 330–1, where the Guermantes' dinner-party acquires the status of a Eucharistic celebration and the invitees are transformed into sculptural re-creations of the original participants in the Last Supper. See *Parsifal*, Act 1 Scene 2, for the dramatization of the Knights' sacred mass. In a description that would be as fitting for the Guermantes as for the Knights of the Grail, Gerd Rienäcker explains of the Grail Brethren of the early part of the opera that, 'it is only in ritual that the community of the knights of the Grail finds and preserves its cohesive strength', but this ritual represents no more than a 'façade of power' (p. 60).
⁵¹ Ashman, p. 12.
⁵² Critics such as Nattiez and Mein have highlighted the parallels between Kundry and the women loved in *A la recherche*. Mein, for example, focuses in particular on Odette, arguing that: 'The "re-incarnations" of as enigmatic a Wagnerian character as the ambivalent Kundry foreshadow the successive "incarnations" of Odette, whom Proust finds equally dual in her association with the transcendental purity of Parsifal on one hand, and the magic of Klingsor on the other. This he conveys in an ironical vein, not without nostalgia, by the two diametrically opposed metaphors of Heaven and Hell respectively, as when, in a manner reminiscent of William Blake, he presents as follows the tiny waiting-room of Mme Swann, with its mutually contrasting fire and "boules-de-neige"; the former by a constant process of "transmutation", with strong overtones of alchemy, reminding the narrator of Klingsor's laboratory, while the latter, said to find themselves "exilé[es] dans l'imparfait du petit salon", inspire the Narrator with such a nostalgia for the country that, through magic of a higher order, they enable him to regain the "Paradise Lost" of Combray, simply by reminding him of a fact of supreme importance to Proust, namely that "L'Enchantement du Vendredi Saint figure un miracle naturel auquel on pourrait assister tous les ans si l'on était plus sage" (*RTP*, I, 635)' (p. 210). The ironic dimension of the analogy could be developed. While the young narrator/protagonist may be filled with nostalgia on considering the 'boules-de-neige', an ironic edge nonetheless intrudes to imply that these symbols of purity are misplaced in Odette's ante-room – '*exilé[es] dans l'imparfait du petit salon*' (my italics). It is as if they generate an impression of purity that does not quite convince. We are reminded of Swann's attempts to impose an identity characterized by purity on to Odette by appreciating her beauty in relation to Botticelli's *Madonna of the Magnificat* or to the pastoral simplicity of Zipporah in the *Life of Moses*. Nattiez widens the association, claiming that: 'Proust associate[s] Odette – and, with her, all the other temptresses, her daughter Gilberte, Mme de Guermantes, Albertine – with Kundry, the prisoner of the magician Klingsor' (p. 31).
⁵³ The narrator feels guilt, in particular, about the pain caused to his mother and grandmother by his failure to work. Significantly, both Parsifal and Amfortas are also weighed down by guilt at what they believe to be their respective matricide

and patricide. Parsifal believes he has killed his mother because of the grief prompted by his succumbing to distractions: 'Your son, your son was then your murderer! / O fool! Blind and blundering fool! / I wandered away, I could forget you, / mother, I could forget you?' (p. 112).

54 Gurnemanz explains to one of the other Knights: 'Yes, under a curse she well may lie. / Now she lives here, / perhaps renewed, / to atone for guilt she may be driven, / some former guilt still unforgiven. / Though she may serve us but as a penance, / yet the noble band of knights is grateful: / good are her deeds, / from them we can tell: / she helps us . . . / herself as well' (p. 88).

55 Nattiez and Mein have both highlighted the association between the Flower Maidens and the 'jeunes filles'. Mein, for example, comments that 'debate continues as to how far Proust may have owed to the translation of the German compound, "Blumen-mädchen" the very conception of "les jeunes filles en fleurs", these figures rich in poetic ambiguity, and hovering, like an exotic vision, between the two worlds of human beings and plants' (pp. 211–12). However, neither critic develops the significance of this association nor the comic elements of the presentation of the aristocratic 'filles-fleurs' suggested previously.

56 Even though the Flower Maidens' words remain on the level of innuendo, with their references to being 'plucked' and about to 'blossom' (p. 108), they are still more overtly sexually aware than the 'jeunes filles'. Metaphorical sources more commonly drawn on in relation to the 'jeunes filles' include images of the stars. These are discussed in Part III of this book.

57 A succession of Flower Maidens attempt to seduce Parsifal with phrases such as 'Let me for you blossom' (p. 108). Kundry, however, banishes them, calling them 'fast-withering flowers' (p. 110).

58 See *Parsifal*, pp. 104–5, where various phrases are sung either by all the Flower Maidens or by two separate choruses.

59 Indeed, for Mein, Kundry represents 'a veritable synthesis of Time' (p. 210). Andrée is the notable exception to this one-dimensional presentation of the 'jeunes filles'.

60 See *JF* II 149 for the conduct of the 'jeunes filles' on the beach at Balbec. The association between Albertine and Kundry is only reinforced by our earliest visions of them: like Kundry galloping along on her horse ('But look, who's wildly riding here!' (*Parsifal*, p. 85), Albertine is an elusive 'bacchante à bicyclette' (*JF* II 228).

61 See Rienäcker, p. 63. Like the fairytale hero, Parsifal is an isolated figure, detached from home, family and, indeed, memory. When first questioned by Gurnemanz, he is unable to say what his name is, where he came from, who his father is or who sent him into the forest. See *Parsifal*, pp. 93–4.

62 See Carolyn Abbate, p. 54. It is Kundry who reminds Parsifal of his past and who reveals to him that his mother has died of grief at his having left her. To restore the Grail to the Brethren thus presents itself as a possible means for him to 'efface' his 'sinful crime' (ibid., p. 113).

63 Abbate, p. 55.

64 Parsifal's significance as a model for emulation or identification may be appreciated only in retrospect by the narrator/writer. The level of awareness of the narrator/protagonist remains elusive.
65 For a discussion of the parallels between Albertine and Eve, see my *Proust's Gods*, pp. 125–8.
66 See above, p. 97.
67 This is arguably a transformation that the narrator/Parsifal can himself not yet forsee.
68 Ashman, p. 12.
69 Robin Holloway highlights some of the parallels that link the various characters in Wagner's opera. This feature was clearly an important influence on Proust: 'It is obvious that Klingsor is a spoilt Amfortas; that Klingsor's self-willed abstention mirrors Parsifal's involuntary temptation and restraint; that Parsifal re-lives Amfortas's adventure but emerges unscathed; and that Kundry is the unchanging instrument of their various progresses': *Debussy and Wagner* (London: Eulenburg Books, 1979), p. 39.
70 Margaret Mein considers the question of whether 'the Narrator (Parsifal) will be able to bring "salvation" retrospectively to Swann (Amfortas) and thereby to the world of *La Recherche* or the realm of the Grail, each, in its individual way, an "inhuman" world to which Art (religious faith) alone can bring redemption, both "kingdoms" inviting comparison with T. S. Eliot's version of "la terre vaste" or "la terre vaine"' (p. 208).
71 This is traced in Rodrigues's discussion.
72 See, in particular, vol. 1 of Proust's collected correspondence.
73 Rodrigues provides further useful insights into the contemporary taste for Wagner, describing how at the turn of the 1890s, after a slow phase of maturation, enthusiasm for Wagner in Europe 'n'est pas simple épiphénomène de la mode mais l'expression d'un monde qui recherche son salut intellectuel et sa rédemption culturelle [. . .] Peu à peu se dégagent les éléments d'une véritable théologie wagnérienne dont les bases théoriques se réduisent à des considérations confuses sur la morale, la religion, jetées par des littérateurs prenant soin de ne pas toucher à la musique' (p. 76). Rodrigues also shows how, as early as the texts of *Les Plaisirs et les jours*, Proust was distancing himself from this idolatry. 'Les excès de la wagnérolâtrie ne le touchent pas', claims Rodrigues (ibid.). He does, nonetheless, chart Proust's early enthusiasm for *Lohengrin*, evidence of which can be detected as early as 1894 (see ibid.).
74 See, for example, *SG* III 212 for Proust's wonderfully comic description of her 'hypersécrétion salivaire' by means of an association with the Greek orator Demosthenes who is reputed to have cured himself of a speech impediment by declaiming against the sea with his mouth full of pebbles.
75 For an analysis of the thematic and aesthetic parallels between the two operas, see Holloway, *Debussy and Wagner*, in particular, chs 4–6, pp. 60–142.
76 Details of each of these works will be provided in the discussion as appropriate. What follows is essentially a summary of these works, with additions and

modifications where appropriate. It provides a springboard to my final analysis of the subtly divergent models of transcendence presented in Wagner's operas.

77 In proposing an answer to why Proust may have favoured *Tristan* above Wagner's other works, Rodrigues describes how: 'Dégagé du symbolisme complexe et de la ferblanterie de la Tétralogie, *Tristan* met en évidence les liens nécessaires entre le bonheur possible et la souffrance consentie' (p. 86). After *Tristan*, Rodrigues has proposed the following as Proust's preferred operas: *Les Maîtres-Chanteurs*, *L'Or du Rhin* and *Parsifal* (p. 85).

78 See ibid., p. 86. The critic is here quoting Jankélévitch's *La Musique et l'ineffable*.

79 Abbate highlights the structural arches that link Proust's and Wagner's works (p. 49), while also commenting on the fact that Wagner's 'control of shape over long expanses of time was one of his great strengths as a dramatist' (ibid., p. 52).

80 Donnan is, however, careful to distinguish between the musical and textual leitmotiv (a term Proust himself used of the recurrent motifs in his own work), on the grounds that 'when a musical leitmotif recurs, the affect is direct; the verbal leitmotiv requires the intermediary step of conceptualization [because of its reliance on words] – at least until the reader's mind has been conditioned to absorb it on an impressionistic level' (p. 171). For a fuller discussion of how this conditioning occurs, see ibid., pp. 170–3. What is key, however, is that it is through metaphor that literature can approximate music. Mein highlights a similar analogy and power: 'In the presence of such an abundance of closely interwoven *motifs*, particularly when Proust uses the leitmotiv contrapuntally – as he does in the 'drame du coucher', at intervals, from the opening sentence of the novel, right through to the climax, and triumphantly towards the close of *Le Temps retrouvé* – he exemplifies the technique of the "stream of consciousness", in a manner enriched by his understanding of Wagner. The worlds of literature and music fuse, and merge into a grand synthesis of all the arts "metamorphosed into one", like the senses for Baudelaire, such is the power of the leitmotiv – at times indeed "visceral" – and so strongly do we feel ourselves to be betwixt and between worlds; or perhaps music and literature have blended to become one, "Et tout le reste est littérature"' (pp. 205–6).

81 Robert Vigneron, 'Structure de *Swann*: Balzac, Wagner et Proust', *French Review*, 19/6 (1946), 370–84 (p. 373).

82 Ibid., p. 375. Hearing the Septet for the first time, the narrator is pulled between a sense of the familiar and the unfamiliar. He realizes, to quote Vigneron, that 'Par rapport à ce septuor, la sonate n'a été qu'un timide essai, bien frêle auprès du chef-d'œuvre triomphal et complet qui se révèle maintenant' (p. 373). This experience thus becomes 'la seconde étape de l'initiation esthétique du protagoniste. Le doute, qui l'avait troublé l'après-midi, a maintenant fait place à la certitude' (p. 375). See Winton [Finch], for a discussion of how revisions to the drafts for this meditation on *Tristan and Isolde* transformed it from 'a rather disjointed appreciation' to an episode 'firmly linked with Marcel's own development, and, with the posing of the puzzle, given a narrative impetus it previously lacked' (pp. 336–7).

83 For rejecting her embraces, Kundry curses Parsifal to wander and not find Amfortas whom he seeks to heal: 'And though you should escape, and search through / every road in the world, / the path that you seek, / that path you'll never discover: / each road and pathway / that leads from my presence, / I now curse them to you: / Wander! Wander! / Share in my fate! / Wander like me evermore' (p. 116). He will fight 'battles and duels' and, like the narrator of *A la recherche*, pass 'through error and through suffering's pathways' (ibid., p. 120).

84 Saint-Loup comments enthusiastically to the narrator: ' "Et ces sirènes, était-ce assez wagnérien, ce qui du reste était bien naturel pour saluer l'arrivée des Allemands, ça faisait très hymne national [. . .]; c'était à se demander si c'était bien des aviateurs et pas plutôt des Walkyries qui montaient." Il semblait avoir plaisir à cette assimilation des aviateurs et des Walkyries et l'expliqua d'ailleurs par des raisons purement musicales: "Dame, c'est que la musique des sirènes était d'un *Chevauchée*! [. . .]" ' (*TR* IV 338).

85 Ashman, p. 8.

86 Gurnemanz describes how 'grateful, all creation sings, / all things that bloom and pass away; / nature her innocence has won, / all is renewed once more this day' (p. 123). In contrast, the sense of renewal at the 'bal costumé' is experienced only by the narrator.

87 Ashman, p. 8. At the end of the novel, the narrator realizes he must renounce everything, including his health, if he is to fulfil his vocation. See *TR* IV, pp. 618–20.

88 See Ashman, p. 20.

89 Isolde is unfaithful to her husband, King Mark, with Tristan, while Tristan's position as one of Mark's favoured knights adds a further element of taboo to the relationship. It also creates a scenario of triangular desire, as analysed by René Girard (*Mensouge romantique*). See *Tristan and Isolde*, Opera Guide Series 6, published in association with English National Opera and The Royal Opera (London: John Calder; NY: Riverrun, 1983). All references to the libretto are from this edition. The scope of the present analysis prevents a detailed exploration of these thematic parallels, confining itself, instead, to a focus on the model of redemption the opera offers.

90 See John Luke Rose, 'A Landmark in Musical History', in *Tristan and Isolde*, p. 9.

91 Ibid., p. 11.

92 Scruton, pp. 128–9.

93 Ibid., p. 130.

94 Arthur Schopenhauer, *The World as Will and Representation*, trans. E. Payne (Indian Hills, CO.: Falcon Wing's Press, 1958), vol. 1, p. 398.

95 In Act 1 Scene 1, Tristan yearns for night in the following terms: 'Oh, were we but / By night enfolded, / The envious day, / So keen and spiteful, / Yet might keep us apart, / But cheat no longer my heart. / For his empty pomp, / And his glittering lies / Mean nought after night / Has blessed our eyes: / And the flickering glare, / The flash of his lightning / Blind our sight no more. / When for

death's dark night, / Loving, we've yearned, / When all her holy / Secrets are learned: / Then daylight's falsehood, / Fame and might / Praise and renown / That shine so bright / Like motes in sunbeams scattered / Are turned to dust and shattered! / And of daylight's idle burning / All that remains is yearning, / That yearning deep / For holy night, / Where endless and always true, / Love brings laughing delight!' (pp. 70–1).

96 In Act 2 Scene 1, Isolde's scarf is the sign to Tristan that he may draw near, while in Act 3 Scene 1, the shepherd's tune is supposed to warn Tristan of the arrival of Isolde's ship.

97 Albertine's persistent corporeality will be discussed in the final part of this book in the context of spiritualism. See below, pp. 130–41.

98 The role of infidelity, jealousy and consequent spying in both operas also suggests thematic links with *A la recherche*. On the plot and character correspondences between the two operas, see Holloway, *Debussy and Wagner*, ch. 4, '*Pelléas* and *Tristan*', pp. 60–75.

99 The dual image also suggests that religion and science, two of the stages in Frazer's model of human evolution, can coincide.

## III RITUALS AND BELIEFS

1 See above, pp. 89–90.
2 See Introduction, pp. 4–12.
3 See Gustav Jahoda, *The Psychology of Superstition* (London: Penguin, 1969), p. 34. Geoffrey Nelson traces the origins of the term 'spiritualism', as understood in the sense of communication with the spirits of the dead, to 1848. At this time, it was used in relation to the claims of the famous Fox sisters in the United States. See Nelson, *Spiritualism and Society* (London: Routledge, 1969), p. 3. Interest in spiritualism also spread in Europe in the nineteenth century. The Society for Psychical Research was founded in London in 1882 and the *Annales de Sciences Psychiques*, based in Paris, date from 1891. Michel Pierssens argues that Proust uses the language of spiritualism 'avec une cohérence et parfois une technicité insuffisamment aperçues' and that he displays 'plus qu'une connaissance ordinaire du vocabulaire et de l'imagerie spirites': 'Proust et la planchette magique', *Critique: Revue Générale des Publications Françaises et Etrangères*, 44/491 (1988), 320–35 (323). This is further borne out by the present discussion. Pierssens's article centres specifically on how spiritualist images and vocabulary are deployed in order to explore 'la question du "retour" de ce que l'on croit disparu – un ancien "moi", des êtres aimés, les choses autrefois familières' (ibid., p. 322).
4 Françoise Askevis-Leherpeux, *La Superstition* (Paris: Presses Universitaires de France, 1988), p. 41.
5 Ibid., pp. 40–1.
6 See Peter Jones, 'Knowledge and Illusion in *A la recherche du temps perdu*', *Forum for Modern Language Studies*, V/4 (1969), 303–22, for a discussion of the various

obstacles to knowledge present in the novel. Jones cites Proust's own list of obstacles, namely, 'l'amour-propre, la passion, l'intelligence, et l'habitude' (P III 474), adding to it two of his own, memory and imagination (p. 308). These obstacles function, in part, because of erroneous association, for example, 'instances of what we take to be love are in fact instances of egotistical desires [. . .]. The narrator believes that when we are in the emotional state we call love, we confuse the desire for physical possession with the only true form of possession, spiritual or mental possession [. . .] by which he means "knowledge"' (ibid., p. 307).

7 Of course, this is not to say that artistic creation is a genuinely 'scientific' project: the work of art is born of inspiration and an individual philosophical and aesthetic vision. Nonetheless, Proust also stresses the role of the intellect in transforming this vision into the work of art. In this, Proust may have been indirectly influenced by the tenets of Naturalism. Although he rejected Zola's emphasis on 'observation', he is certainly engaging in a form of dialogue with those writers who wanted to acquire the prestige of 'science'.

8 Jahoda also includes in this category animistic beliefs. See pp. 10–16 of his study for a full explanation of these categories.

9 The third category will be explored below, pp. 130–41.

10 Don Lewis, *Religious Superstition Through the Ages* (London, Oxford: Mowbrays, 1975), p. 8.

11 This fine line is in part explained by the fact that religions often adapted and incorporated pagan practices (ibid., p. 43).

12 These interdictions are set out in Exodus 34: 26 and Genesis 32: 32 respectively.

13 Jahoda, p. 122.

14 Ibid., p. 123.

15 Unseasonal weather, for example, is, according to Françoise, 'le restant de la colère de Dieu' (G II 446).

16 Interestingly, the term 'coincidence', as we understand it, was not recorded until the end of the seventeenth century (Jahoda, p. 122).

17 At its most active, Françoise's superstition involves an avoidance of certain objects of fear, e.g. she refuses to answer the telephone out of 'une timidité et une mélancolie ancestrales' (*P* III 661).

18 The terms are those of E. A. Wallis Budge in *Amulets and Superstitions* (New York: Dover, 1978 [1930]), p. xxii. See ibid., 18, 'The Cross', pp. 336–49, and ch. 19, 'The Crucifix', pp. 350–3, for a full discussion of Christian talismans.

19 Proust also reminds us here that the same 'madness' may affect all human beings, regardless of intelligence, education or social status.

20 Wallis Budge describes how amulets were commonly used to appeal to divine powers for virility, fecundity, the preservation of the family, success and well-being. Their power was based on the wearer's belief in the triumph of God over Satan, good over evil, law over chaos, light over darkness. Precious stones were incorporated into many amulets: the sapphire, for example, was worn in India and Arabia as a health amulet and as a protection against the Evil Eye, plague

and pestilence. Turquoise was prized in Arab cultures for its colour: called the lucky stone, it was believed to have benevolent powers. Rubies, worn in an amulet, were thought to protect from witchcraft of all kinds, while topaz was worn on the left arm to defend the wearer against the Evil Eye, the symbol, significantly in the context of Swann and Odette's relationship, of jealousy or envy (pp. 321–5).

21. The early version reads simply: 'Sous les innombrables porte-bonheur en saphir, trèfles en email, médaillons en or, philippines en rubis qui l'entouraient comme des symboles de superstition, des gages de tendresse, des souvenirs' (I 1035–6).
22. Eliade, *Images and Symbols*, p. 127.
23. According to Jean Piaget, 'la superstition est une manifestation du réalisme enfantin'. It reveals a belief, common in childhood, that one can influence the external world, whether through 'la magie par participation des gestes et des choses' (as, for example, when one steps only on every other paving-stone), or through 'la magie par participation de la pensée et des choses' (the child believes a look or thought can modify reality), or through 'la magie par participation d'intentions'. In this last case, physical objects are endowed with life and obey the child's will. Quoted in Askevis-Leherpeux, pp. 68–70.
24. Elisabeth Ladenson, *Proust's Lesbianism* (Cornell: Cornell University Press, 1999), p. 53. Alison Finch notes, more generally, that Proust sought 'in his expansion of *A la recherche*, to amplify characteristics or situations marked by ambiguity and uncertainty, ranging from mistaken identity to proliferation of rumour, or from Albertine's lies to manifestations of bisexuality' (Winton [Finch], p. 254).
25. Stéphane Chaudier, *Proust et le langage religieux: La Cathédrale profane*, Recherches proustiennes 2 (Paris: Honoré Champion, 2004), p. 388. Chaudier inserts this within a religious paradigm, arguing that the desire for 'l'interpénétration des âmes' (P III 888) is equivalent to a desire for transparency, indeed, for complete knowledge of the Other or for what he terms 'la négation de la différence' (p. 388). Biblical wisdom, however, grants this power to God alone. Chaudier thus follows Philippe Sollers's interpretation of *A la recherche*: 'C'est en compétition ouverte avec Gomorrhe que toute la *Recherche* est construite': 'Proust et Gomorrhe', in *Théorie des exceptions* (Paris: Gallimard, 1986), p. 79.
26. Although not explicitly identified as a superstition on Swann's part, his (misguided) belief that Odette will not lie to him when wearing her medallion acquires the status of such a belief in turn.
27. Askevis-Leherpeux, pp. 50–1.
28. See ibid., pp. 55–6.
29. See ibid., pp. 94–7.
30. See above, p. 34.
31. Françoise's convictions form part of a coherent cosmology in contrast to the more superficial alignment of the various women loved in the novel. Nonetheless, all have recourse to pre-existing and widespread beliefs.

32 Although Proust offers penetrating insights into female characters in the novel, the woman loved always remains to some extent other. Had he conformed in his text to the stereotype of the superstitious woman, therefore, empathy and thus knowledge concerning the limitations of knowledge would have become problematic.

33 The narrator's first sighting of Gilberte at Tansonville is also the first time he hears her name: 'Ainsi passa près de moi ce nom de Gilberte, donné comme un talisman qui me permettrait peut-être de retrouver un jour celle dont il venait de faire une personne' (S I 140). This talisman seems to work, for the narrator does indeed find Gilberte again, but having apparently completed this specific task, its power extends no further. It is on this basis that Wallis Budge distinguishes talismans from amulets, the latter being intended to perform a single task alone (pp. 13–14).

34 In this discussion, spiritualism is understood in the specific sense of the practice of communication with the spirits of the dead, especially via a medium. Although some commentators have distinguished ghosts from spirits, the first term referring to spontaneous appearances of the spirits of the dead, the latter to those who are wilfully evoked (for example by a medium), all are included here, given the distinction drawn in the text – by metaphorical association with the spiritualist intertext – between the voluntary and involuntary evocations of memory.

35 One might argue that the narrator/protagonist never genuinely considers spiritualism as an option, that this is never any more than a figure of speech. However, given the popularity of seances at the time and Proust's own knowledge of them, as set out by Pierssens, it is likely that the narrator's interest is genuine. Victor Graham, in contrast, argues that 'generally speaking, Proust has no use for spiritualism' (*The Imagery of Proust*, p. 157). The discussion that follows counters this assertion by illustrating its successive appeal as literal belief system and metaphorical intertext.

36 Jahoda's third category of superstition comprises occult experiences, such as visions of ghosts, forebodings of death and disaster and manifestations of the supernatural, such as poltergeists etc. (p. 14).

37 The body elsewhere becomes a source of anxiety for the narrator. See, for example, his disappointment in Bergotte's corporeality; below, pp. 142–3.

38 With its echoes of spirit rappings, the practice of the narrator's grandmother, when in Balbec, of knocking on the 'cloison' that separates her from the narrator, in response to his signal, further prefigures her death. See *JF* II 29.

39 Jahoda, pp. 84–5, summarizing the theories of Whiting and Child proposed in: J. W. M. Whiting and I. L. Child, *Child Training and Personality: A Cross-Cultural Study* (New Haven: Yale University Press, 1953).

40 Chaudier charts this process through the patterns of maternal profanation that run throughout the novel. These include the profane re-enactment of his mother's kiss with Albertine as well as examples of the profanation of (maternal) 'judéité' by both the narrator and Charlus. See pp. 360–5.

41 The narrator's acceptance of his grandmother's death is achieved in the course of the second trip to Balbec; *Albertine disparue* charts his progress from an initial

reluctance to accept Albertine's death to a detailed meditation on grief and loss.

42  The extract in question does not explicitly identify the narrator's grandmother as a ghost and, indeed, the details that follow are more strongly associated with memories of her. However, the suddenness of her appearance and the narrator's use of the verb 'voir' grants the experience the flavour of a supernatural apparition.

43  Vieda Skultans, *Intimacy and Ritual: A Study of Spiritualism, Mediums and Groups* (London: Routledge, 1974), p. 4.

44  See ibid., pp. 36, 47.

45  The narrator claims that his curiosity about those unknown aspects of her life which prompt his jealousy has not faded because: 'l'être ne meurt pas tout de suite pour nous, il reste baigné d'une espèce d'aura de vie qui n'a rien d'une immortalité véritable mais qui fait qu'il continue à occuper nos pensées de la même manière que quand il vivait' (*AD* IV 92). It is as if, he claims, the person is simply on holiday. For evidence of Proust's/the narrator's ambivalent attitude to religion, see Chaudier, part 2, pp. 91–195.

46  The perspicacity of Proust's portrait of grief is confirmed by other studies, whether literary, psychological or psychoanalytical. Freud, for example, in his *On Murder, Mourning and Melancholia* (1917), charts how, in the wake of the loss of a loved 'object', reality demands that the libido – that is, the emotional attachment – be withdrawn from the loved one. He recognizes the pain and difficulty of this process, however. Indeed, these emotions may reach such a level of intensity that the bereaved person turns away from reality and clings to the object by refusing to believe it is no longer present. See Sigmund Freud, *On Murder, Mourning and Melancholia* (London: Penguin, 2005). Freud's account has influenced many later analyses of the nature of grief. Significant among these, argues John Archer, is 'the view that grief is an active process involving the struggle to give up the emotional and internal attachment to a love object, a process which takes up much time and energy (later called "grief work")': *The Nature of Grief: The Evolution and Psychology of Reactions to Loss* (London, NY: Routledge, 1999), p. 16. Archer's discussion also highlights the temptations of obsessive 'rumination' (pp. 112 and 120), the unproductive counterpart to 'grief work', to which the narrator, at least provisionally, succumbs. His analysis of the grief process, including stages such as 'numbness and disbelief' and 'yearning and preoccupation' – a stage which, significantly, can find a cathartic channel in writing – is also dramatized in Proust's presentation (see ibid., pp. 68–78).

47  Rapping and voices are common spirit manifestations.

48  Certainly, Aimé's credibility is compromised by the fact that he elicits a confession from the 'blanchisseuse' regarding her sexual exploits with Albertine only by entertaining her lavishly, then going to bed with her himself (*AD* IV 105–6). Likewise, Andrée's suspected involvement with Albertine casts a shadow over her apparent frankness in responding to the narrator's questions about their sexuality. See *AD* IV 129. See also Wassenaar, pp. 201–5, for a discussion of how the 'effect of Aimé's letter is to introduce, not much-needed information, but a systematic degradation of Albertine's desires. [. . .] Degradation is to be

taken in many senses at once: as the natural decay of memory, its supplementation by fresh experiences, but also as a gradual abdication of mourning, Marcel's abandoning of the state of abandonment' (pp. 201–2).

49 Wassenaar continues: 'What is so hard to read here is not that Marcel should be in pain, but that pains should *take the form of jealousy*, and that our hitherto reliably ironic, detached narrator should have lost control, to the extent of lying blatantly to us' (pp. 186–8). Wassenaar's analysis of *Albertine disparue* offers one of the most original and complex analyses of the narrator's grief (and the self-justificatory impulses that define it) to appear in critical literature on Proust. See, in particular, ibid., ch. 5, 'Under Cover of Mourning: The Ethics of Vulnerability', pp. 171–208.

50 C. S. Lewis's *A Grief Observed* provides a first-hand account of bereavement that further confirms the accuracy of Proust's vision. Despite divergent motivations – Lewis's aim is to offer an 'honest dissection of grief', the 'negation of self-pity' and a distancing from 'the conventional posture of the mourner' – his perspectives nonetheless chime with Proust's own. (See *A Grief Observed* (London and Boston: Faber & Faber, 1966), p. 50. The quotations above, regarding Lewis's motivations, are extracts from reviews of the text included in this edition.) Lewis's evocation of the unexperienced (and thus merely potential) memories of which death deprives the surviving partner in a couple extends the pattern identified by Proust here, with its suggestion that death consigns certain experiences to the realm of the definitively unknown: 'You have stripped me even of my past, even of the things we never shared. I was wrong to say that the stump was recovering from the pain of the amputation. I was deceived because it has so many ways to hurt me that I discover them only one by one' (ibid., p. 52). Like Proust's narrator uncovering progressively more areas where knowledge evades him – uncovering, indeed, his persistent externality to Albertine's experiences – the writer's pain is constantly reshaped and renewed.

51 Skultans, pp. 30–1.

52 The presence of an alternative means of communion with the dead – that promised by 'l'abbé X***' – further implies the narrator's non-alignment with spiritualist thought.

53 One further reference to a medium appears in this volume, prompted by the narrator's perspective on the soldiers on leave from the front as representatives of (imminent) death. It is therefore as if they have been evoked by a medium. See TR IV 336–7.

54 For the introduction of this metaphorical paradigm in other thematic contexts in the novel, see SG III 203 for its ironic use to expose the pretences of social interaction, and G II 488–9 for a similarly ironic challenge to contemporary orientalist stereotypes.

55 Skultans, p. 16.

56 Ibid., pp. 270–1.

57 The earlier aesthetic meditations in *La Prisonnière* seem tentatively to hint at a new, if surprising, realization on the narrator's part of the artist's existence as

a normal human being: 'comme il était singulier que le pressentiment le plus différent de ce qu'assigne la vie terre à terre, l'approximation la plus hardie des allégresses de l'au-delà se fût justement matérialisée dans le triste petit bourgeois bienséant que nous rencontrions au mois de Marie à Combray!' (*P* III 765).

58  See Skultans, p. 36.
59  See Colin Davis, 'Hauntology, Spectres and Phantoms', État présent, in *French Studies*, 59/3 (2005), 373–9. Hauntology does not concern itself with literal ghosts. For Derrida, it 'supplants its near homonym, ontology, replacing the priority of being and presence with the figure of the ghost as that which is neither present nor absent, neither dead nor alive' (ibid., p. 373). This spectre is 'a deconstructive figure [. . .] making established certainties vacillate' (ibid., p. 376). Abraham and Torok represent the opposing view, seeking to unravel secrets in the text of which the text itself may be unaware, 'but which the reader or critic may be able to elicit' (ibid., p. 375). Abraham and Torok thus 'seek to return the ghost to the order of knowledge' (ibid., p. 378). This 'tension between the desire to understand and the openness to what exceeds knowledge' (ibid., p. 379) extends far beyond Proust's ghostly metaphors into the very textures of language and meaning in the novel.
60  Skultans, p. 32.
61  Ibid.
62  See Albouy, 'Images et structures mythiques', pp. 984–7, for an alternative view of Proust's analysis of Vinteuil's music which situates it within, not a spiritualist intertext, but an Orphic schema.
63  See the discussion of *Parsifal* in Part II of this book for an analysis of the narrator's valorization of music.
64  '[C]omme je le sus plus tard, ses autres œuvres, n'avaient toutes été par rapport à ce septuor que de timides essais, délicieux mais bien frêles, auprès du chef-d'œuvre triomphal et complet qui m'était en ce moment révélé [. . .] de même, si je considérais maintenant non plus mon amour pour Albertine, mais toute ma vie, mes autres amours n'y avaient été que de minces et timides essais qui préparaient, des appels qui réclamaient ce plus vaste amour . . . l'amour pour Albertine' (*P* III 756–7).
65  Graham highlights Proust's introduction of the spiritualist intertext in relation to the appreciation of Vinteuil's music. However, the complex and changing roles ascribed to the different participants in this 'seance' are not addressed. Graham states simply that 'the performer stands between the composer and the listener as a sort of re-creator and his movements are like those of the body of a medium in a seance' (*The Imagery of Proust*, p. 41).
66  Early images in the novel suggest the young narrator's misguided belief in the divine, unattainable status of the artist. Drawing on classical mythology, Bergotte becomes a god passing down his oracles to mankind (S I 99), while La Berma is a 'Déesse dévoilée' (*JF* I 435).
67  See *P* III 759–68.
68  No such images appear in *Du côté de chez Swann*, while two appear in *Sodome et Gomorrhe* and one in each of *La Prisonnière* and *Le Temps retrouvé*.

[69] This point is cogently argued by Chaudier who counters critical claims that the narrator must renounce the material world in favour of 'la vraie vie' that is art: 'la vraie vie', he proposes, is 'pressentie et éprouvée par le *corps*, analysée et conquise par l'esprit, révélée et traduite par l'art, la vraie vie exprime la joie d'un rapport retrouvé au réel' (p. 141).

[70] This culminates in a rejection of Bergotte's posthumous fate. The author's books are ranged in booksellers' windows on the evening of his funeral: 'On l'enterra, mais toute la nuit funèbre, aux vitrines éclairées, ses livres, disposés trois par trois, veillaient comme des anges aux ailes éployées et semblaient pour celui qui n'était plus, le symbole de sa résurrection' (*P* III 693). The image is clearly celebratory, and yet an underlying hint that the symbol of Bergotte's immortality is being deflated into a symbol of commercial opportunism suggests that the narrator is seeking a more satisfying form of transcendence than this conventional conception of immortality through art: that is, a spiritual and temporal transcendence in the work of art, not endurance in the minds of his readers.

[71] '"C'est ainsi que j'aurais dû écrire, disait-il. Mes derniers livres sont trop secs, il aurait fallu passer plusieurs couches de couleur, rendre ma phrase en elle-même précieuse, comme ce petit pan de mur jaune"' (*P* III 692). The only other 'prestidigitateur' explicitly referred to in the novel is the doctor, Professor Dieulafoy, who attends the narrator's grandmother and who, in a decorous sleight of hand, whisks away his payment without anyone noticing (*G* II 638). The subtle 'rapprochement' that this common incarnation effects between the doctor and Bergotte may be a means of underlining this mature view of Bergotte's work as lacking substance.

[72] Several moments of voyeurism – at Montjouvain, for example, or in Jupien's brothel – extend this dialectic to imply the narrator's 'externality' to certain forms of knowledge. More subtly, too, the narrator's meditation on the carafes that children put in the Vivonne in order to try to catch fish hints variously at the traps laid by perception, the elusiveness and ungraspability of the external world: the carafes are 'remplies par la rivière, où elles sont à leur tour encloses, à la fois "contenant" aux flancs transparents comme une eau durcie, et "contenu" plongé dans un plus grand contenant de cristal liquide et courant, [et] évoquaient l'image de la fraîcheur d'une façon plus délicieuse et plus irritante qu'elles n'eussent fait sur une table servie, en ne la montrant qu'en fuite dans cette allitération perpétuelle entre l'eau sans consistance où les mains ne pouvaient la capter et le verre sans fluidité où le palais ne pourrait en jouir' (*S* I 166). The apparently transparent (in both a literal and abstract sense) may still lead us into perceptual error, as the use of oxymoron ('l'eau durcie') only underlines. That even the young narrator/protagonist senses these epistemological difficulties is signalled by the simultaneous but conflicting responses this vision prompts: it is at once tantalizingly 'délicieuse' and 'irritante'.

[73] The novel, like Proust's own, wavers between the literal and metaphorical in its presentation of the supernatural. The female protagonist, Jeanne, is described as 'ensorcelée' in the context of her submission to the 'satanic' priest, 'l'abbé de

la Croix-Jugan' ('le démon en habit de prêtre', p. 663): J. Barbey d'Aurevilly, *L'Ensorcelée*, in *Œuvres romanesques complètes*, Bibliothèque de la Pléiade (Paris: Gallimard, 1964). The intrusion of genuinely supernatural episodes (as, for example, when the shepherd who has supposedly cursed Jeanne shows her husband an encounter with the priest in an apparently magical mirror, p. 678) nonetheless generates an attitude of ambivalence in the reader as to whether her 'possession' is psychological or magical.

74  This is not an exhaustive list of the images of witchcraft and sorcery that appear in the novel. Further examples include the pain and helplessness the narrator feels when his beloved grandmother is ill, for this prompts a description of the thermometer as a 'sorcière' (G II 595). Further aesthetic reflections also turn to this intertextual source: the young Elstir, as M. Biche, reveals his immature pretension by describing a work by another artist, saying 'c'en est sorcier' (S I 251); and in *Le Côté de Guermantes*, the narrative projects us forward to a moment in Venice when the narrator will experience a moment of aesthetic appreciation of a sight that does not conventionally belong to the world of art. In keeping with the collapsing of aesthetic hierarchies so common in the novel, a vision of an old woman brushing a young girl's hair is inserted within a 'cadre': 'D'ailleurs l'extrême proximité des maisons aux fenêtres opposées sur une même cour y fait de chaque croisée le cadre où [. . .] une jeune fille se laisse peigner les cheveux par une vieille à figure [. . .] de sorcière' (G II 860).

75  The phrase appears in Charles Baudelaire's 'Ébauche d'un épilogue pour la deuxième édition des "Fleurs du mal"', in *Les Fleurs du mal et autres poèmes* (Paris, Garnier-Flammarion, 1964), p. 214. Baudelaire famously introduces the image of sorcery into his essay on Théophile Gautier: 'Manier savamment une langue, c'est pratiquer une espèce de sorcellerie évocatoire', in *Œuvres complètes*, Bibliothèque de la Pléiade, 2 vols (Paris: Gallimard, 1976), vol. 2, p. 118. We may also recall the opening lines of Mallarmé's poem, 'Prose': 'Hyperbole! De la mémoire / Triomphalement ne sais-tu / Te lever, aujourd'hui grimoire / Dans un livre de fer vêtu', in Stéphane Mallarmé, *Œuvres complètes*, Bibliothèque de la Pléiade (Paris: Gallimard, 1945), p. 55.

76  The image of the artist as a fraudulent sorcerer is, of course, a common one in literature, ranging from the character Scapin in Molière's *Les Fourberies de Scapin* to the vitriol directed against the artist by Gide's Strouvilhou in *Les Faux-monnayeurs*. But like Gide himself seeking an authenticity of representation in this novel, Proust renews the image of sorcery, transforming it into a metaphor that conveys the creative transformations of the artist's vision.

77  Charles W. Olliver, *Handbook of Magic and Witchcraft* (Twickenham: Tiger Books, 1996 [1928]), p. 115.

78  Gilles de Rais is the source for the fairytale character, Bluebeard.

79  'Je descendis de voiture pour donner au cocher l'adresse de Brichot. Du trottoir je voyais la fenêtre de la chambre d'Albertine, cette fenêtre autrefois toujours noire le soir quand elle n'habitait pas la maison, que la lumière électrique de l'intérieur, segmentée par les pleins des volets, striait de haut en bas de barres

d'or parallèles. Ce grimoire magique, autant il était clair pour moi et dessinait devant mon esprit calme des images précises, toutes proches, et en possession desquelles j'allais entrer tout à l'heure, était invisible pour Brichot resté dans la voiture, presque aveugle, et eût, d'ailleurs, été incompréhensible pour lui' (P III 833–4).

80 Olliver, p. 115.
81 'The principle which forms the very essence of the Devil, the idea of opposition, also underlies the whole ceremonial and ritual of Black Magic and Black Masses' (ibid.).
82 Graham attributes a social dimension to Proust's allocation of magical roles in the novel, with the aristocracy being likened to fairies while 'the comparison of witches or sorcerers is on a less noble plane [. . .] and Proust reserves it for servants or common folk' (*The Imagery of Proust*, p. 157). Although valid to an extent, a darker undercurrent, as we have seen, nonetheless defines the rituals of aristocratic society.
83 To take just one example of Charlus's taste for the scatological, he takes delight in referring to M. de Cambremer as the marquis de Cambremerde (*SG* III 475).
84 [. . .] 'je fus envahi pendant quelques instants par un sentiment trouble et bientôt dissipé de désir et de mélancolie' (*AD* IV 226).
85 Jan Lauts, *Carpaccio: Paintings and Drawings*, complete edn, trans. Erica Millman and Marguerite Kay (London: Phaidon, 1962), pp. 27–8. This is reflected in the narrator's own description of the painting, which focuses, not on the exorcism, but on 'la rive ou fourmillent les scènes de la vie vénitienne de l'époque. Je regardais le barbier essuyer son rasoir, le nègre portant son tonneau, les conversations des musulmans, des nobles seigneurs vénitiens en larges brocarts, en damas, en toque de velours cerise' (*AD* IV 226).
86 See Malcolm Bowie, 'Proust and the Art of Brevity', in *The Cambridge Companion to Proust*, ed. Richard Bales (Cambridge: Cambridge University Press, 2001), pp. 216–29 on the importance and, indeed, pleasures of the small details that are easily missed when confronted with the grand narrative sweep of *A la recherche* or, to use Bowie's terms, the stylistic 'micro-dramas taking place in a grandly unfolding festal pageant' (p. 229).
87 Olliver, p. 113, quoting Eliphas Lévi.
88 Elsewhere, too, Proust hints at the possibility of social revolution. With its wall of windows, the dining-room in the Grand Hôtel at Balbec is transformed into an aquarium 'devant la paroi de verre duquel la population ouvrière de Balbec, les pêcheurs et aussi les familles de petits bourgeois, invisibles dans l'ombre, s'écrasaient au vitrage pour apercevoir, lentement balancée dans des remous d'or, la vie luxueuse de ces gens, aussi extraordinaire pour les pauvres que celle de poissons et de mollusques étranges' (*JF* II 41). The image concludes with the following open question: 'une grande question sociale, de savoir si la paroi de verre protégera toujours le festin des bêtes merveilleuses et si les gens obscurs qui regardent avidement dans la nuit ne viendront pas les cueillir dans leur aquarium et les manger.' (*JF* II 41–2).

89  The narrator's grandfather is able to divine the Jewish origins of the narrator's friends: 'Avant de les avoir vus, rien qu'en entendant leur nom [. . .] il devinait non seulement l'origine juive de ceux de mes amis qui l'étaient en effet, mais même ce qu'il y avait quelquefois de fâcheux dans leur famille' (S I 90).

90  'L'habitude d'être obligé de recourir à l'observation personnelle et à la déduction pour connaître les petites affaires des maîtres, ces gens étranges qui causent entre eux et ne leur parlent pas, développe chez les "employés" [. . .] un plus grand pouvoir de divination que chez les "patrons".' (SG III 219). Interestingly, this extract suggests that the narrator appreciates that the servants' powers of divination are based on observation and deduction, but this is the only context, at this stage in the novel, where he does not see this power as an inexplicable, quasi-supernatural one. It also represents an evolution in understanding from his earlier astonishment at Françoise's divinatory capacity. See G II 363 for the first hint that the narrator realizes Françoise's apparent powers may simply be the product of information passed between the servants of different households.

91  Charlus's divinatory powers are implicitly suggested when we read that his 'discernement divin' tells him that Cottard is not 'de sa sorte' (SG III 313).

92  Albertine stops confiding in the narrator about her acquaintances and experiences because she has 'deviné un sentiment inquisitional' in him. See P III 566.

93  In fact, it is the art critic or 'consumer' of art to whom the role of would-be diviner appears to be attributed. The narrator imagines how Elstir's paintings are scattered throughout the country and how the owner of one of these paintings would be 'enfermé comme un astrologue, interroge[ant] un de ces miroirs du monde qu'est un tableau d'Elstir' (G II 424).

94  Olliver, pp. 165, 166.

95  Ibid., p. 167. For example, from an examination of the clouds and winds, in conjunction with a consideration of past conditions, one might deduce whether a particular day was auspicious for setting sail.

96  As Albouy suggests, the image aligns her with the moon, while Proust's first description of Saint-Loup associates him with the sun: his skin is '"aussi blonde et les cheveux aussi dorés que s'ils avaient absorbé tous les rayons du soleil". Saint-Loup est le Soleil et il aime Rachel, qui est la Lune. Façon mythologique de lire le récit de leurs amours! . . .' ('Images et structures mythiques', p. 974).

97  That his powers of prediction are as yet underdeveloped is suggested by his failure to read Andrée correctly. He initially believes her to be healthy, when, in fact, he will later discover that this impression of health comes only from her proximity to the other 'jeunes filles', 'comme les planètes empruntent leur lumière [à d'autres]' (JF II 296).

98  Indeed, he describes how 'nous nous imaginons les différentes reines de la société poursuivant leur route dans le ciel à une distance infinie' (G II 672–3). See C. G. H. Mann, 'The Moon and the Sun in *A la recherche du temps perdu*', *Nottingham French Studies*, 26/1 (1987), 66–76, for a telling analysis of the symbolism that links Albertine to the moon, which 'speaks of romance, but of impermanence' (p. 69), and the narrator's mother to the sun, which 'outshines the moon (strength) and returns every day and without any visible variation (constancy)' (p. 70).

[99] The stars also become a metaphor for the object of homosexual desire. Of Charlus, when speaking to one of Mme de Surgis le Duc's handsome sons, we read: 'dans ses prunelles s'inscrivaient comme de distantes et mystérieuses étoiles' (SG III 102). This desiring gaze is then inverted when Charlus becomes the object of the attention of some ruffian in the street. Charlus is, in this scenario, 'un astre' 'accompagné de son satellite' (P III 709).

[100] See Graham, *The Imagery of Proust*, pp. 146–7, for further uses of astronomy as a metaphorical source in the novel.

[101] A convenient recourse to the principle of fate also permits the narrator to abdicate responsibility for the irrational, jealousy-prompted actions that define his relationships with women, and especially Albertine. He refuses, for example, to leave Albertine and Saint-Loup on the train for a brief moment while he accompanies Bloch to greet the latter's father, on the grounds (unknown to Bloch) that the narrator does not wish to leave Albertine alone with Saint-Loup. Having lamented how 'on devrait toujours s'expliquer franchement', he concedes that 'Il n'y avait rien à faire qu'à s'incliner devant ce *fatum* qui avait voulu que la présence d'Albertine m'empêchât de le reconduire et qu'il pût croire que c'était au contraire celle de gens brillants, laquelle, l'eussent-ils été cent fois plus, n'aurait eu pour effet que de me faire occuper exclusivement de Bloch et réserver pour lui toute ma politesse' (SG III 487–8).

[102] See Chaudier, pp. 461–2.

[103] See above, pp. 154–5.

[104] For a further example of these reiterative metaphors, see *TR* IV 478: the narrator refers back, in a reminder to the reader of his earlier misunderstanding of the notion of divination and, indeed, of artistic creation, to the experiences which he now knows will form the substance of the work he is to create but whose purpose he was unable to 'divine' at the time: 'Et je compris que tous ces matériaux de l'œuvre littéraire, c'était ma vie passée; je compris qu'ils étaient venus à moi, dans les plaisirs frivoles, dans la paresse, dans la tendresse, dans la douleur, emmagasinés par moi sans que je devinasse plus leur destination, leur survivance même, que la graine mettant en réserve tous les aliments qui nourriront la plante'.

[105] Proust explicitly addresses the opposition, but mutual dependency, of inspiration and effort in *Contre Sainte-Beuve* by means of a discussion of the interaction of instinct and intellect: 'si l'intelligence ne mérite pas la couronne suprême, c'est elle seule qui est capable de la décerner. Et si elle n'a dans la hiérarchie des vertus que la seconde place, il n'y a qu'elle qui soit capable de proclamer que l'instinct doit occuper la première' (p. 216).

[106] The metaphors are Proust's own. Saint-Loup explains: 'Je reconnais que c'est très beau le moment où ils montent, où ils vont *faire constellation*, et obéissent en cela à des lois tout aussi précises que celles qui régissent les constellations [. . .] Mais est-ce que tu n'aimes pas mieux le moment où [. . .] ils *font apocalypse*, même les étoiles ne gardant plus leur place? Et ces sirènes, était-ce assez wagnérien, ce qui du reste était bien naturel pour saluer l'arrivée des Allemands, ça faisait très hymne national [. . .]; c'était à se demander si c'était bien des aviateurs et pas plutôt des Walkyries qui montaient' (*TR* IV 337–8).

## CONCLUSION

1. Eliade, *Myth and Reality*, pp. 136, 138.
2. Jahoda, p. 100.
3. See Lucien Lévy-Bruhl, *Les Fonctions mentales dans les sociétés inférieures* (Paris: Presses Universitaires de France, 1951).
4. See Victor Segalen, *Essai sur l'exotisme: une esthétique du Divers* (Paris: Livre de Poche, 1986). For Segalen, this impossibility is to be celebrated, however, whereas Proust offers a rather more ambivalent approach.
5. References to the magic lantern are not included in the distribution tables that feature in the Introduction, as this optical device is not discussed in any of the main chapters that constitute the present study. See Michel Prat, 'Proust et la lanterne magique de Schopenhauer', *Revue de littérature comparée*, 218/2 (1981), 195–207; and Howard Moss, *The Magic Lantern of Marcel Proust* (New York and London: Macmillan, 1962) for further discussion.
6. Eliade, *Myth and Reality*, p. 191.
7. See ibid., p. 192.
8. Ibid., p. 188.

# BIBLIOGRAPHY

### WORKS BY PROUST

Contre Sainte-Beuve, précédé de Pastiches et mélanges et suivis de Essais et articles, Bibliothèque de la Pléiade (Paris: Gallimard, 1971).

Jean Santeuil, précédé de Les Plaisirs et les jours, Bibliothèque de la Pléiade (Paris: Gallimard, 1971).

A la recherche du temps perdu, Bibliothèque de la Pléiade, 4 vols (Paris: Gallimard, 1987–9).

Correspondance de Marcel Proust, ed. P. Kolb, 21 vols (Paris: Plon, 1970–93).

### SELECT BIBLIOGRAPHY OF CRITICAL AND OTHER WORKS

Abbate, C., 'Parsifal: Words and Music', in Parsifal, Opera Guide Series 34 (London: John Calder; NY: Riverrun, 1986), pp. 43–58.

Ackerman, R., The Myth and Ritual School: J. G. Frazer and the Cambridge Ritualists (NY: Garland Science, 1990).

Albouy, P., 'Quelques images et structures mythiques dans la Recherche du temps perdu', Revue d'Histoire Littéraire, 71 (1971), 972–87.

Archer, J., The Nature of Grief: The Evolution and Psychology of Reactions to Loss (London, NY: Routledge, 1999).

Ashman, Mike, 'A Very Human Epic', in Parsifal, Opera Guide Series 34 (London: John Calder; NY: Riverrun, 1986), pp. 7–14.

Askevis-Leherpeux, F., La Superstition (Paris: Presses Universitaires de France, 1988).

Auerbach, E., Mimesis: The Representation of Reality in Western Literature, trans. W. Trask (Princeton: Princeton University Press, 1968).

Bailey, P., Proust's Self-Reader: The Pursuit of Literature as Privileged Communication (Birmingham, AL: Summa, 1997).

Baird, B., The Art of the Puppet (New York: Macmillan, 1965).

Bakhtin, M., Rabelais and his World, trans. Hélène Iswolsky (Bloomington: Indiana University Press, 1984).

Barbey D'Aurevilly, J., *L'Ensorcelée*, in *Œuvres romanesques complètes*, Bibliothèque de la Pléiade (Paris: Gallimard, 1964).
Barchilon, J. and Flinders, P., *Charles Perrault*, Twayne World Authors Series 639 (Boston: Twayne, 1981).
Baudelaire, C., *Les Fleurs du mal et autres poèmes* (Paris: Garnier-Flammarion, 1964).
—— *Œuvres complètes*, Bibliothèque de la Pléiade, 2 vols (Paris: Gallimard, 1976).
Beckett, S., *Proust* (London: Chatto & Windus, 1931).
Bedriono, E., *Proust, Wagner et la coïncidence des arts* (Tübingen: Gunter Narr Verlag; Paris: Editions Jean-Michel Place, 1984).
Bergson, H., *Le Rire: Essai sur la signification du comique* (Paris: Presses Universitaires de France, 1975).
Bersani, L., *Marcel Proust: The Fictions of Life and Art* (NY: Oxford University Press, 1965).
Bettelheim, B., *The Uses of Enchantment: The Meaning and Importance of Fairy Tales* (London: Penguin, 1991 [1975]).
Biard, J. D., *The Style of La Fontaine's Fables* (Oxford: Blackwell, 1966).
Blackham, H. J., *The Fable as Literature* (London: Athlone, 1985).
Boni, S., 'La Grand-mère et Albertine: Figures wagnériennes', *Bulletin Marcel Proust*, 50 (2000), 103–27.
Borchmeyer, D., 'Recapitulation of a Lifetime', in *Parsifal*, Opera Guide Series 34 (London: John Calder; NY: Riverrun, 1986), pp. 15–22.
Bowie, M., *Freud, Proust and Lacan: Theory as Fiction* (Cambridge: Cambridge University Press, 1987).
—— *Proust Among the Stars* (London: HarperCollins, 1998).
—— 'Proust and the Art of Brevity', in *The Cambridge Companion to Proust*, ed. Richard Bales (Cambridge: Cambridge University Press, 2001).
Bradbury, M., *Possibilities: Essays on the State of the Novel* (Oxford: Oxford University Press, 1973).
Brunet, E., *Le Vocabulaire de Proust*, Travaux de linguistique quantitative 18, 3 vols (Geneva: Slatkine-Champion, 1983).
Bucknall, B., *The Religion of Art in Proust*, Illinois Studies in Language and Literature 60 (Urbana: University of Illinois Press, 1969).
Buisine, A., 'Marcel Proust: Le Côté de l'Orient', *Revue des Sciences Humaines* 90 (1989), 123–44.
Carter, W. C., *The Proustian Quest* (NY, London: New York University Press, 1992).
Chaudier, S., *Proust et le langage religieux: La Cathédrale profane*, Recherches proustiennes 2 (Paris: Honoré Champion, 2004).
Chernowitz, M. E., *Proust and Painting* (New York: International University Press, 1945).
Cocking, J. M., *Proust: Collected Essays on the Writer and his Art* (Cambridge: Cambridge University Press, 1982).
*Collins Dictionary and Thesaurus* (Glasgow: HarperCollins, 2000).
Conze, E. (ed.), *Buddhist Scriptures* (Harmondsworth: Penguin, 1976).
Coudert, R., *Proust au féminin* (Paris: Grasset, 1998).

Coupe, L., *Myth*, New Critical Idiom Series (London, NY: Routledge, 1997).
Davis, C., 'Hauntology, Spectres and Phantoms', État présent, *French Studies*, 59/3 (2005), 373–9.
Delarue, P., 'Les Contes merveilleux de Perrault et la tradition populaire', *Bulletin folklorique de l'Île-de-France*, January–March (1961).
*Dictionnaire historique de la langue française* (Paris: Dictionnaires le Robert, 1992).
Donnan, T., 'Proust "reprit à la musique son bien": A Study in Analogies between Wagnerian and Proustian Composition', *Stanford French Review*, 13/2–3 (1989), 159–74.
Eells, E., *Proust's Cup of Tea: Homoeroticism and Victorian Culture* (Aldershot: Ashgate, 2002).
Eliade, M., 'Les Savants et les contes de fées', *NRF*, 4 (1956), 884–91.
—— *Myths, Dreams and Mysteries* (London: Collins/Fontana, 1968).
—— *Myth and Reality*, World Perspectives Series 21, trans. Willard R. Trask (London: Allen & Unwin, 1964).
—— *Images and Symbols: Studies in Religious Symbolism*, trans. Philip Mairet (Princeton, NJ: Princeton University Press, 1991).
—— *The Myth of the Eternal Return: or, Cosmos and History*, Bollingen Series XLVI, trans. Willard R. Trask (Princeton, NJ: Princeton University Press, 1991 [1954]).
Faber, R., 'The Apostle and the Poet: Paul and Aratus', *Clarion*, 42/13 (1993), http://spindleworks.com/library/rfaber/aratus.htm (accessed 10 July 2004).
Fraisse, L., *L'Esthétique de Marcel Proust* (Paris: SEDES, 1995).
Franz, M.-L. von, *An Introduction to the Interpretation of Fairy Tales* (Dallas: Spring Publications, 1970).
Frazer, J. G., *The Golden Bough*, 3rd edn, 12 vols (London: Macmillan, 1911–15).
Freud, S., *On Murder, Mourning and Melancholia* (London: Penguin, 2005).
Genette, G., *Discours du récit* (Paris: Seuil, 1972).
—— *Palimpsestes: La Littérature au second degré* (Paris: Seuil, 1982).
Girard, R., *Mensonge romantique et vérité romanesque* (Paris: Grasset, 1961).
Graham, V. E., 'Marcel Proust and the *Mille et Une Nuits*', *Canadian Review of Comparative Literature*, Winter, 1 (1974), 89–96.
—— *The Imagery of Proust*, Language and Style Series 2 (Oxford: Blackwell, 1966).
Guyau, A., 'Proust et la fable', *Bulletin de la société des amis de Marcel Proust*, 18 (1978), 685–9.
Hindus, M., *The Proustian Vision* (NY: Columbia University Press, 1958).
Holloway, R., *Debussy and Wagner* (London: Eulenburg Books, 1979).
—— 'Experiencing Music and Imagery in *Parsifal*', in *Parsifal*, Opera Guide Series 34 (London: John Calder; NY: Riverrun, 1986), pp. 23–42.
Hughes, E. J., *Marcel Proust: A Study in the Quality of Awareness* (Cambridge: Cambridge University Press, 1983).
—— 'Proust and Social Spaces', in *The Cambridge Companion to Proust*, ed. Richard Bales (Cambridge: Cambridge University Press, 2001), pp. 151–67.
Jahoda, G., *The Psychology of Superstition* (London: Penguin, 1969).
Johnson, J. T., 'The Painter and his Art in the Works of Marcel Proust' (doctoral dissertation, University of Wisconsin, 1964).

Jones, P., 'Knowledge and Illusion in *A la recherche du temps perdu*', *Forum for Modern Language Studies*, V/4 (1969), 303–22.
Jullien, D., 'Ailleurs ici: Les *Mille et Une Nuits* dans *A la recherche du temps perdu*', *Romanic Review*, 79 (1988), 466–75.
—— *Proust et ses modèles: Les* Mille et Une nuits *et les* Mémoires *de Saint-Simon* (Paris: Corti, 1989).
Jung, C. G., *Métamorphoses de l'âme et ses symboles* (Paris: LGF, 1996).
—— 'The Phenomenology of the Spirit in Fairytales', in *The Collected Works of C. C. Jung*, vol. 9, 1 (London: Routledge, 1959).
Jurkowski, H., *A History of European Puppetry: From its Origins to the End of the 19th Century* (Lewiston, Queenston, Lampeter: Edwin Mellen, 1996).
Kawakami, A., 'Stereotype Formation and Sleeping Women: The Misreading of *Madame Chrysanthème*', *Forum for Modern Language Studies*, 38/3 (2002), 278–90.
Keller, L., 'Proust au-delà de l'impressionnisme', in S. Bertho (ed.), *Proust et ses peintres* (Amsterdam: Rodopi, 2000), pp.57–70.
Kennedy, V., *Edward Said: A Critical Introduction* (Oxford: Polity, 2000).
Kleist, H. von, 'On the Marionette Theatre', trans. Idris Parry, *http://southerncross review.org/9/kleist.htm*.
Kneller, J. W., 'The Musical Structure of Proust's "Un Amour de Swann"', *Yale French Studies*, 4 (1949), 55–62.
Kostis, N., 'Albertine: Characterization through Image and Symbol', *PMLA*, 84 (1969), 125–35.
La Fontaine, J. de, *Fables*, Hachette French Classics, ed. Francis Tarver (London: Hachette, 1898).
—— *Fables* (Paris: Gallimard, 1964).
Ladenson, E., *Proust's Lesbianism* (Cornell: Cornell University Press, 1999).
Larzul, S., *Les Traductions des 'Mille et Une Nuits': Étude des versions Galland, Trébutien et Mardrus, précédé de 'Traditions, traductions, trahisons' par Claude Bremond* (Paris: L'Harmattan, 1996).
Lauts, J., *Carpaccio: Paintings and Drawings*, complete edn, trans. E. Millman and M. Kay (London: Phaidon, 1962).
*Le nouveau petit Robert* (Paris: Le Robert, 1993).
Leriche, F., 'Proust, An "Art Nouveau" Writer?', in Armine Kotin Mortimer and Katherine Kolb (eds), *Proust in Perspective: Visions and Revisions* (Urbana: University of Illinois Press, 2002), pp. 189–212.
Lévi-Strauss, C., *Pensée sauvage* (Paris: Plon, 1962).
Lewis, C. S., *A Grief Observed* (London, Boston: Faber & Faber, 1966).
Lewis, D., *Religious Superstition Through the Ages* (London, Oxford: Mowbrays, 1975).
Lüthe, M., *The Fairytale as Art Form and Portrait of Man*, trans. J. Erikson (Bloomington: Indiana University Press, 1984).
MacKenzie, R., 'Proustian Doubles: Patterns of Duality and Multiplicity in *A la recherche du temps perdu*', *Forum for Modern Language Studies*, 38/2 (2002), 219–301.

Mallarmé, S., *Œuvres complètes*, Bibliothèque de la Pléiade (Paris: Gallimard, 1945).
Mann, C. G. H., 'The Moon and the Sun in *A la recherche du temps perdu*', *Nottingham French Studies*, 26/1 (1987), 66–76.
Mardrus, J. C. (ed.), *Le Livre des Mille Nuits et Une Nuit, Traduction littérale et complète du texte arabe*, 16 vols (Paris: Charpentier et Fasquelle, 1899–1904).
Maya, K., *L' 'Art caché' ou le style de Proust* (Tokyo: Keio UP, 1997).
McGinnis, R., 'L'inconnaissable Gomorrhe: à propos d'*Albertine disparue*', *Romanic Review*, 81 (1990), 92–104.
McGlaherty, J., *Fairy Tale Romances: The Grimms, Basile, and Perrault* (Urbana, Chicago: University of Illinois Press, 1991).
Mein, M., 'Proust and Wagner', *Journal of European Studies*, xix (1989), 205–22.
Melnick, D., 'Proust, Music, and the Reader', *Modern Languages Quarterly*, 41 (1980), 181–92.
Miguet-Ollagnier, M., 'Le Don des *Mille et Une Nuits* dans *Sodome et Gomorrhe*', *Revue d'Histoire Littéraire*, 93 (1993), 903–18.
Miller, M., *Nostalgia: A Psychoanalytical Study of Marcel Proust* (Boston: Houghton Mifflin, 1956).
Moss, H., *The Magic Lantern of Marcel Proust* (New York, London: Macmillan, 1962).
Mothe, J.-P., *Du Sang et du sexe dans les contes de Perrault*, Collection l'Œuvre et la Psyché (Paris: L'Harmattan, 1999).
Mourgues, O. de, *La Fontaine: Fables* (London: Edward Arnold, 1960).
Mouton, J., *Proust*, Les Ecrivains devant Dieu 19 (Bruges: Desclée de Brouwer, 1968).
Murray, J., 'The Mystery of Others', *Yale French Studies*, 34 (1965), 65–72.
Nattiez, J.-J., *Proust as Musician*, trans. D. Puffett (Cambridge: Cambridge University Press, 1989).
Nelson, G. K., *Spiritualism and Society* (London: Routledge, 1969).
Olliver, C. W., *Handbook of Magic and Witchcraft* (Twickenham: Tiger Books, 1996 [1928]).
Otten, M., 'Proust et l'art du sélam', *Les Lettres romanes*, 39 (1985), 73–82.
*Oxford English Dictionary* (Oxford: Clarendon, 1994).
*Oxford Paperback Thesaurus* (Oxford: Oxford University Press, 1994).
Pasco, A. H., 'Albertine's Equivocal Eyes', *Australian Journal of French Studies*, 5 (1968), 257–62.
Perrault, C., *Contes* (Paris: Gallimard, 1981).
Pierssens, M., 'Proust et la planchette magique', *Critique: Revue générale des publications françaises et etrangères*, 44/491 (1988), 320–35.
Pommier, J., *La Mystique de Marcel Proust*. (Paris: Droz, 1939).
Prat, M., 'Proust et la lanterne magique de Schopenhauer', *Revue de littérature comparée*, 218/2 (1981), 195–207.
Rienäcker, G., 'Discursions into the Dramaturgy of *Parsifal*', in *Parsifal*, Opera Guide Series, 34 (London: John Calder; NY: Riverrun, 1986), pp. 59–70.
Rivers, J. E., *Proust and the Art of Love: The Aesthetics of Sexuality in the Life, Times and Art of Marcel Proust* (New York: Columbia University Press, 1980).

Robinson, C., *Scandal in the Ink: Male and Female Homosexuality in Twentieth-Century French Literature* (London: Cassell, 1995).

Rodrigues, J.-M., 'Genèse du wagnérisme proustien', *Romantisme: revue du 19ème siècle*, 17/57 (1987), 75–88.

Rose, J. L., 'A Landmark in Musical History', in *Tristan and Isolde*, Opera Guide Series 6 (London: John Calder; NY: Riverrun, 1981), pp. 9–16.

Said, E., *Orientalism: Western Conceptions of the Orient* (Harmondsworth: Penguin, 1991 [1978]).

Schœntjes, P., *Recherche de l'ironie et ironie de la Recherche* (Gent: Rijksuniversiteit te Gent, 1993).

Schopenhauer, A., *The World as Will and Representation*, trans. E. Payne (Indian Hills, CO.: Falcon Wing's Press, 1958).

Scruton, R., *Death-Devoted Heart: Sex and the Sacred in Wagner's Tristan and Isolde* (Oxford: Oxford University Press, 2004).

Segal, R. A. (ed.), *Jung on Mythology*, Key Readings (London: Routledge, 1998).

Segalen, V., *Essai sur l'exotisme: une esthétique du Divers* (Paris: Livre de Poche, 1986).

Senn, H., 'Proust and Melusine: From Fairy Magic to Personal Mythology', *Southern Folklore Quarterly*, 43/3–4 (1979), 267–75.

Seznec, J., *Marcel Proust et les dieux* (Oxford: Clarendon, 1962).

Shattuck, R., *Proust's Binoculars: A Study of Memory, Time and Recognition in A la recherche du temps perdu* (London: Chatto & Windus, 1964).

—— *Proust's Way: A Field Guide to In Search of Lost Time* (London: Penguin, 2000).

Skultans, V., *Intimacy and Ritual: A Study of Spiritualism, Mediums and Groups* (London: Routledge, 1974).

Slater, M., *Humour in the Works of Proust* (Oxford: Oxford University Press. 1979).

Sollers, P., 'Proust et Gomorrhe', *Théorie des exceptions* (Paris: Gallimard, 1986).

Soriano, M., *Les Contes de Perrault: Culture savante et traditions populaires*, Collection Tel 22 (Paris: Gallimard, 1977).

Speaight, G., *Punch and Judy: A History* (London: Studio Vista, 1970).

Splitter, R., *Proust's Recherche: A Psychoanalytic Interpretation* (Boston and London: Routledge, 1981).

Stendhal, *La Chartreuse de Parme*, in *Romans et nouvelles*, Bibliothèque de la Pléiade (Paris: Gallimard, 1952).

Tadié, J.-Y., *Lectures de Proust* (Paris: Armand Colin, 1971).

Topping, M., '*Les Mille et Une Nuits* proustiennes', Essays in French Literature, 35/36 (November 1998–9), 113–30.

—— *Proust's Gods: Christian and Mythological Figures of Speech in the Works of Marcel Proust* (Oxford: Oxford University Press, 2000).

—— 'Andromeda's Mysterious Saviour: The Absent Hero in Proust's *A la recherche du temps perdu*', *Dalhousie French Studies*, 63 (Summer 2003), 53–8.

Urbain, J.-D., '*I travel, therefore I am*: The "Nomad Mind" and the Spirit of Travel', trans. C. Forsdick, *Studies in Travel Writing* 4 (2000), 141–64.

Vallée, C., *La Féerie de Marcel Proust* (Paris: Fasquelle, 1958).

Vernant, J.-P., *Myth and Society in Ancient Greece* (London: Methuen, 1982).

Vigneron, R., 'Structure de Swann: Balzac, Wagner et Proust', *French Review*, 19/6 (1946), 370–84.
Wallis Budge, E. A., *Amulets and Superstitions* (New York: Dover, 1978 [1930]).
Warner, M., *From the Beast to the Blonde: On Fairy Tales and their Tellers* (London: Vintage, 1995).
Wassenaar, I., *Proustian Passions: The Uses of Self-Justification for* A la recherche du temps perdu (Oxford: Oxford University Press, 2000).
Weiner, M. A., 'Zwieback and Madeleine: Creative Recall in Wagner and Proust', *Modern Languages Notes*, 95 (1980), 679–84.
Whiting, J. W. M. and Child, I. L., *Child Training and Personality: A Cross-Cultural Study* (New Haven: Yale University Press, 1953).
Winton, A., *Proust's Additions: The Making of* A la recherche du temps perdu, 2 vols (Cambridge: Cambridge University Press, 1977).
Zima, P.-V., Le Désir du mythe: Une lecture sociologique de Marcel Proust (Paris: Nizet, 1973).

# INDEX

*Note*: Principal subjects such as Proust, the narrator, *A la recherche du temps perdu*, myth, metaphor and the supernatural are indexed only where general or theoretical observations are made. Works by other artists are listed by title and can be found in their alphabetical positions. These, and the names of fairytale and legendary characters, are given in French where the original source is French; otherwise, they are listed in the English form. Noun headwords are understood to include related ideas (including adjectival and verbal forms).

Abbate, Carolyn 99, 100, 190 n. 62, 192 n. 79
Adam 99
  *see also* Bible; Christianity
Aegisthus 82
agnosticism 133
Aimé 134, 198 n. 48
*Aladin ou la Lampe merveilleuse* 44, 54, 178 n. 51
  *see also Mille et Une Nuits*
Albertine 6, 10, 18, 20, 35, 36–41, 44, 45–9, 53, 55, 57–8, 64, 65, 76, 84, 85, 90, 97–101, 105, 111–12, 129, 130, 132–6, 137–9, 144, 145, 146–7, 148–9, 151, 152–3, 154, 155–6, 157, 173 n. 6, 174 n. 19, 176 n. 38, 177 nn. 43 & 44, 189 n. 52, 190 n. 60, 191 n. 65, 194 n. 97, 197 nn. 40 & 41, 198 n. 48, 199 n. 50, 200 n. 64, 202 n. 79, 204 nn. 92 & 98, 205 n. 101

Albouy, Pierre 170 n. 49, 172 n. 73, 200 n. 62, 204 n. 96
*Ali-Baba* 23, 44, 45, 49–50, 53, 178 n. 51
  *see also Mille et Une Nuits*
Amfortas 93, 99, 100–1, 109, 112, 188 n. 46, 189 n. 53, 191 nn. 69 & 70, 193 n. 83
  *see also Parsifal*
Andrée 134, 190 n. 59, 198 n. 48, 204 n. 97
  *see also* Albertine; 'jeunes filles'
Andromeda 30, 174 n. 18
Archer, John 198 n. 46
Areopagus 82, 185 n. 22
Argencourt, M. de 115–16, 180 n. 65
Argonauts 30
aristocracy 37, 44, 45, 53, 61, 76–8, 79, 93–6, 153, 181 n. 76, 203 n. 82
  *see also* individual character names

# Index

art nouveau 181 n. 79
Ashman, Mike 92–3, 100, 109
Askevis-Leherpeux, Françoise 119, 127, 129
astrology (including planets; stars) 3, 9, 13, 119, 150–1, 153–5, 156–8, 159, 162, 171 n. 67, 190 n. 56, 204 nn. 93, 97 & 98, 205 nn. 99 & 106
astronomy 154, 157, 205 n. 100

bacchante 58
Baird, Bil 184 n. 13
Bakhtin, Mikhail 8, 76, 114
Balbec 46, 48, 54, 60, 68, 107, 144, 152, 154, 170 n. 55, 190 n. 60, 197 nn. 38 & 41, 203 n. 88
'bal costumé' 17, 27, 67, 76, 109, 115, 136, 144, 193 n. 86
Balzac, Honoré de 55, 104, 106
*Barbe-Bleue, La* 24, 32–4, 38–9, 173 n. 8, 175 nn. 30, 31, 32 & 33, 176 nn. 33, 37, 39 & 41, 202 n. 78
  see also Perrault
Barchilon, Jacques 55, 177 n. 43
Basile, Giambattista 174 n. 17
Baudelaire, Charles 146, 202 n. 75
*Belle au bois dormant, La* 10, 24, 26, 29–30, 37–40, 57, 67, 68, 174 n. 17, 177 n. 43, 181 nn. 75 & 78
  see also Perrault
*Belle et la Bête, La* 29, 35–6, 64, 180 n. 72
  see also Perrault
Bergotte 16, 21, 135, 142–3, 151–2, 157, 187 n. 35, 197 n. 37, 200 n. 66, 201 nn. 70 & 71
Bergson, Henri 78, 119, 183 n. 8
Berma, La 69, 142, 151–2, 187 n. 35, 188 n. 38, 200 n. 66
Bettelheim, Bruno 34, 39, 42, 63, 64, 175 n. 33

Biard, Jean-Dominique 166 n. 15, 186 n. 34
Bible 38, 99, 121, 173 n. 6, 176 n. 41, 195 n. 12
  see also Christianity
Bloch, Albert 49, 171 nn. 63 & 65, 205 n. 101
Borchmeyer, Dieter 98, 99
*Boris Godounov* (Modest Mussorgsky) 113–14
Bowie, Malcolm 159–60, 177 n. 48, 187 n. 36, 203 n. 86
Bradbury, Malcolm 91
Brichot, professeur 21, 145, 171 n. 63, 186 n. 29, 202 n. 79
Brothers Grimm 41
Bucknall, Barbara 169 n. 44
Buddhism 9–10, 169 nn. 42 & 43
Buisine, Alain 178 n. 50

Cambremer, M. de 7, 21, 22, 81, 82, 87–8, 101, 103, 172 n. 72, 185 n. 22, 186 n. 32, 203 n. 83
Cambremer, Mme de 21, 22, 77–8, 79, 101–3, 175 n. 29
  mother-in-law of 103
Carter, William 57, 58
*Cendrillon* 24, 26, 29–30, 60, 64, 180 n. 71, 181 n. 76
  see also Perrault
Charlus, baron de 20, 21, 22, 31, 32, 34, 45, 48–53, 55, 148, 151, 171 n. 63, 173 n. 6, 174 n. 20, 179 nn. 53 & 55, 186 n. 29, 203 n. 83, 204 n. 91, 205 n. 99
*Chartreuse de Parme, La* (Stendhal) 187 n. 35
*Chat botté, Le* 24, 61–2, 72, 180 n. 69
  see also Perrault
Chaudier, Stéphane 126, 132, 156, 196 n. 25, 197 n. 40, 198 n. 45, 201 n. 69
Chernowitz, Maurice E. 182 n. 82
Child, Irvin 131–2

Christ(ianity) 82, 97, 98, 99, 109, 123, 129, 178 n. 50, 182 n. 87, 189 n. 50, 195 n. 18
Clytemnestra 82
Combray 25, 37, 44–5, 46, 48, 53, 54, 55, 59, 71, 74, 93, 95, 102, 104, 153, 173 n. 4, 178 n. 50, 189 n. 52, 200 n. 57
Comte, Auguste 119, 167 n. 20
*Contes de ma mère l'oye*
see Perrault
Cottard, M. 204 n. 91
Cottard, Mme 21
Coupe, Laurence 22–3, 32, 58, 165 n. 8
Courvoisier, vicomte de 148
Cubism 181 n. 79

Darwin(ism) 119, 167 n. 20
Davis, Colin 200 n. 59
Debussy, Claude 18, 20, 75
see also *Pelléas et Mélisande*
Decamps, Alexandre-Gabriel 50, 51
Delarue, Paul 177 n. 43
Demosthenes 191 n. 74
destiny 68, 111, 150, 151, 153–6, 157, 158, 159, 163, 171 n. 67
Devil
see Satan
Dieulafoy, Professor 201 n. 71
divination 3, 119, 150, 151–3, 157, 158, 159, 161, 170 n. 57, 171 n. 67, 204 nn. 89, 90, 91, 92 & 93, 205 n. 104
Doncières 13, 79, 150, 158
Donnan, Thomas 106, 183 n. 3, 192 n. 80
Doré, Gustave 176 n. 33
*Dormeur éveillé, Le* 24, 43, 44, 178 n. 51
see also *Mille et Une Nuits*
Dostoevsky, Fyodor 145
'drame du coucher' 12, 132, 173 n. 4, 192 n. 80

Eells, Emily 167 n. 20
Eliade, Mircea 4, 5, 7, 8, 25, 28, 29, 108, 109, 119, 125, 130, 161, 163, 168 nn. 39, 40 & 41
Elstir 17, 21, 29, 36, 66, 69, 77, 104–5, 107, 120, 126, 142, 182 n. 85, 188 n. 38, 202 n. 74, 204 n. 93
Enlightenment 167 n. 19
*Ensorcelée, L'* (Jules Barbey d'Aurevilly) 145, 201 n. 73
Eve 99, 191 n. 65
see also Bible; Christianity

*Fables* (La Fontaine) 2, 5, 6, 7, 22, 74, 76, 80, 81–91, 101, 103, 109, 113, 118, 166 nn. 14, 15 & 18, 193 n. 2, 184 n. 17, 185 nn. 18 & 22, 186 nn. 30 & 31
 Animaux malades de la peste, Les 187 n. 35
 Chameau et les Bâtons flottants, Le 87, 88, 172 n. 72, 186 n. 32
 Colombe et la Fourmi, La 186 n. 29
 Deux Pigeons, Les 87, 89–91, 185 n. 24
 Grenouille et le Rat, La 84, 85
 Grenouille qui veut se faire aussi grosse que le Bœuf, La 83–4, 85
 Grenouilles qui demandent un Roi, Les 83
 Homme et la Couleuvre, L' 87
 Lièvre et les Grenouilles, Le 185 n. 27
 Lion et le Rat, Le 186 n. 29
 Meunier, son Fils et l'Âne, Le 85–87, 90
fairy godmother 37, 42, 55, 60, 63, 64, 170 n. 55, 180 n. 71
fairy queen 6, 56, 59–64, 145, 171 n. 62

# Index

fairytale (general) 5, 9, 14–15, 16, 24–73, 94, 112, 127, 156, 161, 162, 171 n. 59, 174 n. 10, 178 n. 49, 182 n. 83, 188 n. 46
  duality and disguise 5, 26, 40, 41, 49–50, 60, 67, 94, 100, 112, 138, 162, 173 n. 8, 182 n. 84
  hero 27–8, 58, 174 n. 12
  and metamorphosis 27, 32, 35–7, 59–60, 62, 67
  and oedipal complex 63–4, 180 nn. 72 & 74
  as quest for the absolute 24–5
  and social mobility/boundaries 60, 62, 64, 67, 173 n. 3, 174 n. 20, 181 n. 76
  and transgression 28, 32–4
  and the 'unpromising' 26–7, 58, 60, 72
  *see also* magic; Perrault
*Faux-Monnayeurs, Les* (André Gide) 202 n. 76
Flinders, Peter 55, 177 n. 43
Flower Maidens 2, 94–8, 188 nn. 43 & 48, 190 nn. 55, 56, 57 & 58
  *see also* Parsifal
Forcheville, M. de 126
Fortuny, Mariano
  fabrics 149
*Fourberies de Scapin, Les* (Molière) 202 n. 76
Françoise 12, 21, 40, 121–3, 134, 151, 157, 170 nn. 54 & 55, 173 nn. 4 & 6, 195 nn. 15 & 17, 196 n. 31, 204 n. 90
*François le Champi* (George Sand) 71, 179 n. 54
Franz, Marie-Louise von 41
Frazer, Sir James 6, 119–20, 129, 167 nn. 20 & 21, 194 n. 99
Freud, Sigmund 9, 126, 165 n. 7, 168 n. 35, 177 n. 48, 198 n. 46
Fromentin, Eugène 50
Fromm, Erich 111 n. 46

Gautier, Théophile 202 n. 75
Girard, René 175 n. 29, 193 n. 89
God 147, 195 n. 20, 196 n. 25
  *see also* Bible; Christianity
gods 151, 152
Goncourt brothers 21
Graham, Victor 43, 44, 178 n. 50, 185 n. 18, 197 n. 35, 200 n. 65, 203 n. 82, 205 n. 100
Grail, Holy 2, 5, 74, 93, 94, 96, 100, 101, 109–10, 112, 188 nn. 42 & 46, 191 n. 70
  Brethren of the Knights of 8, 9, 96, 97, 108, 109, 189 n. 50, 190 n. 62
  *see also* Parsifal
*Grisélidis* 24, 30–1, 34, 174 n. 19, 175 n. 22
  *see also* Perrault
Guermantes, le côté de 57
Guermantes, les 92, 93–4, 96, 97, 115, 123, 147, 178 n. 50, 186 n. 29, 189 n. 50
Guermantes, M. de 77, 93, 153, 186 n. 28, 187 n. 37
Guermantes, Mme de 6, 9, 17–8, 21, 24, 59–64, 76, 77, 78, 102, 120, 123–4, 127, 145, 153, 154–5, 157–8, 171 n. 62, 173 n. 2, 180 n. 65, 181 n. 77, 187 n. 37, 189 n. 52
Guermantes, prince de 32, 67, 174 n. 20
Guermantes, princesse de 7, 81, 188 n. 47
  Mme Verdurin as 62, 83, 89, 115, 171 n. 63
Gurnemanz 96, 188 n. 42, 190 nn. 54 & 61, 193 n. 86
  *see also* Parsifal
Guyau, André 183 n. 2

Hahn, Reynaldo 101
Hardy, Thomas 145

Haroun Al Raschid, calife 51
    see also Mille et Une Nuits
Hinduism 9
Holloway, Robin 188 n. 46, 191 nn.
    69 & 75
homosexuality 22, 29, 30–2, 44–53,
    148–9, 152, 162, 167 n. 20, 174
    nn. 18, 20 & 21, 175 nn. 22, 23,
    24 & 26, 176 n. 37, 179 n. 55,
    186 n. 28, 187 n. 36
Hughes, Edward 174 n. 16, 181 n. 76

idolatry 82
Impressionism 65–6, 67, 79, 181 n. 79

Jahoda, Gustav 120–1, 122, 124, 126,
    162, 194 n. 3, 195 nn. 8 & 16,
    197 nn. 36 & 39
Jankélévitch, Vladimir 105
'jeunes filles' 26, 98, 126, 142, 154,
    190 nn. 55, 56, 59 & 60, 204
    n. 97
    see also individual character names
Johnson, J. Theodore 182 n. 82
Jones, Peter 194 n. 6
Judaism 152, 204 n. 89
Judas 99
    see also Bible; Christianity
Jullien, Dominique 178 n. 50
Jung, Carl-Gustav 4, 26, 32, 38, 122,
    165 n. 7, 173 n. 7
Jupien 31, 32, 44, 49, 51, 52, 53, 148,
    174 n. 20, 201 n. 72
    niece of 148
Jupiter 83
Jurkowski, Hendryk 184 n. 17

Kawakami, Akane 176 n. 40
Keller, Luzius 181 n. 79
Kleist, Heinrich von 77–8, 183
    nn. 7 & 8
Klingsor 2, 92–4, 97, 100, 188 nn. 42,
    43 & 46, 191 n. 69
    see also Parsifal

Kundry 11, 97–101, 107, 189 n. 52,
    190 nn. 57, 59, 60 & 62, 193
    n. 83
    see also Parsifal

Ladenson, Elisabeth 126
La Fontaine, Jean de
    see Fables
Larzul, Sylvette 179 n. 54
Lauts, Jan 149
Léa 47
legend 1, 2, 3, 4, 5, 6, 7, 12, 15–16,
    17, 18, 22, 55, 61, 72, 74–117,
    118, 159, 161, 162, 169 n. 42
Léger, Fernand 57
Legrandin, M. 21, 136, 180 n. 67
Lemaire, Suzanne 101
Leriche, Françoise 181 n. 79
lesbianism
    see homosexuality
Lévy-Bruhl, Lucien 162
Lewis, C. S. 199 n. 50
Lewis, Don 120
Life of Moses (Sandro Botticelli) 82,
    189 n. 52
Lohengrin 191 n. 73
    see also Wagner
Loti, Pierre 176 n. 40
Lüthe, Max 24–9, 173 nn. 3 & 6, 174
    n. 12, 182 n. 84
Luxembourg, M. de 85, 186 n. 28

Madonna of the Magnificat (Sandro
    Botticelli) 82, 189 n. 52
Maeterlinck, Maurice 113
magic (general) 3, 6, 14, 16–17,
    58–9, 112, 119, 120, 126, 127,
    142–50, 159, 162, 163, 167
    n. 21, 170 n. 55, 171 n. 65,
    173 n. 1, 182 n. 88, 196 n. 23,
    203 n. 82
    black magic and the occult 3, 14,
        119, 120, 141, 142, 146, 147–9,
        159, 161, 168 n. 32, 203 n. 81

of the conjuror/illusionist 36–7,
142–3, 144, 146, 171 n. 59, 201
n. 71
and fairytale 24–73, 170 n. 56, 181
n. 77
lantern 163, 175 n. 31, 206 n. 5
possession and exorcism 60,
149–50, 171 n. 59, 202 n. 73,
203 n. 85
sorcery and witchcraft 48, 142,
144–7, 150, 155, 171 nn. 59 &
62, 202 nn. 73, 74, 75 & 76, 203
nn. 79 & 82
Malherbe, François 86
Malinowski, Bronislaw 126
Mallarmé, Stéphane 146, 202 n. 75
Martinville, clochers de 68, 145
Mein, Margaret 106, 183 n. 3, 188
n. 40, 189 n. 52, 190 nn. 55 &
59, 191 n. 70, 192 n. 80
*Mémoires d'Outre-Tombe* (François
René Chateaubriand) 171 n. 64
memory (general) 7–10, 130, 133, 159,
163, 168 nn. 36 & 39
involuntary 8, 9, 10, 17, 25, 53–4,
55, 57, 71, 76, 109, 116, 122,
123, 133, 136, 144, 145, 157,
168 n. 40, 169 n. 44, 171 n. 64,
173 n. 4, 178 n. 50, 197 n. 34
as return to origins 9
Méséglise, le côté de 57
mesmerism 119
metaphor (general) 11–12, 13, 28,
29, 55–6, 65–72, 105–6, 109,
120, 146, 151, 161–2, 170
nn. 51 & 52, 192 n. 80, 205
n. 104
as demythicized myth 6–7, 9, 161
and involuntary memory 8, 9, 25,
116, 168 n. 40
mediated v. unmediated 20, 172
n. 70, 184 n. 10
oscillation between literal and
metaphorical evocations of myth
11, 12–20, 119, 130, 159, 197
n. 35, 201 n. 73
Mill, John Stuart 119
*Mille et Une Nuits, Les* 1, 6, 11, 14,
18, 22, 24, 29, 42–55, 56, 58,
178 n. 50
Galland translation 46–7, 53, 179
n. 54
Mardrus translation 46–7, 53, 179
n. 54
*see also* titles of individual tales
Miller, Milton 177 n. 48
Mnemosyne 168 n. 36
Monet, Claude 66
Monteriender, comtesse de 21, 140
Montjouvain 184 n. 14, 201 n. 72
morality 187 n. 36
Morel, Charlie 32, 64–5, 69, 144, 148,
151–2, 174 n. 20
Morienval, Mme de 91
*Mort de Sardanapale* (Eugène
Delacroix) 179 n. 55
Mothe, Jean-Pierre 31, 34, 176 n. 37,
180 n. 74
Mourgues, Odette de 166 n. 15
Musset, Alfred de 89
mysticism 169 n. 44
myth 3–12, 22, 58, 155, 161–4, 166
n. 9, 167 n. 19, 168 nn. 32 & 39,
169 n. 49
of the artist 7
and communication 5–7, 10, 119,
130, 161, 163
cosmogonic 4
eschatological 9
and initiation 163, 168 n. 40
and renewal 7, 8–9, 23, 109
as self-creation 4–5, 10, 17, 119,
130, 163
statistical occurrences of in *A la
recherche* 12–22
as symbol 6
and time 7–10, 25, 68, 70, 71–2,
119, 130, 161, 163, 168 n. 40

mythology, classical 30, 168 n. 36, 170 n. 49, 182 n. 87, 200 n. 66
see also individual mythological figures

Nanda Anshen, Ruth 3
narrator (of *A la recherche*)
   father 28
   grandfather 151, 152, 204 n. 89
   grandmother 13, 28, 46–7, 60, 79, 97, 102, 130–3, 134, 135, 139, 173 n. 2, 175 n. 32, 179 n. 52, 180 n. 73, 187 n. 37, 189 n. 53, 197 nn. 38 & 41, 201 n. 71, 202 n. 74
   great-aunt (Léonie) 44, 46, 53, 155
   mother 12, 28, 46–7, 93–4, 97, 132, 134, 156, 173 n. 2, 175 n. 32, 179 n. 54, 180 n. 73, 189 n. 53, 197 n. 40, 204 n. 98
   mythical quest 3, 4, 6, 9, 11, 12–20, 22–3, 72, 74–6, 92, 106, 108, 113, 116–17, 118, 130, 158, 161, 162, 164
   parents 142
Nattiez, Jean-Jacques 96, 104, 106, 107, 108, 183 n. 3, 189 n. 52, 190 n. 55
Nelson, Geoffrey 132, 194 n. 3
Norpois, M. de 69, 70

*Odalisque à l'esclave* (Jean Auguste Dominique Ingres) 179 n. 55
Odette 17, 21, 27, 35, 62, 69, 81–5, 93, 97, 99, 120, 123, 124–6, 127, 128–9, 139–40, 170 n. 54, 173 n. 6, 184 n. 16, 185 n. 20, 189 n. 52, 196 nn. 20 & 26
Olliver, Charles 146, 147, 152
Orestes 82
Orientalism 6, 43, 49, 199 n. 54
   see also Said, Edward
Orpheus 170 n. 49, 200 n. 62

paganism 82
pantheism 82
Paris 9, 22, 50, 51, 54, 67, 74, 79, 93, 94, 96, 108, 109, 111, 114, 123, 131, 144, 156, 159, 194 n. 3
*Parsifal* (work)/Parsifal (protagonist) 2, 5, 9, 11, 74, 89, 91–2, 92–101, 103, 104, 105, 106, 107, 108–10, 112, 172 n. 71, 188 nn. 40, 43, 46 & 48, 189 n. 53, 190 nn. 57, 61 & 62, 191 nn. 64, 67, 69 & 70, 192 n. 77, 193 n. 83, 200 n. 63
   see also Wagner
*Patriarche di Grado esorcisant un possédé* (Carpaccio) 149–50
Paul, Saint 82, 185 n. 21
*Peau d'Âne* 30–1, 72, 174 n. 9, 181 n. 76
   see also Perrault
*Pelléas et Mélisande* 16, 75, 89, 102–3, 113–14, 172 n. 71
   see also Debussy
Perrault, Charles
   *Contes de ma mère l'oye* 1, 8, 11, 26, 29, 30, 31, 32, 35, 38, 40, 42, 62, 64, 72, 162, 173 nn. 3 & 8, 174 n. 17, 176 nn. 33 & 41, 177 n. 43, 45 & 46, 180 n. 74
   see also titles of individual tales
*Petit Chaperon rouge, Le* 24, 40–1, 177 nn. 45 & 46
   see also Perrault
*Petit Poucet, Le* 24, 26, 37, 58, 67, 71, 173 n. 8, 180 n. 63
   see also Perrault
*Phèdre* (Jean Racine) 142, 187 n. 35
phrenology 119
Piaget, Jean 196 n. 23
Pierssens, Michel 194 n. 3, 197 n. 35
planets
   see astrology
Pommier, Jean 169 n. 44

Poseidon 30
Proust, Marcel
  as myth-maker 4–10
  /the narrator-writer's aesthetic 'quest' 3, 5, 6, 22, 72–3, 75–6, 92, 101, 108, 113, 114–15, 118, 130, 162–3, 164
  *Contre Sainte-Beuve* 167 n. 20, 205 n. 105
  *Correspondance* 167 n. 20, 191 n. 72
  *Essais et articles* 167 n. 20
  *Jean Santeuil* 167 n. 20, 175 n. 31
  *Pastiches et mélanges* 167 n. 20
  *Plaisirs et les jours, Les* 167 n. 20, 191 n. 73
  puppet theatre 2, 8, 13–14, 16, 73, 74, 75, 76–80, 81, 84, 90, 95, 109, 113, 115–17, 118, 165 n. 5, 182 n. 1, 183 nn. 5, 6 & 9, 184 nn. 10 & 13, 184 n. 16
  distinction between 'Guignol' and 'Polichinelle' 183 n. 5, 184 n. 11

Rabelais, François 114
Racan, Honorat de Bueil, seigneur de 86–7
*Rachel quand du Seigneur* 7, 81, 89–91, 127, 153–4, 171 n. 65, 187 n. 38, 204 n. 96
redemption 2, 11, 97, 98, 100–1, 105, 108, 109, 160, 188 n. 40, 191 n. 70
Reinäcker, Gerd 189 n. 50, 190 n. 61
*Riquet à la houppe* 24, 35–6, 173 n. 8, 176 n. 38
  see also Perrault
ritual 3, 4, 8, 9, 14, 15, 16, 17, 76, 78, 80, 81, 94, 95, 96, 109, 113, 116, 162, 165 nn. 32 & 35, 171 n. 59, 189 n. 50, 203 n. 82
  and belief 118–60
Rivers, Julius E. 174 n. 21, 175 nn. 24 & 26
Robinson, Christopher 175 n. 23

Rodrigues, Jean-Marc 102, 105, 183 n. 3, 191 nn. 71 & 73, 192 n. 77
Rose, John Luke 110

(sado-)masochism 31–2, 51–3, 77, 175 n. 26
Said, Edward 5, 166 n. 17
  see also Orientalism
Sainte-Euverte, Mme de 139, 147, 181 n. 77, 184 n. 16
Saint-Loup, Robert de 18, 21, 22, 51, 60–1, 64, 120, 126, 134, 154, 159–60, 171 n. 65, 173 nn. 1 & 6, 184 n. 15, 193 n. 84, 204 n. 96, 205 nn. 101 & 106
Satan 148, 165 n. 5, 195 n. 20, 203 n. 81
Schéhérazade 43
  see also *Mille et Une Nuits*
Schopenhauer, Arthur 109, 110–12
science 6–7, 119, 120, 122, 127, 129, 150, 152, 155, 157, 158, 162, 163, 194 n. 99, 195 n. 7
Scruton, Roger 2, 110–11
Segalen, Victor 163, 206 n. 4
*Sesame and Lilies* (John Ruskin) 45
*Simbad le Marin embarquant à Bassora avec toutes ses richesses* 44, 178 n. 51
  see also *Mille et Une Nuits*
Skultans, Vieda 133, 136–8
Sollers, Philippe 196 n. 25
Soriano, Marc 72, 162, 173 n. 8, 177 nn. 45 & 46
Speaight, George 76, 182 n. 1, 183 n. 9
spiritualism 3, 6, 12, 14, 15, 119, 120, 130–41, 159, 161, 172 n. 69, 194 n. 97, 197 nn. 34, 35 & 38, 199 nn. 52 & 53, 200 nn. 62 & 65
  and bereavement 133–6
  as metaphor for the artistic enterprise 136–41

Splitter, Randolph 176 n. 34, 177 n. 48
stars
    see astrology
Stermaria, Mlle de 60, 155–6, 170 n. 55
supernatural (general) 3–4, 11–12, 119, 149–50, 162
    narrator's understanding of 59
    oscillation between natural and supernatural 153
    oscillation between scientific and supernatural 152, 155, 156–7, 158, 172 n. 67
    power of art 163
    statistic occurrences of in *A la recherche* 12–22
superstition 3, 14, 17–18, 119–30, 158–9, 161, 162, 168 n. 32, 197 n. 36
    as cosmology 120, 121–4
    and gender 127–9, 197 n. 32
    personal 121, 126–8, 196 n. 26
    socially shared 120, 123–6, 127–8, 170 n. 54
Surgis le Duc, Mme de
    sons of 205 n. 99
Swann, Charles 26, 35, 37, 44, 69, 80, 81–5, 92–3, 97, 99, 100–1, 120, 125, 126, 128–9, 139–41, 147, 155, 157, 173 n. 6, 180 n. 67, 184 n. 16, 185 nn. 20 & 26, 187 n. 37, 189 n. 52, 191 n. 70, 196 nn. 20 & 26
Swann, Gilberte 76–7, 90, 154, 155, 189 n. 52, 197 n. 33
Swann, les 24, 92
Swann, Mme
    see Odette

Tadié, Jean-Yves 53–4, 55, 178 n. 50, 179 n. 56
Taoism 125

technological advances
    car travel 57–9, 71, 179 n. 59
    telephone 56–7, 130–1
Terence (Publius Terentius Afer) 170 n. 50
Theophilus, Saint 122
*Tristan and Isolde* 2, 5, 16, 74, 75, 89, 91–2, 101, 102, 104, 108, 109, 110–13, 169 n. 48, 192 nn. 77 & 82, 193 nn. 89 & 95, 194 n. 96
    see also Wagner
Turgot, Anne Robert Jacques 167 n. 20
Turquie, ambassadrice de 21, 81, 85, 185 n. 28, 186 n. 29

Urbain, Jean-Didier 58, 179 n. 62

*Valkyrie, The* 22, 108, 193 n. 84, 205 n. 106
    see also Wagner
Vallée, Claude 11–12, 28, 170 nn. 51, 52 & 53
Venice 18, 54, 58, 156, 202 n. 74
Verdurin, les 145, 147, 185 n. 22, 186 n. 32
Verdurin, Mme 21, 27, 60, 61–2, 64, 69, 83–4, 144, 184 n. 16
    see also princesse de Guermantes
Vermeer, Jan 143
Vernant, Jean-Pierre 167 n. 19
Vico, Giambattista 167 n. 20
Vigneron, Robert 107–8, 192 n. 82
Villeparisis, Mme de 21, 60–2, 63, 68, 170 n. 55, 173 n. 6, 180 n. 67
Vinteuil, M. (including Septet and Sonata) 16, 26, 54–5, 69–70, 75, 80, 82, 104, 105, 106, 108, 137, 139–40, 145, 174 n. 10, 184 n. 16, 192 n. 82, 200 nn. 62, 64 & 65
Vinteuil, Mlle 31, 34
    lover of 143

Viviane, la fée 61
  *see also* Grail
Vivonne, la 201 n. 72

Wagner, Richard 2, 8, 10–11, 16, 18, 20, 22, 75, 76, 89, 91–113, 118, 172 n. 71, 191 nn. 69 & 73, 192 nn. 76, 77, 79 & 80, 193 n. 84
  *see also Lohengrin, Parsifal, Tristan and Isolde* and *The Valkyrie*
Wallis Budge, E. A. 195 nn. 18 & 19, 197 n. 33

Warner, Marina 27, 32, 42, 72, 174 n. 17, 175 n. 30, 176 nn. 33 & 41, 178 n. 49
Wassenaar, Ingrid 135, 172 n. 68, 198 n. 48, 199 n. 49
Whiting, John 131–2
Winton [Finch], Alison 185 n. 28, 196 n. 24

Zobéide, *Histoire de la belle* 24, 44, 48, 51–3, 178 n. 51
  *see also Mille et Une Nuits*